PAST BODIES

Past Bodies

Body-Centered Research in Archaeology

edited by

Dušan Borić and John Robb

Oxbow Books
Oxford & Philadelphia

Published in the United Kingdom in 2008 by
OXBOW BOOKS
10 Hythe Bridge Street, Oxford OX1 2EW

and in the United States by
OXBOW BOOKS
908 Darby Road, Havertown, PA 19083

Reprinted in paperback 2014

Paperback Edition: ISBN 978-1-78297-542-7
Digital Edition: ISBN 978-1-78297-543-4

A CIP record for this book is available from the British Library

For a complete list of Oxbow titles, please contact:

UNITED KINGDOM
Oxbow Books
Telephone (01865) 241249, Fax (01865) 794449
Email: oxbow@oxbowbooks.com
www.oxbowbooks.com

UNITED STATES OF AMERICA
Oxbow Books
Telephone (800) 791-9354, Fax (610) 853-9146
Email: queries@casemateacademic.com
www.casemateacademic.com/oxbow

Oxbow Books is part of the Casemate Group

*Front cover: Clay model of a sleeping lady from the Ħal Saflieni Hypogeum, Malta.
National Museum of Archaeology, Valletta. ©2014 Daniel Cilia/Heritage Malta*

Table of Contents

List of Contributors

PROFESSOR DOUGLASS BAILEY
Department of Anthropology
San Francisco State University
1600 Holloway Avenue
San Francisco, California 94132, USA
Email: dwbailey@sfsu.edu

DR. DUŠAN BORIĆ
Department of Archaeology
University of Cambridge
Downing Street
Cambridge CB2 3DZ, United Kingdom
Email: db231@cam.ac.uk

DR. CHRIS FOWLER
School of Historical Studies
University of Newcastle Upon Tyne
Armstrong Building
Newcastle Upon Tyne NE1 7RU, United Kingdom
Email: c.j.fowler@ncl.ac.uk

DR. SUSAN GILLESPIE
Department of Anthropology
University of Florida
P.O. Box 117305
Gainsville, Florida 32611–7305, USA
Email: sgillesp@ufl.edu

PROFESSOR ROSEMARY JOYCE
Department of Anthropology
University of California, Berkeley
232 Kroeber Hall
Berkeley, California 94720–3710, USA
Email: rajoyce@berkeley.edu

DR. LAMBROS MALAFOURIS
McDonald Institute for Archaeological Research
University of Cambridge
Downing Street
Cambridge CB2 3ER, United Kingdom
Email: lm243@cam.ac.uk

DR. CAROLINE MALONE
School of Geography, Archaeology and
Palaeoecology
Elmwood Avenue
Queen's University
Belfast BT7 1NN United Kingdom
Email: c.malone@qub.ac.uk

DR. PRESTON MIRACLE
Department of Archaeology
University of Cambridge
Downing Street
Cambridge CB2 3DZ, United Kingdom
Email: ptm21@cam.ac.uk

SLOBODAN MITROVIĆ
Department of Anthropology
Graduate Center CUNY
365 Fifth Avenue
New York, NY 10016, USA
Email: smitrovic@gc.cuny.edu

PROFESSOR ROBIN OSBORNE
Faculty of Classics
University of Cambridge
Sidgwick Site
Cambridge CB3 9DA, United Kingdom
Email: ro225@cam.ac.uk

DR. KATHARINA REBAY
Department of Archaeology
University of Cambridge
Downing Street
Cambridge CB2 3DZ, United Kingdom
Email: kr302@cam.ac.uk

DR. JOHN ROBB
Department of Archaeology
University of Cambridge
Downing Street
Cambridge CB2 3DZ, United Kingdom
Email: jer39@cam.ac.uk

PROFESSOR NAN ROTHSCHILD
Department of Anthropology
Columbia University
452 Schermerhorn Extension
1200 Amsterdam Ave.
New York, New York 10027–7003, USA
Email: nar8@columbia.adu

DR. MARIE LOUISE STIG SØRENSEN
Department of Archaeology
University of Cambridge
Downing Street
Cambridge CB2 3DZ, United Kingdom
Email: mlss@cam.ac.uk

Dr. Simon Stoddart
Department of Archaeology
University of Cambridge
Downing Street
Cambridge CB2 3DZ, United Kingdom
Email: ss16@cam.ac.uk

Dr. Sarah Tarlow
School of Archaeology and Ancient History
University of Leicester
University Road
Leicester LE1 7RH, United Kingdom
Email: sat12@le.ac.uk

1

Body theory
in archaeology

Dušan Borić and John Robb

Context: A Nascent Archaeology of the Body

The body in archaeology is both omnipresent and invisible. Bodily matters are tangible in the archaeological record in a way most other theoretical centralities never appear to be. Ancient bodies surround us, in representations, in burials, in the nourished senses behind foodways, in hands holding tools, in the responsive presences centred within architecture and monuments. This omnipresence reflects both the position of the body in the centre ground of social theory and its materiality and concreteness.

Yet, invisibility: in spite of this, there is surprisingly little published work on the body in archaeology. Three traditions of study have raised this theme. The oldest is the art-historical study of how the body has been represented in the arts, particularly in Classical art. Secondly, critical discussion of the body is implicit in the tradition, now over two decades old, of gender and feminist archaeology, which problematises the relationship between the physical body and ascribed or performed genders. A decade more recently, the introduction of phenemonological thought to archaeology raised the issue of how experience is an embodied process and launched diverse lines of inquiry into the archaeology of the sensing body. Each of these has made important contributions, but they have remained bounded enclaves within archaeological theory, at odds with one another theoretically, and limited by their own purview. For example, prehistorians have generally repudiated the canonical study of body representations; approaches to the body deriving from feminism have rarely been extended even to questions of other dimensions of identity such as age (but see Gilchrist 2000; Moore and Scott 1997), and the phenomenological 'archaeology of the senses' remains focused upon a narrow range of prehistoric topics.

The 'body's career in archaeology' (to paraphrase Csordas 1999) remains shadowy and understated. There is increasing interest and a smattering of journal articles on the topic, but they tend to be disparate rather than integrated. Among book-length treatments, Rautman's edited *Reading the Body* (1999) and Montserrat's edited *Changing Bodies, Changing Meanings. Studies on the Human Body in Antiquity* (1998) are principally works on gender, and works such as Bailey's *Prehistoric Figurines* (2005) and Sofaer's *The Body as Material Culture* (2005) focus upon particular topics. Hamilakis, Pluciennik and Tarlow's *Thinking through the Body* (2001) provided a key introductory work, but one which has been undeservedly poorly circulated. Meskell and Joyce's co-authored *Embodied Lives* (2003) is the most prominent book-length treatment. It provides essential reading; yet it presents one of a number of possible theoretical viewpoints, and deals principally with questions of death and representation in high civilisations. Aside from this, there is remarkably little literature available upon what is increasingly widely acknowledged to be a key topic in current archaeological theory.

Different books serve our needs in different ways. To take an example, Gero and Conkey's *Engendering Archaeology* (1991) was a collection of disparate essays, some of which have stood the test of time better than others, and in many ways it has been superseded by more theoretically nuanced and in-depth studies. Yet, as the first widely read introduction to gender archaeology, it stimulated archaeological thought much more effectively than any monographic treatment presenting a single perspective with meticulous documentation and hair-splitting theoretical acuteness. Ten or fifteen years from now, the archaeology of the body will need the latter. What it needs now is something more broad, varied and synthetic, to provoke the imagination and map out new territories: something bringing together the diverse strands of an emerging perspective to provide a guide to the range of possibilities, both in terms of theoretical approach and methods. This is the purpose of this volume.[1]

Theorising Past Bodies

One may ask the following question: are physical bodies simply shells for the hidden true nature within, where the configuration of one's features masks the true person inside? Contrary to such a view, one of the great American novelists, Saul Bellow, argued for a refreshed phrenology, focusing, for instance, on the human head as characterological map. He describes the features of the body in a belief that human flesh has no secrets: the decay of one's body reads the decay of one's soul for Bellow. Marilyn Strathern once remarked that the body is a museum of one's life. And, one may add, bodies are also museums of long-term historical processes that continue to structure the conditions of social existence in every corner of the globe. It is true that the mere difference in facial features or the colour of one's skin or eyes in a very physical way structure the reality of social interactions. We may safely assume that in the past, social conditions of existence relied on the appearance and form of the corporeal body and meanings that gave rise to or rules and control that they were subject to.

Despite its apparent relevance, it is only in the last couple of decades that the body became one of the central theoretical topics of current sociological, philosophical and anthropological debates, strongly influencing certain strands of research in other related disciplines, including archaeology or the Classics. In this way, these fields of study through the newly chosen focal point – the body, serving as a sort of theoretical proxy – readdressed and recharged much older themes and debates, such as materialism, essentialism, subjectivity and self-identity, social basis of behaviour, ideology, social inequalities, sex/gender differences, etc. Yet, this peculiar discovery of the body by social theory in particular can closely be related to the wider cultural and political context of the present-day, described by some authors as late capitalist consumer society (Featherstone 1990, 1991) or high modernity (Giddens 1990). The increasing individualism of the present-day culture is centred around the body, as a

primary signifier, with its resultant commodification through the capitalist mode of production. The legitimate question hence is whether all this 'fuss about the body' (Bynum 1995) is a mere reflection of our current social and historical condition?

Two main strands of thought in body theory were previously identified as naturalistic and social constructionist views of the body. Both have been found guilty of either undermining the social reality in which the bodies are immersed as the case is with naturalistic approaches or by subjugating the physical body to the inescapable rule of discursive formations as with social constructionist approaches. Consequently, there have been attempts to transcend and overcome these naturalist and discursive essentialisms by stressing unfinishedness of the body at birth (Turner 1992), phenomenology of embodiment and lived experience (Csordas 1999; cf. Merleau-Ponty 1962; Turner 1984), processes of subjectification (Giddens 1991) and the need to take the coroporeality of the body seriously (Shilling 1993: *passim*).

We envision that the way this collection of works on past bodies may enrich the field of body theory is by looking at how the attitudes toward the body changed historically, focusing on both important differences and similarities in the ways embodied individuals lived their lives in particular historical and social contexts (e.g., Bynum 1995; Elias 1994; Meskell 2002).

Here, we would like to try identifying main trends for intellectual inspiration of archaeologists in their difficult task of tacking between, on the one hand, sophisticated theoretical nuances that various bodies of social theory and anthropology provide, and, on the other hand, the plenitude of not easily decipherable material and textual data that are the core edifice of our discipline. In this way, it becomes instructive to see the patterning of association between a particular type of theory and the quality of data for particular chronological periods at archaeologists' disposal. We will try to list specific bodies of theory that archaeologists working with particular chronological periods have found relevant and have utilised to date. We will also try to indicate briefly some possible shortcomings of certain approaches and to suggest what perspectives might have remained under-explored.

1) One social theorist that has appealed widely to archaeologists is Pierre Bourdieu (1990; see Bourdieu and Wacquant 1992). His concepts of *habitus*, i.e., ingrained practices that constitute a particular life-way on an infra-conscious level, and *doxa* for many archaeologists have had the immediacy of the familiar. After all, in an attempt to recognise particular patterns in the accumulative nature of the archaeological record, often

without elaborate mortuary or representational data, it is these ingrained daily practices that archaeologists remain hopeful in identifying as evidence for the existence of people's specific daily routines. The use of the notion of routinised, repeated bodily practices has had its application in diverse archaeological accounts that ranged from micromorphological analyses of building floors in the Near Eastern tells (e.g., Mathews *et al.* 1997) to discussions on the formation of self-identity among Bronze Age warriors (e.g., Treherne 1995). Yet, a critique of Bourdieu's notion of *doxa* as the main principle structuring the societies of the Ancients has been raised. It has been argued that it limits the understanding of pre-modern societies to the sets of highly scripted routines instead of exploring an active intention and agency (cf. Smith 2001). In Adam Smith's words, 'we must actively resist the construction of rigid boundaries that set the ancient apart from the modern as an ontologically distinct "other"' (Smith 2001: 157).

An additional aspect of Bourdieu's theory that remains attractive for archaeologists relates to the question of subjectification in the past as a historical trajectory of an ever-increasing emphasis on the bounded individual. Sociologists, such as Bourdieu and Giddens (1991), in their accounts build on the assumed differences between pre-modern, traditional societies and what Giddens calls 'high modernity'. In European Prehistory, Julian Thomas (1991: 142) and Paul Treherne (1995: 122) capitalise on this argument when postulating the change from identities more anchored in a social group than within an individual as characteristic of the Neolithic period, while arguing for a greater awareness about the bounded entity of an individual self in the Copper and Bronze Ages of European Prehistory. Without denying important diachronic changes in the processes of subjectification, Giddens's sharply postulated difference between moderns and pre-moderns regarding the notions of body, individuality and self-identity can again be subject to criticism for its rather essentialist and deterministic dichotomy of separating 'native' and 'modern' bodies. One might need to abandon altogether the search for the origins of individuation and subjectification, seeing no essential differences between moderns and pre-moderns (Berger 1990; Shilling 1993: 180). Even the typically rehearsed point about the Western idea of the boundedness of self is a rhetorically exaggerated, more apparent than real difference. Thus, in a Western society, similarly to various groups of 'pre-moderns,' one can identify figurations of mutually interdependent individuals (Elias 1994, 1983: 209). At the same time, to claim this is not to deny varying regimes of different cultural contexts in imposing boundaries to the constitution of

self and politics of individuation (e.g., Bynum 2001; papers in Lambek and Strathern 1998; Meskell 1996: 13).

Most recently, agency theory has strongly influenced a lot of archaeological writing about the conduct of past bodies (e.g., Dobres and Robb 2000). These discussions of agency in archaeology can again be traced back to the writings of Bourdieu (1990) but also Giddens (1979) and previous philosophical writings on intentionality and free-will subject. The predicament of cause-effect in agency theory has important moral implications for the accountability of the agent. Yet, in archaeology, the agenda of agency theory has been appropriated in emphasising the importance of acting individuals and their relations to dominant structures, which individuals are shaped by and which they create at the same time. Agency theory has helped archaeologists in discussing practical engagements in the world as well as in the analytical dissection of the scale on which agency of subjects may operate: from an individual to the agency of social groups and the material world that surrounds us. And, it is exactly the question of materiality that has most recently been discussed in relation to the body and material things, while one anthropological work has played an especially important role: *Art and Agency* by Alfred Gell (1998). Although Gell was concerned primarily with art objects and the idea of their agency, his discussion became a seminal work for discussing the agency of objects and material culture in general. Can material things have agency (and intentionality) or only second-class agency via a mediating subject as argued by Gell? Should the term be confined strictly to the acting (human?) subject? Can animals be said to have human-equivalent agency? All these questions depend on a particular ontological perspective. Very often, recent discussions of agency theory in archaeology have conflated two quite separate ideas of agency and intentionality: our own Western ontology of intentionality and agency, on the one hand, and quite diverse ontologies of the non-Western peoples and possibly also those human groups who inhabited the past, on the other hand. In order to understand what might have harmed, cured, affected, pleased or killed bodies in the past we need to search for and reconstruct specific ontologies of intentionality and agency in our case-studies. Only in this way will we understand in what ways were bodies in the past lived and died.

2) Another critical influence for the way in which (mainly) prehistoric archaeologists discuss the body in the past are ethnographic and anthropological studies. The most influential in this respect has been the work of Marilyn Strathern in Melanesia, to the point that the warnings have been raised that the

personhood in European Prehistory, and Neolithic in particular, acquired 'a Melanesian flavour' (Jones 2005: 195)! Several recent accounts probe various bodies of archaeological data with Strathern's (1988) and Roy Wagner's (1991) concepts of *dividual* and *fractal* persons (e.g., Fowler 2004; Chapman 2000). This is certainly the most useful way to defamiliarise characteristically Western conception of the bounded individual. Yet, here as well one may raise the critique that the difference between the West and its 'others' is frequently overemphasised. Both individuality and dividuality are properties of humans and, as LiPuma argues, '*persons emerge precisely from that tension between individual and dividual aspects/relations*' (LiPuma 1998: 57).

3) The next significant influence for many archaeologists in discussing past bodies is of course Michael Foucault. In his earlier writings, Foucault envisions past bodies as mere social constructions of a historically dominant *episteme* that strongly governs individual lives (Foucault 1970). In those accounts that adopted this kind of social constructionist position in archaeology, the body is seen as a passive tool of control over the society. It is merely a means for the playing out of larger structures that deliver fixed meanings: 'the *body as artefact*' and 'the *body as the scene of display*' as Lynn Meskell argues (1996: 6–7, 1998). In such accounts of past bodies all one encounters are 'faceless blobs' to use Ruth Tringham's catchphrase (1991). And social constructionist accounts of past bodies in archaeology have been presented frequently along with a Marxian conception of ideology as false consciousness.

It is only fair to remember that in his later writings, Foucault himself turned to the question of subject by discussing techniques of the self and care for the self (Foucault 1985, 1986, 1988). It is the appropriate conduct in terms of the techniques of the self that he identified as critical for moral existence. Body is central in this context as well as individual and social agency. This concept of the techniques of self is based on the ancient Greek conception of *paraskeuē*, i.e., equipment that aids one when 'confronting and coping with external events and internal passions' (cf. Rabinow 2005: 10). For instance, in his discussion of the constitution of Bronze Age warriors' identity through specific practices, the use of particular types of artefacts for the care of the body, and in the development of a particular ethos, Paul Treherne (1995) identifies such practices of the care for self within the European Bronze Age. And such an approach may have a great applicability across various archaeological case studies.

4) The perspective that dominates more recent accounts about the body in the past and tries to rectify the inadequacies of the social constructionist perspectives focuses on *embodiment*, i.e., the way people lived their lives in the past (see Csordas 1999). Such paradigm belongs to the phenomenological tradition of thought and can be traced to the writings of Merleau-Ponty (1962). The paradigm of embodiment in the discussion of lived bodies in archaeology has most explicitly been applied recently by Lynn Meskell in the context of dynastic Egypt and by Rosemary Joyce in the Mesoamerican context (Joyce 1996; Meskell 1999, 2002; Meskell and Joyce 2003). These authors combine both archaeological and textual data in their analyses, something not always easily done in prehistoric case studies. This approach also evokes aspects of performative and gender theory as discussed by Judith Butler (1990, 1993) and Elizabeth Grosz (1994). The embodiment paradigm in archaeology certainly helps put faces on those previously mentioned 'faceless blobs' from the past and it importantly resonates with the concerns of third wave feminism for underprivileged sites of inquiry, be it the lives of children, disabled and other 'etceteras' of ordinary life (e.g., Gilchrist 2000; Moore and Scott 1997), trading grand narratives for microhistories (cf. Ginzburg 1993; Lyotard 1984). Yet, it could be that the paradigm of embodiment also suffers from its share of methodological problems. For instance, one could say that through the paradigm of embodiment, the *stability* is preferred to the *processuality* of bodily configurations. The individual frequently remains constituted in advance with a given set of parameters.

5) Voices of Americanists that work with Amazonian ethnography, for instance, warn against 'human exceptionalism' that predominates in the paradigm of embodiment. What Amazonian ethnography evokes is the idea of instability of bodies that are constructed as 'relational configurations', where the self-image is reshaped through constant processuality that characterises social reality (Taylor 1996; Viveiros de Casto 1998, 2004). The defining feature between different classes of animate and inanimate beings is, then, the capacity for metamorphosis (Vilaça 2005; cf. Ingold 2000a, 2000b). Such perspective acknowledges an unstable reality of perpetual change that affects both the bodies of humans, animals, and other-than human beings.

This conceptualisation of unstable and shifting physical bodies that are perpetually threatened and prone to change may not be only the feature of Amazonian ethnography. Several archaeological discussions that focus on the mutability of the body form and its relation to social identity have primarily come from the scholars working on prehistoric societies (Borić 2005; Conneller 2004; Miracle and Borić this volume; Yates 1990) or those working on social contexts rich in iconography, added by written sources (e.g., Meskell and Joyce 2003). The theme runs in many other cultural and chronological contexts. For instance, the fear of metamorphosis and instability of the body form has been explored by Caroline Walker Bynum in the context of medieval Europe, the topic present in popular fables about werewolves around the year AD 1300 as well as in the theological discussions of St. Augustine whose teachings strongly denied the existence of such transformations (Bynum 2001). The same theme also appears in the modernist age, in the work of Franz Kafka, who calls the emergent cough that led to his death, the 'animal' inside (Benjamin 1968: 132). Kafka remains obsessed with the transformation from human form into the state of animality, i.e., death.

It is not here the place to explore this subject further, but we use it to emphasise the point that instead of drawing only on differences between specific periods of the past in conceptualising and theorising bodies, one may also change the perspective and explore what themes and ways of conceptualising the body remain the same across social, cultural and temporally distinct contexts. Furthermore, for specific regional traditions, or 'culture areas', we may also explore the long-term persistence of specific ways of living and caring about one's body, similar to the parallels that Michael Rowlands (1998) makes between the traditional focus on the body through metaphors of protection and feeding and bodily practices in legitimising power of current political leaders in sub-Saharan Africa.

In sum, a number of accounts that focus on the past bodies by both social theorists and those archaeologists who make the use of existing aspects of specific sociological and anthropological bodies of theory have been focusing on drawing differences in the construction of bodies between different periods in the past, and between the past and the present. And, there is no doubt about the importance of such studies to understand the variability of bodily practices for the construction of specific identities in the past and the present. However, too frequently these accounts have drawn sharp demarcation lines between what is considered the conditions of 'modern' social reality and those of pre-modern, traditional, pre-industrial societies, arguing for radically different ways of being a person on different ends of this rather arbitrary temporal barrier. We would suggest that we perhaps also need to focus on those aspects of body, identity and processes of subjectification that represent a common tread between different epochs. Thus, can we suggest some joint themes and provide a fruitful comparative perspective? Furthermore, can we follow specific trajectories of attitudes toward the body in specific regional contexts, focusing both on changes

and similarities that become apparent in the treatment of one's body in life and death over the long-term?

The purpose and organisation of the book

The articles in this volume span the entire range of human societies from the hunter-gatherers of the Upper Palaeolithic through modern British populations. The bulk of them refer to the European sequence, but there are important discussions of Near Eastern, North American and Mesoamerican cases as well. The variety of the volume has three important theoretical implications. First, it underscores the productive richness of the concept of the body in archaeology. Secondly, it shows that the archaeology of the body is not the monopoly of a single province of archaeology, particularly the data-rich neighbourhoods. A major barrier to every theoretical advance in the last twenty-five years has been the prejudice, still widely current, that 'theory (or symbols, or gender, or agency, or social relations, or ritual experience…) are all very well, but you can only do them where you have texts (or pyramids, or figurines, or megaliths….) – not in my field'. By introducing the archaeology of the body with case studies spanning the range of human societies and archaeological situations, we make it more likely that an interested seeking analytical strategies will find something useful to her/his particular situation. Finally, it means that papers articulate with, and juxtapose, a range of theoretical approaches within archaeology and cognate disciplines which have been associated with particular topics such as the Aegean Bronze Age, Classical sculpture or Mesoamerican political iconography.

The volume is organised into four sections, which group papers by general themes or approach in order to draw attention to cross-disciplinary linkages. The first section presents introductory or general perspectives; the goal is to mark out the landscape for readers new to the topic. It includes this general introduction to social theories of the body and an overview of relevant archaeological methodologies. The second section presents studies of the represented body and the third studies of the body in death; it is hoped that such groupings will help readers see both commonalities and divergences in how the body has been approached in different traditions of archaeology, history and art history. The final section contains studies which cut across traditional domains of study such as representation and burial and focus upon the socially contextualised body at particular historical moments. In the end, critical notes on the field are provided by Chris Shilling.

Note

1   This volume is a collection of essays resulting from two symposia. Both were held under the auspices of the Leverhulme Research Programme 'Changing Beliefs of the Human Body.' This research programme, based at Cambridge University, brings together researchers in Archaeology, Anthropology, Classics and History to compare studies of how beliefs and practices involving the human body changed at key points in human history from the Palaeolithic through the present. Both symposia involved a stimulating mixture of programme participants and outside speakers. The first, 'Past Bodies,' was held in Cambridge on January 13, 2006. The second, 'Acting and Believing: An Archaeology of Bodily Practices', was held at the Society for American Archaeology meetings at San Juan, Puerto Rico, on April 4, 2006. Not all of the oral presentations reached this volume. Yet, we are grateful to the participants of both symposia for their active and stimulating discussions, which are to some degree represented on the pages that follow.

Bibliography

Benjamin, W. 1968. *Illuminations*. New York: Schocken Books.

Berger, P. 1990. *The Sacred Canopy. Elements of a Sociological Theory of Religion*. New York: Anchor Books.

Borić, D. 2005. Body metamorphosis and animality: volatile bodies and boulder artworks from Lepenski Vir. *Cambridge Archaeological Journal* 15(1): 35–69.

Bourdieu, P. 1990. *The Logic of Practice*. Cambridge: Polity Press

Bourdieu, P. and Wacquant, L.J.D. 1992. *An Invitation to Reflexive Sociology*. Chicago: University of Chicago Press.

Butler, J. 1990. *Gender Trouble: Feminism and the Subversion of Identity*. London: Routledge.

Butler, J. 1993. *Bodies that Matter: On the Discursive Limits of 'Sex'*. London: Routledge

Bynum, C. 1995. Why all the fuss about the body. *Critical Inquiry* 22: 1–33.

Bynum, C.W. 2001. *Metamorphosis and Identity*. New York: Zone Books.

Bailey, D. 2005. *Prehistoric Figurines*. London: Routledge.

Chapman, J.C. 2000. *Fragmentation in Archaeology. People, Places and Broken Objects in the Prehistory of South-eastern Europe*. London: Routledge.

Conneller, C. 2004. Becoming deer: Corporeal transformations at Star Carr. *Archaeological Dialogues* 11(1): 37–56.

Csordas, T.J. 1999. The body's career in anthropology. In *Anthropological Theory Today*, edited by H. Moore, pp. 172–205. Cambridge: Polity.

Dobres, A-M. and Robb, J. (eds) 2000. *Agency in Archaeology*. London: Routledge.

Elias, N. 1994. *The Civilizing Process: The History of Manners and State Formation and Civilization*. Oxford: Basil Blackwell.

Featherstone, M. 1990. *Consumer Culture and Postmodernism*. London: Sage Publications.

Featherstone, M. 1991. The body in consumer culture. In *The Body: Social Process and Cultural Theory*, edited by M. Featherstone, M. Hepworth and B. Turner, pp. 170–196. London: Sage Publications.

Foucault, M. 1970. *The Order of Things. An Archaeology of the Human Sciences*. London: Routledge.

Foucault, M. 1985. *The Use of Pleasure: The History of Sexuality*, vol. 2. London: Penguin Books.

Foucault, M. 1986. *The Care of the Self: The History of Sexuality*, vol. 3. London: Penguin Books.

Foucault, M. 1988. Technologies of the self. In *Technologies of the Self: A Seminar with Michel Foucault*, edited by L.H. Martin, H. Gutman, and P.H. Hutton, pp. 16–49. London: Tavistock.

Fowler, C. 2004. *The Archaeology of Personhood: An Anthropological Approach*. London: Routledge.

Gell, A. 1998. *Art and Agency. An Anthropological Theory*. Oxford: Clarendon Press.

Gero, J. and Conkey, M. (eds) 1991. *Engendering Archaeology: Women and Prehistory*. Oxford: Blackwell.

Giddens, A. 1979. *Central Problems in Social Theory: Action, Structure and Contradiction in Social Analysis*. Berkeley: University of California Press.

Giddens, A. 1990. *The Consequences of Modernity*. Cambridge: Polity Press.

Giddens, A. 1991. *Modernity and Self-Identity*. Cambridge: Polity Press.

Gilchrist, R. (ed.) 2000. *Human Lifecycles/World Archaeology* 31(3). London: Routledge.

Ginzburg, C. 1993. *The Cheese and the Worms*. Baltimore: Johns Hopkins University Press.

Grosz, E. 1994. *Volatile Bodies: Toward a Corporeal Feminism*. Bloomington: Indiana University Press.

Hamilakis, Y., Pluciennik, M. and Tarlow, S. 2001. *Thinking through the Body. Archaeologies of Corporeality*. New York: Kluwer Academic/Plenum Publishers.

Ingold, T. 2000a. A circumpolar night's dream. In *The Perception of the Environment. Essays on Livelihood, Dwelling and Skill*, edited by T. Ingold, pp. 89–110. London: Routledge.

Ingold, T. 2000b. Totemism, animism and the depiction of animals. In *The Perception of the Environment. Essays on Livelihood, Dwelling and Skill*, edited by T. Ingold, pp. 111–131. London: Routledge.

Jones, A. 2005. Lives in fragments? Personhood and the European Neolithic. *Journal of Social Archaeology* 5(2): 193–224.

Joyce, R.A. 1996. The construction of gender in Classic Maya monuments. In *Gender and Archaeology*, edited by R.P. Wright, pp. 167–195. Philadelphia: University of Pennsylvania Press.

Lambek, M. and Strathern, A. (eds) 1998. *Bodies and Persons. Comparative Perspectives from Africa and Melanesia*. Cambridge: Cambridge University Press.

LiPuma, E. 1998. Modernity and forms of personhood in Melanesia. In *Bodies and Persons: Comparative Perspectives from Africa and Melanesia*, edited by M. Lambek and A. Strathern, pp. 53–80. Cambridge: Cambridge University Press.

Lyotard, J.-F. 1984. *The Postmodern Condition: A Report on Knowledge*. Minneapolis: University of Minnesota Press.

Matthews, W., French, C., *et al.* 1997. Microstratigraphic traces of site formation processes and human activities. *World Archaeology* 29 (2): 281–308.

Merleau-Ponty, M. 1962. *The Phenomenology of Perception*. London: Routledge and Kegan Paul.

Meskell, L. 1996. The Somatization of archaeology: institutions, discourses, corporeality. *Norwegian Archaeological Review* 29(1): 1–16.

Meskell, L.M. 1998. The irresistible body and the seduction of archaeology. In *Changing Bodies, Changing Meanings. Studies on the Human Body in Antiquity*, edited by D. Montserrat, pp. 139–161. London: Routledge.

Meskell, L.M. 1999. *Archaeologies of Social Life: Age, Sex, Class, etc. in Ancient Egypt*. Oxford: Blackwell.

Meskell, L.M. 2002. *Private Life in New Kingdom Egypt*. Princeton, NJ: Princeton University Press.

Meskell, L.M. and Joyce, R.A. 2003. *Embodied Lives: Figuring Ancient Maya and Egyptian experience*. London: Routledge.

Montserrat, D. (ed) 1998. *Changing Bodies, Changing Meanings. Studies on the Human Body in Antiquity*. London: Routledge.

Moore, J. and Scott, E. (eds) 1997. *Invisible People and Processes: Writing Gender and Childhood into European Archaeology*. London: Leicester University Press.

Rabinow, P. 2003. *Anthropos Today. Reflections on Modern Equipment*. Princeton and Oxford: Princeton University Press.

Rautman, A.E. (ed) 1999. *Reading the Body. Representations and Remains in the Archaeological Record*. Philadelphia: University of Pennsylvania Press.

Rowlands, M. 1998. The embodiment of sacred power in Cameroon Grassfields. In *Social Transformations in Archaeology. Global and Local Perspectives*, edited by K. Kristiansen and M. Rowlands, pp. 410–428. London: Routledge.

Smith, A.T. 2001. The limitations of doxa: Agency and subjectivity from an archaeological point of view. *Journal of Social Archaeology* 1(2): 155–171.

Shilling, C. 1993. *The Body and Social Theory*. London: Sage Publications.

Sofaer, J.R. 2005. *The Body as Material Culture: A Theoretical Osteoarchaeology*. Cambridge: Cambridge University Press.

Strathern, M. 1998. *The Gender of the Gift. Problems with Women and Problems with Society in Melanesia*. Berkeley: The University of California Press.

Taylor, A.C. 1996. The soul's body and its states: An Amazonian perspective on the nature of being human. *Journal of the Royal Anthropological Institute* (N.S.) 2: 201–15.

Thomas, J. 1991. *Rethinking the Neolithic*. Cambridge: Cambridge University Press.

Treherne, P. 1995. The warrior's beauty: the masculine body and self-identity in Bronze-Age Europe. *Journal of European Archaeology* 3(1): 105–44.

Tringham, R.E. 1991. Households with faces: The challenge of gender in prehistoric architectural remains. In *Engendering Archaeology: Women and Prehistory*, edited by J. Gero and M. Conkey, pp. 93–131. Oxford: Blackwell.

Turner, B.S. 1984. *The Body and Society. Explorations in Social Theory*. Oxford: Basil Blackwell.

Turner, B.S. 1991. Recent developments in the theory of the body. In *The Body: Social Processes and Cultural Theory*, edited by M. Featherstone, M. Hepworth and B. Turner. London: Sage Publications.

Turner, B.S. 1992. *Regulating Bodies*. London: Routledge.

Vilaça, A. 2002. Making kin out of others in Amazonia. *Journal of the Royal Anthropological Institute* (N.S.) 8: 347–65.

Vilaça, A. 2005. Chronically unstable bodies: Reflections on Amazonian corporalities. *Journal of the Royal Anthropological Institute* (N.S.) 11: 445–64.

Viveiros de Castro, E. 1998. Cosmological deixis and Amerindian perspectivism. *Journal of the Royal Anthropological Institute* (N.S.) 4: 469–88.

Viveiros de Castro, E. 2004. Perspectival anthropology and the method of controlled equivocation. *Tipití* 2(1): 3–22.

Wagner, R. 1991. The fractal person. In *Big Men and Great Men: Personifications of Power in Melanesia*, edited by M. Strathern and M. Godelier, pp. 159–173. Cambridge: Cambridge University Press.

Yates, T. 1990. Archaeology through the looking-glass. In *Archaeology after Structuralism. Post-Structuralism and the Practice of Archaeology*, edited by I. Bapty and T. Yates, pp. 154–202. London: Routledge.

2

The corporeal politics
of being in the Neolithic

Douglass Bailey

Introduction

From the middle of the sixth to the middle of the fifth millennium cal BC, in a region straddling the Danube in southern Romania and northern Bulgaria, small communities of people lived a partially settled life, herding, farming and gathering, burying their dead in cemeteries (investing disproportionate amounts of energy and objects in the burials of certain individuals), and making occasional, short-term use of insubstantial architecture (small semi-subterranean pit-houses or surface level buildings).[1] These lives were lived against the background of a jumble of created and curated material culture (pots, jewellery, bone and stone tools), refuse and discard, interventions into nature (hunted, conserved, bred, slaughtered animals; collected and cultivated plants), varying environmental conditions (topographies, hydrologies, climates), innumerable, brief unrecorded, unrecoverable conversations, arguments and agreements, and the silent looks and glances, sneers, grumbles and groans that constitute human sociality. In among this clutter of bits and pieces of daily life (of ceremony and routine), the most archaeologically obvious engagements with the human body are the ways that it was treated after death and the ways in which it was modelled in clay.[2] While discussions of the funerary ceremonies of this region have proposed reconstructions of social structure and demography, they offer very little insight into the role of the body in daily life. Compared to the inhumation of dead bodies within ostentatious, explicitly charged community ceremonies, anthropomorphic figurines work in a very different way, saturating daily life and regularly presenting people with tangible and viewable representations of the human body.[3]

In other regions at this time, people lived in similar ways, though with easily recognisable, minor differences in the specific material manifestations of living; variations in pottery design and decoration are two, well studied examples; the morphology of figurines is another. As with ceramic form and decoration (and undoubtedly with many more ephemeral activities, behaviours, customs and styles of being), the figurines produced in this region of the lower Danube have a particular form which sets them apart from fired clay representations made in other parts of southeastern Europe. Most characteristic are their bulbous body morphology (almost pneumatic), the absence (in almost every case) of faces or heads, and the limited descriptive detail of the body surface. When we look at these figurines, what do we see? Are we looking, as Marija Gimbutas (1982, 1989, 1991) and many others have claimed, at goddesses or gods or participants in cultic ceremonies? Are we looking at portraits of the people who made these objects or representations of particular members of a community?

When I look at or handle these figurines, I am struck by the similarity of body morphology, of inflated torsos, of long triangular necks, of heads and faces never modelled. Though no two figurines are exactly alike, a common corporeal morphology is repeated through most of them. The variation that is present in the region's figurine inventory is limited and local specialists are content in their three-part categorisation based on body position (Berciu 1966; Haşotti 1985, 1986, 1997; Vajsov 1987, 1992a, 1992b). If these figurines are representations of people, then they are representations of a very few people. If they are of goddesses or gods, then the pantheon is very exclusive indeed. How should

we understand these figurines? Should we think about deities, of people, or of some more expansive concept which might inform on local people's perceptions of themselves and of the world and people that surround them?

Understanding figurines

Figurines stimulate people (modern and Neolithic) to think and, especially, to draw inferences about themselves and about other people.[4] Part of the facility of figurine-as-stimulus-to-think is borne from the enabling processes of miniaturisation. In many cases, the making of something small includes a process of abstraction: the reduction of size accompanied by the reduction of the number of features represented. Important (though perhaps subconscious) decisions are made about what should be included in the reduced representations and what should not be reproduced.

As miniature representations, figurines encourage their prehistoric (and modern) spectators to draw inferences about what is not represented, of what is absent. This process of representational absence is important and complex and draws on the psychoanalysis of loss (of Lacan 1973 and Freud 1899) and the experimental psychology of Richard Gregory (especially his work on illusions and the efforts that the human brain makes in trying to understand visual illusions [Gregory 1968, 1980, 1997]) (Bailey 2007).

One of the consequences of representational absence, and indeed of working with miniatures in general, is that when people make, look at and handle miniature representations, they gain access to other worlds. For example, when the contemporary artist Michael Ashkin describes what happens to him when he works on his miniature landscape art, he speaks about a narcotic effect which allows him access to other places beyond the here and now of his workshop or gallery. Similar effects are familiar to people who tend *bonsai* trees, or who work on highly detailed reduced scale models of boats and trains (Bailey 2005: 33–4). In a series of extraordinary experiments, the psychologist and architect Alton Delong showed that when subjects played computer games on small television screens or imagined themselves to be in miniature buildings, the subjects' brain activities changed; people played better, brains processed more information more quickly, and their perceptions of time changed; time appeared to pass more quickly when people imagined themselves in miniature places (Delong 1981, 1983). In brief, therefore, when people engage the miniature, they gain access to other worlds and alternative realities.

When we define Neolithic figurines in terms of miniaturisation, abstraction and absence, and then add the rhetorical potency that representations of the human body possess (e.g., dolls), we move the debate some distance beyond traditional anecdotal explanations which limit interpretation to untestable suggestions of figurine function (e.g., goddess, votive, doll). I have argued at length elsewhere that we are better to understand figurines as philosophies, as objects that make people question who they are, what they look like, how they are similar to some but different from others (Bailey 2005). Can we say anything more about this philosophising? Can we be more specific about what thoughts people were having and about who was doing the thinking? What ideas were being stimulated and what do these thoughts tell us about the particularities of living (and the people who were living) in southeastern Europe during the Neolithic? One potentially fruitful way to attack these questions is to think about Neolithic figurines in terms of the concept of stereotypes and the process of stereotyping.

Stereotypes

What are stereotypes, what is stereotyping, and how might a knowledge of stereotyp(ing) contribute to a better understanding of Neolithic figurines? Commonly invoked in a negative sense when linked to racist and bigoted opinion, stereotypes get a very bad press. A deeper understanding reveals the concept as a potent interpretive tool for thinking about social interaction.[5] In simplest terms, stereotypes are conventional, formulaic and oversimplified conceptions or images which propose a set of fixed, unvarying ways to understand the world around us. Founded on simplification, generalisation, exaggeration or distortion, stereotypes (re)present cultural attributes as natural essences. As simplified representations, they conform to fixed morphologies and smooth otherwise naturally occurring irregularities. Used in social psychology and psychiatry, the concept plays on its Ancient Greek referents (*stereos* meaning rigid, and *tupos* meaning trace) and applies to the frequent, mechanical repetition of the same gesture, posture or speech that is symptomatic of disorders like *dementia praecox* (Leyens *et al.* 1994: 9).

At the broader level of social psychology, stereotypes are implicit in human nature and human sociality. They are critical tools with which people make sense of the world around them and of their relations with others whom they encounter, interact with and are dependent on (McGarty *et al.* 2002b: 198). As the material of shared beliefs, stereotypes propose and confirm relations between groups. By regulating diverse individual perceptions, they smooth social interaction and ensure group survival (Leyens *et al.* 1994: viii, 3, 13, 19). Stereotypes work within people's conceptions of what is normal or natural. They are part of the ways in which communities create and sustain a shared sense of the proper limits of what is accepted as legitimate and right. Stereotypes enable the construction of social groups by maintaining and reproducing the norms and conventions of behaviour, identity and value (Picking 2001: xiv, 5). People see themselves sharing the same characteristics and perceptions with others in their group; thus stereotypes enable people to make sense of the world in a particular way (Leyens *et al.* 1994: 18, 71).

Stereotypes as generalisations and fictions

Stereotypes are lazy devices that linger on the surfaces of phenomena (Leyens *et al.* 1994: 92). They generalise, smooth, simplify, arrest and fix. They reduce complexity down to artificial categories and make different individuals interchangeable. They smooth and hide

ambivalences. As the psychologist Michael Pickering puts it, stereotypes categorise people and in doing so they 'evacuate the specific historicality' of individual events, thoughts and behaviours (Pickering 2001: 43, 45). In these senses, stereotypes are fictions and illusions. They do not record reality, but create a record of constructed perceptions within existing relations of power(s) and of order(s). Though stereotypes give the impression of precision (through their exploitation of processes of categorisation), such precision is nothing more than an illusion (Pickering 2001: 1–4).

In addition, stereotypes are energy-savers. They help people handle and understand the extraordinary complexity of perceiving the world about them; they help people process information efficiently (Allport 1954; Hamilton 1981; McGarty *et al.* 2002a: 4; and see McGarty 1999). They are efficient devices through which people distinguish themselves from others. The judgements and expressions of difference which construct and thus project distinction between groups

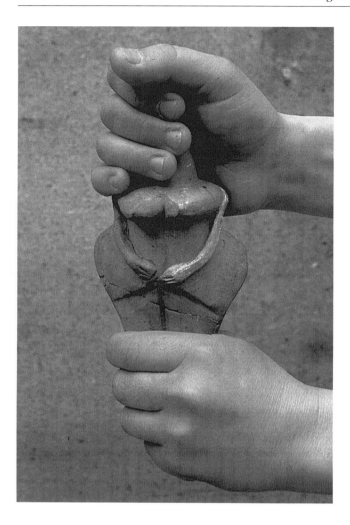

(between us and them) are expressions and orderings of power (Pickering 2001: 5).

Stereotypic illusion imposes a sense of order on otherwise unordered social worlds. Stereotypes seek to deny the existence of flexibility of thought and of judgement which flows in and around categories of people (Pickering 2001: 43). To similar degrees, stereotypic illusion contributes to human understanding of many dimensions of life: of places (i.e., the country-side, the wild, the urban, Germany), of things (meat, vegetables, beer), of emotions (anger, grief, lust), and, most especially, of people (us, them). Critically, stereotypes prevail when distinctions and order are otherwise unstable (Pickering 2001: 43). This is a wonderful paradox; the clearest impressions (i.e., stereotypic illusions) of stability and categorisation hide the greatest instabilities, fluidities and flexibilities. Stereotypes are the thin veneer that covers the raw chip-board of reality. They obscure the ceaseless,

tumultuous making of the world. By injecting a purifying essence into reality, stereotypes interfere with the continuous transformations of social reality. Stereotypes fossilise people's thinking about the Other and exclude alternative ways of seeing and understanding, and the resulting inflexibility soothes and comforts people and reinforces their beliefs that the existing relations of power are necessary and fixed (Pickering 2001: 3, 43).

Stereotypes are especially potent for understanding the relationships among different groups of people. In 1970, the social psychologist Henri Tajfel carried out what has become a seminal experiment on inter-group behaviour, particularly on the ways that people who belong to one group view people belonging to other groups and, most importantly, how people privilege the members of their own group at the expense of members of other groups (1970). In his study Tajfel divided up a group of 64 boys from a comprehensive school in Bristol into groups of eight; though he told the boys that membership in the different groups was based on each boy's achievement in a test that Tajfel had set for them, the creation of the study groups was entirely random. Once established in their separate groups, the boys were presented with a series of options by which they could award benefits (money) either to all boys in all groups or only to boys in their own group. Significantly, the boys choose to award benefits to boys who were members of their own groups at the expense of boys who were members of the other groups. Furthermore, comparison of the total amount of benefit accumulated by individual boys showed, first, small distinctions within one's own group (boys awarded the individual members of their groups similar amounts) and, second, large distinctions between one's own group and each of the other groups. Tajfel's study probed the mechanics of intergroup behaviour and demonstrated that one of the most power factors affecting a person's perception of other people was that person's membership in a group which s/he had been told or shown to be distinct from the members of other groups.

Sitting in a longer tradition starting with Allport (1954) and then accelerating in the 1970s and 1980s (see reviews by Hamilton *et al.* 1990; Hamilton and Mackie 1993: 2; Messick and Mackie 1989), Tajfel's work demonstrated that one of the most important reasons for inter-group discrimination could be found in nothing more complex than the categorisation of individuals into groups, even when group membership was nothing more than the random assignment of an individual to a group. Of importance in this debate is the recognition that stereotypes often form and are employed to distinguish between a group that a person belongs to (i.e., the ingroup) and a second group which has a different membership (i.e., the outgroup). Furthermore, not only do people direct benefits more regularly to members of their own group (as Tajfel's seminal study suggested), but they also tend to view outgroups in less favourable terms than those with which they view their ingroup (Doise *et al.* 1972; Haslam *et al.* 2002: 159; Tajfel 1969, 1981).

Understood as fictions, as interruptions of reality, and as judgements on difference and distinction, intergroup distinctions which employ stereotypes reveal very little (if any) information about the group, person, place, or thing that is the target of stereotyping (the outgroup). The perception and representation that a member of the ingroup make of the outgroup are products of the ingroup alone and need have little relation to the ways that other groups see that outgroup or to the way in which members of the outgroup see themselves. It follows, then that a study of the stereotyping (and stereotypic representations) provides vital important information about the group doing the stereotyping, specifically about ingroup insecurities, fears, concerns, and world-views. Following this logic, the group represented through the stereotype (i.e., the outgroup) has no objective reality outside of the perceptions and projections of the ingroup. Significantly then, to study stereotypes is to study those who are creating the stereotypes and not those who are being stereotyped.

The rhetoric of stereotypes

What is the rhetoric of a stereotype? What is it about them that makes them succeed in the ways that they do to create distinctions between groups? Stereotypes propose relations through representation and they do this through any available informative media (spoken, material, representational). Stereotypes are manifest in everyday objects; their regular, routine and repeated presences in daily life contribute to their rhetorical success. Stereotypic representation need not be intended as stereotypic, but can emerge as consequence and contingency. Stereotypes form most easily at the level of the common place and emerge most powerfully through what is taken for granted (Leyens *et al.* 1994: 45). Importantly, the illusionary realities which stereotypes construct gain strength through iteration; people treat a repeated and consistent set of information as if it were part of an original authentic reality (Leyens *et al.* 1994: 42). Through (re)-iterations of an emergent set of relations, people fashion a sense of belonging in the world; people position themselves along descriptive dimensions of differentiation. In addition, successful stereotypes are consensual: they are shared beliefs.

They are not merely impressions that one person holds of others, but they are impressions that are held and shared by a group of people (Haslam 1997; Haslam *et al.*1996a, 1996b, 1998, 2002; McGarty *et al* 2002a; Reicher *et al.* 1997).

Furthermore, stereotypic expressions of difference and similarity most often reduce to the isolation of variation of body action or body morphology. Stereotypes work best on physical characteristics, though they also work well on behaviour (Brewer 1988; Leyens *et al.* 1994: 20); of course behaviour can be defined as nothing more than recognisable patterns of bodily movement. Stereotypes succeed as visual manifestations, particularly when they feed on the appearances of the body, body morphology, surface politics of the body, and social dramas in which the body plays a central role. Though representations of the body are not the only media that contribute to the production and reproduction of the body, they are one of the most powerful (Pickering 2001: 32).

Outgroup homogeneity

As noted, stereotypes work through generalisation and oversimplification. In particular, stereotype formation discourages the recognition or accurate reproduction of variability among the individuals within a stereotyped group, most clearly in the perception of outgroups (Judd and Park 1988; Linville *et al.* 1986, 1990; Park and Rothbart 1982; Quatronne and Jones 1980; Wilder 1984). As Steven Stroessner and Diane Mackie put it, an important part of stereotype formation is the stripping out of variability from outgroups (Stroessner and Mackie 1993: 64; see also Linville *et al.* 1986; Park and Hastie 1987; Park and Judd 1990). Stereotypic representation of outgroups under-represents the actual variation that exists within that outgroup and thus creates false representations of outgroup homogeneity (and indeed this can be seen in Tajfel's Bristol study where the distinction between the awards made to individuals in the outgroups was significantly lower than the variation between awards made to in- and outgroups). What causes this inaccurate representation of outgroups as homogenous?

Studying the ways in which people who belong to the ingroup perceive members of an outgroup, Stoessner and Mackie have shown that the moods of the people doing the perceiving affect the accuracy of their perceptions of an outgroup's internal variability (Stoessner and Mackie1992, 1993). Stoessner and Mackie have documented important differences in the perceptions formed by neutral-mood people when compared with perceptions formed by people either with positive-moods (happy) or negative-moods (sad). In the Stroessner and Mackie study, groups of subjects were shown one of three movies: a comedy (positive/happy); a documentary about child cancer (negative/sad); and a programme about putting corks in wine bottles (neutral). Subjects were then given descriptions of men whose behaviours either were very similar (men doing similar things in similar ways for similar reasons) or were very heterogeneous (doing a wider range of things in a wider range of ways for a wider range of reasons). The subjects were then asked to rate the similarity of the men from these groups. Stroessner and Mackie analysed the subjects' perceptions of similarity among the men and compared the perceptions formed by subjects who were happy, who were sad, and who were mood-neutral.

If the mood of the subject had had no affect on the subject's perception of the variation in the men's behaviour, then one would have expected there not to have been any significant differences among the three mood groups in their perceptions of the homogeneous or heterogeneous men (i.e., all three mood groups would have accurately perceived the homogeneity of one group's behaviour and the heterogeneity of the other). For the mood-neutral group, the prediction held; the subjects accurately perceived that the men in the heterogeneous group were similar and that the men in the other group were different. However, when Stroessner and Mackie analysed the happy and sad subjects' perceptions, the prediction did not hold. Both the sad and the happy subjects perceived the homogenous group to be as similar/diverse as the heterogeneous group. Furthermore, both the sad and happy subjects perceived the ranges of similarity within both groups to be similar (i.e., both the happy and the sad subjects unrepresented the diversity among behaviour in the heterogeneous group). Stroessner and Mackie concluded that subjects' moods affected their perceptions of individuals in outgroups, particularly the degree of variation among outgroup individuals.

Thinking with stereotypes about figurines

What if we think again about our pneumatic figurines from the lower Danube in the spirit of stereotypes and stereotyping? First, we would have to accept that to see figurines as stereotypes is not to study a woman, child, goddess, priest or acolyte but to study records of someone's perceptions of others. It is to gain an insight into the person or group of people who created those figurines (an ingroup). Furthermore, thinking of figurines in terms of stereotypes forces us to ask questions about what judgments were being made,

about who were making these judgements, about how those making the judgements had assumed the rights to judge, and, finally about what authority those judgements possessed and what media and conceits were employed to project that authority. Stereotypes help us think (today) about the Neolithic and about Neolithic figurines in the same way, as I have argued, that figurines helped people in the Neolithic think about themselves, though the latter philosophising was a more unconscious process. Thinking with stereotypes moves us beyond questions of figurine use. It does not matter how these figurines were used, how they were disposed of, or with what explicit intention they were originally shaped, decorated and fired. If figurines have a value to us, then it is in showing us how they worked within ongoing, never-ending (though not necessarily intentional or planned) everyday constructions and reconstructions of people's silent and inherent understandings of who they were/were not.

Working through the rhetoric of stereotype and perceptions of outgroups makes us think about the people who made figurines, though not in the traditional sense of identifying a particular, potential crafts-person or master-artisan. We move beyond the tired and empty queries: were they men; were they women; were they shamans or other special members of communities who had special statuses, linked to special knowledges; were they children; were they potters; were they artists; or were they priests/priestesses? Any one of these suggestions may be correct and, just as possibly all of them may be incorrect. It does not matter, because these suggestions are not explanations. They are anecdotal proposals that have neither any means of assessment nor any real contribution to make to a critical understanding of the people who lived in the Hamangia communities of the lower Danube in the fifth millennium cal BC.

By thinking with stereotypes, however, we begin to think about the perceptions that a figurine maker had about himself or herself and about other people who lived around them and who lived in other places. We begin to wonder about the inferences that a Neolithic person made when he or she looked at and held a figurine. If, as will very likely be the case, we cannot uncover those specific Neolithic thoughts, then can we identify the types of things that people were thinking about? Were they thinking about differences and similarities? Were they thinking about ingroups or outgroups? Or was it a much more subtle series of thoughts, unnoticed and unannounced, that filtered down and rested at the base of people's understanding of their worlds, and sedimented into deep, inter-grading strata of belonging, of inclusion and exclusion?

An older question, 'Who made these figurines?' becomes an investigation of how perceptions of individuality, difference and similarity eroded through these sediments of accumulated understanding of living.

By thinking with stereotypes, we begin to see the Neolithic in new ways. Are figurines but one of many symptoms of the emergence of one variation of sociality and being? Are we better served to think about life in southeastern Europe in terms of categorisation, but of categorisation not only of people and their bodies, but also of things, places, thoughts and emotions? Certainly, there is nothing specific to the fragment of the region which I am focusing on in this chapter that excludes the role of stereotypes and stereotyping in earlier or later periods, nor is it legitimate to assume that issues of corporeal differentiation were static or standard in the many different moments and many differently shaped loci of being in the Neolithic. However, there is something particular about the durable, expressive materiality of categorisation across this region during this period, and there is something significant about the strength of the unintended consequences resulting from the new materiality (of miniature, modelled, fired clay) and especially about the role that the body played in these processes. One comes to sense the illusory power of generalisations about people (via the surfaces and morphologies of the body), about groups (via the adoption by many people of architecture and building aggregation – i.e., houses and villages), and at a more general level about emerging patterns of behaviour that fix, order and control the otherwise unstable, fleeting and ephemeral (of voice and gesture and representation in perishable media) in a lasting and affective [sic] manner via a durable and direct media.

Conclusion: a corporeal politics of being

The conclusion is not that Hamangia figurines should be interpreted as Hamangia stereotypes. To do so would be to revert to the unassessability and reduction of explanation by anecdote.[6] Rather, the proposal is think through the concept of stereotype and the process of stereotyping and thus to approach the material from a new and informative angle. To do so is to recognise the complexity of representation, especially when what is being represented is the human form. At a basic level, it is clear that the suggestions of representational equation between particular bodies represented in Neolithic figurines and any real (or spiritual) Neolithic beings are irrelevant, dangerously misguided, and will lead only to false reconstructions of Neolithic individuals or groups. Furthermore, it is also clear that figurines

provide a previously under-appreciated source of information about the ways that Neolithic people thought about themselves, but particularly about the ways that people thought about others and the ways that they sought to categorise, homogenise and simplify what was otherwise the jumbled clutter of chaotic and dynamic instability that makes up everyday life.

Regardless of the origins of the technological, cognitive or sensory abilities that elide in the making, viewing and handling of anthropomorphic figurines across southeastern Europe in the Neolithic, there are significant consequences (most probably unintended) that follow the emergence of body representation that runs through the Neolithic and of which figurines are one (preserved and thus recoverable) part. A consequence is that corporeality occupies a significant position on the stage of the political constitution and, more importantly, contestation of life in the region over a substantial period, from 6500–3500 cal. BC. Through its representation, decoration, inhumation, the human body courses through the Neolithic pulse. Even without attempting to reconstruct unrecoverable choreographies, performativities, and proxemics, it is clear that in this period of time in this region of the world, life, living, and being each engaged human corporeality in a material way not recognised in earlier or later periods or in other regions.

The Hamangia figurines saturated Hamangia communities with particular images and senses of being human. In other regions of southeastern Europe at this time similar saturations of different images and of varying senses took place. Despite the difference in the particularities of image, there is a significant commonality: the manifestation of the body in the widely available, mundane medium of modelled and fired clay. While there is variation in the representation of the body in different regions at this time, it is the unrealised potential for formal variation that the medium of clay offers the modeller which is most striking. Though Hamangia figurines are an extreme example of this similarity and repetition of form (what other archaeologists once may have wished to identify as a master's signature or a cultural canon), the inventories of figurines across the region are marked by restricted corporeal variation. This homogeneity has found traditional explanatory safety within culture-historical paradigms which accept formal similarity among artefacts as a reflection of community cohesion. An understanding of the false representation of outgroup homogeneity within stereotyping and intergroup categorisation turns this logic on its head. Perhaps corporeal forms in figurines represent outgroups and are not reflections of ingroup identity (i.e., Hamangia figurines do not represent

Hamangia people). Furthermore, if we argue that figurines represent not the people who modelled them or other members of their social or political groups (but members of other people in outgroups), then we can go further and suggest that these representations of members of outgroups inaccurately portray variation in corporeal form among members of that outgroup; indeed, this is the lesson to take from the psychology of stereotype work by Stroessner and Mackie (and others) on the perception and representation of outgroup homogeneity.

Regardless of the validity of these suggestions (which some might find anecdotal and thus of little explanatory value), the important note is that from 6500 cal. BC, the human body as an object had become a significant factor in the way that people thought about themselves, but particularly, how they thought about others (and indeed the facts that they were seeing and handling, on a daily basis, coherent images of those others, fashioned in a mundane medium of quotidian life – fired clay). Furthermore, the limited formal range of the created corporeal morphologies which are manifest in anthropomorphic figurines not only within one region, but also across southeastern Europe suggests a flattening out and smoothing of variation in the ways that people thought of themselves and of others. This is a Neolithic move towards generalisation about the Neolithic self and about Neolithic communities and it fits in well with the contemporary emergence of alterations to the physical and social landscapes: the construction of buildings for communal activities and as foci for membership within small groups; the aggregation of buildings into villages as foci of memberships within larger groups. The adaptation of schedule-dependent agricultural activities (such as large-scale cultivation, tending, harvesting and processing of cereal grains) adds to this new conception of a period which may be best understood, not in terms of economic revolution, but in terms of a corporeal politics of being.

Why had such a corporeal politics of being not appeared before 6500 cal. BC? Undoubtedly, the cognitive abilities and socio-political conditions had existed at least since the arrival of Anatomically Modern Humans in Europe. What had not came into use before this time was a set of materials and technologies which (while not of themselves causing the emergence of social groups such as households or villages) had important and extraordinarily long-lasting, cumulative consequences on how people perceived/constructed their worlds. The question of why these materials and technologies combined at this time and in this region needs a separate discussion, though the likelihood is that a combination of processes and events (emulation,

adaptation, adoption) led to the more gradual sequence than the term revolution was ever equipped to infer. In this context, the appearance of Venus figurines or anthropomorphic cave art in the Upper Palaeolithic can be seen as evidence for the perceptions of self and of other at a time when people possessed the same cognitive abilities as did people of the Neolithic, but at a time and in contexts in which the technological, economic, and climatic conditions were not conducive to the development of stable social groupings such as villages and (eventually in the later Bronze and early Iron Ages) proto-towns and towns. At the end of the Neolithic (i.e., after 3500 cal. BC), anthropomorphic figurines disappear from the lives of the people who lived in this region. What happened? Is it enough to write that population changed, that new groups surged into the region with different sets of material culture? It may be more useful to suggest that the material and political registers-of-being shifted towards media other than fired clay. However, it seems highly unlikely that after the beginning of the Neolithic (in southeastern Europe at least) the body as a rhetorically efficient mechanism for personal and social definition ever moved very far from the centre of political and personal essences of being.

Notes

1   I am writing about the Hamangia Culture (5500–4500 cal. BC); see Berciu (1966), Haşotti (1997) and Bailey (2005: 45–65) for a fuller description.

2   Though I am not dealing with it here, the many other ways that body courses through life are equally important, if not so easily recoverable (e.g., proxemics, choreography, performance).

3   In fact in Hamangia contexts, figurines cut across the mundane reality of daily life and the scripted performances of mortuary ceremony. Figurines have been found in burials and in non-mortuary contexts.

4   For a full discussion of the interpretation of figurines see Bailey (2005).

5   Research on stereotypes and stereotyping in social psychology is substantial and the literature is plentiful. For good introductions see McGarty *et al.* (2002c), Leyens *et al.* (1994) and Pickering (2001); see also Miller (1982), Ashmore and Del Boca (1981), Brigham (1971), and Lippmann (1922).

6   Indeed, one of the peer-reviewers of this volume wanted me to add a section at the end of my paper where I would apply the ideas that I raised about stereotypes and psychological studies to Neolithic figurines. S/he wanted me to draw some clear conclusions about Neolithic society. But this is precisely what I am arguing against. The conclusion that the work on stereotypes draws us to confront is, in fact, that we cannot draw the types of conclusions about the past which the reviewer wanted. Just as figurines are parts of the construction of fictive outgroups (which never really existed in any Neolithic flesh-and-blood), so also

is our own creation of a Neolithic past a construction of a fictive outgroup ('Neolithic people') that never existed in any coherent sense; coherence and clean conclusions are nothing better than misguided attempts to strip out variability from the messiness of reality in the effort to take refuge in the soft smoothness of false homogeneity. The call to create homogenising conclusions comes from our own insecurities, concerns and fears of the unordered and jagged, of the chaotic and unmeaningful, and of what George Bataille termed *informe* (Bois and Krauss 1997). From my position, I see more value in the formless than in the tidiness of closure and anecdote, and, thus, I have declined to draw the seductive, simple, but ultimately hollow conclusions about Neolithic society or individuals that the anonymous reviewer wanted me to spoon-feed to the reader.

Bibliography

Allport, G.W. 1954. *The Nature of Prejudice*. Reading, MA: Addison-Wesley.

Ashmore, R.C. and Del Boca, F.C. 1981. Conceptual approaches to stereotypes and stereotyping. In *Cognitive Processes in Stereotyping and Intergroup Behaviour*, edited by D.L. Hamilton, pp. 1–35. Hillsdale, NJ: Lawrence Erlbaum.

Bailey, D.W. 2005. *Prehistoric Figurines: Representation and Corporeality in the Neolithic*. London: Routledge.

Bailey, D.W. 2007 The anti-rhetorical power of representational absence: faceless figurines in the Balkan Neolithic. In *Material Beginnings: a Global Prehistory of Figurative Representation*, edited by C. Renfrew and I. Morley, pp. 117–26. Cambridge: McDonald Institute.

Berciu, D. 1966. *Cultura Hamangia*. București: Editura Academiei Republicii Populare Romine.

Brigham, J.C. 1971. Ethnic stereotypes. *Psychological Bulletin* 76: 15–38.

Bois, Y-A. and Krauss, R.E. 1997. *Formless: a User's Guide*. Cambridge, MA: MIT Press.

Brewer, M.B. 1988. A dual model of impression formation. In *A Dual Model of Impression Formation: Advances in Social Cognition*, edited by T.K. Srull and R.S. Wyer, pp. 1–35. Hillsdale: Erlbaum.

Delong, A.J. 1981. Phenomenological space-time: toward an experiential relativity. *Science* August 7, 1981: 681–2.

Delong, A.J. 1983. Spatial scale, temporal experience and information processing: an empirical examination of experiential reality. *Man-Environment Systems* 13: 77–86.

Doise, W., Csepeli, G., Dann, H.D., Gouge, C., Larsen, K. and Ostell, A. 1972. An experimental investigation into the formation of intergroup representations. *European Journal of Social Psychology* 2: 202–4.

Freud, S. 1899. *The Interpretation of Dreams*. (1998 trans by J. Crick). Oxford: Oxford University Press.

Gimbutas, M. 1982. *The Goddesses and Gods of Old Europe, 6500–3500 BC, Myths and Cult Images*. Berkeley: University of California Press.

Gimbutas, M. 1989. *The Language of the Goddess*. San Francisco: Harper Collins.

Gimbutas, M. 1991. *The Civilization of the Goddess: the World of Old Europe*. San Francisco: Harper Collins.

Gregory, R. 1968. Perceptual illusions and brain models. *Proceedings of the Royal Society* 171: 279.

Gregory, R. 1980. Perceptions as hypotheses. *Philosophical Transactions of the Royal Society B* 290: 181–97.

Gregory, R. 1997. Knowledge in perception and illusion. *Philosophical Transactions of the Royal Society of London B* 352(1): 121–8.

Hamilton, D.L. (ed.) 1981. *Cognitive Processes in Stereotyping and Intergroup Behaviour*. Hillsdale, NJ: Erlbaum.

Hamilton, D.L. and D.M. Mackie 1993. Cognitive and affective processes in intergroup perception: the developing interface. In *Affect, Cognition, and Stereotyping*, edited by D.M. Mackie and D.L. Hamilton, pp. 1–11. San Diego, CA: Academic Press.

Hamilton, D.L., Sherman, J.W. and Ruvolo, C.M. 1990. Stereo-typed-based expectancies: effects on information processing and social behavior. *Journal of Social Issues* 46: 35–69.

Haslam, S.A. 1997. Stereotyping and social influence: foundations of stereotype consensus. In *The Social Psychology of Stereotyping and Group Life*, edited by R. Spears, P.J. Oakes, N. Ellemers and S.A. Haslam, pp. 119–43. Oxford: Blackwell.

Haslam, S.A., Oakes, P.J., McGarty, C., Turner, J.C., Reynolds, K.J., and Eggins, R. 1996a. Stereotyping and social influence: the mediation of stereotype applicabililty and sharedness by the views of ingroups and outgroup members. *British Journal of Social Psychologyy* 35: 369–97.

Haslam, S.A., Oakes, P.J., Turner, J.C. and McGarty, C. 1996b. Social identity, self-categorisation and the perceived homogeneity of ingroups and outgroups: the interaction between social motivation and cognition. In *Handbook of Motivation and Cognition Volume 3*, edited by R.M. Sorrentino and E.T. Higgins, pp. 198–222. New York: Guilford.

Haslam, S.A., Turner, J.C., Oakes, P.J., McGarty, C. and Reynolds, K.J. 1998. The group as a basis for emergent stereotype consensus. *European Review of Social Psychology* 9: 203–39.

Haslam, S.A., Turner, J.C., Oakes, P.J., Reynolds, K.J. and Doosje, B. 2002. From personal pictures in the head to collective tools in the world: how shared stereotypes allow groups to represent and change social reality. In *Stereotypes as Explanations: the Formation of Meaningful Beliefs about Social Groups*, edited by C. McGarty, V.Y. Yzerbyt and R. Spears, pp. 157–85. Cambridge: Cambridge University Press.

Hașotti, P. 1985. Noi descoperiri privind plastica Hamangia. *Pontica* 18: 25–34.

Hașotti, P. 1986. Observați asupra plasticii culturii Hamangia. *Pontica* 19: 9–17.

Hașotti, P. 1997. *Epoca Neolitică în Dobrogea*. Constanța: Muzeul de Istorie Națională și Arheologie.

Judd, C.M. and Park, B. 1988. Out-group homogeneity: judgements of variability at the individual and group level. *Journal of Personality and Social Psychology* 54: 778–88.

Lacan, J. 1973. *The Four Fundamental Concepts of Psychoanalysis*. (1977 trans by A. Sheriden). New York: Norton.

Leyens, J-P., Yzerbyt, V. and Schadron, G. 1994. *Stereotypes and Social Cognition*. London: Sage.

Linville, P.W., Fischer, G.W and Salovey, P. 1990. Perceived distributions of the characteristics of in-group and out-group members: empirical evidence and a computer simulation. *Journal of Personality and Social Psychology* 57: 165–88.

Linville, P.W., Salovey, P. and Fischer, G.W. 1986. Stereotyping and perceived distributions of social characteristics: an application to ingroup-outgroup perception. In *Prejudice,*

Discrimination and Rascism, edited by J.F. Dovidio and S.L. Gaernter, pp. 127–63. Orlando: Academic.

Lippmann, W. 1922. *Public Opinion.* New York: Harcourt Brace.

McGarty, C. 1999. *Categorisation and Social Psychology.* London: Sage.

McGarty, C., Yzerbyt, V.Y. and Spears, R. 2002a. Social, cultural and cognitive factors in stereotype formation. In *Stereotypes as Explanations: The Formation of Meaningful Beliefs about Social Groups,* edited by C. McGarty, V.Y. Yzerbyt, and R. Spears, pp. 1–15. Cambridge: Cambridge University Press.

McGarty, C., Spears, R. and Yzerbyt, V.Y. 2002b. Conclusions: stereotypes are selective, variable and contested explanations. In *Stereotypes as Explanations: The Formation of Meaningful Beliefs about Social Groups,* edited by C. McGarty, V.Y. Yzerbyt and R. Spears, pp. 186–199. Cambridge: Cambridge University Press.

McGarty, C., Yzerbyt, V.Y. and Spears, R. (eds) 2002c. *Stereotypes as Explanations: The Formation of Meaningful Beliefs about Social Groups.* Cambridge: Cambridge University Press.

Messick, D.M. and Mackie, D.M. 1989. Intergroup relations. *Annual Review of Psychology* 40: 45–81.

Miller, A.G. (ed.) 1982. *In the Eye of the Beholder: Contemporary Issues in Stereotyping.* New York: Praeger.

Park, B. and Hastie, R. 1987. The perception of variability in category development: instance- versus abstraction-based stereotypes. *Journal of Personality and Social Psychology* 53: 621–35.

Park, B. and Judd, C.M. 1990. Measures and models of perceived group variability. *Journal of Personality and Social Psychology* 59: 173–91.

Park, B. and Rothbart, M. 1982. Perception of out-group homogeneity and levels of social categorisation: memory for subordinate attributes of in-group and out-group members. *Journal of Personality and Social Psychology* 42: 1051–68.

Pickering, M. 2001. *Stereotyping: The Politics of Representation.* Basingstoke: Palgrave.

Quattrone, G.A. and Jones, E.E. 1980. The perception of variability within in-groups and out-groups: implications for the law of small numbers. *Journal of Personality and Social Psychology* 38: 141–52.

Reicher, S.D., Hopkins, N. and Condor, S. 1997. Stereotype construction as a strategy of influence. In *The Social Psychology of Stereotyping and Group Life,* edited by R. Spears, P.J. Oakes, N. Ellemers and S.A. Haslam, pp. 94–118. Oxford: Blackwell.

Stroessner, S.J. and Mackie, D. 1992. The impact of induced affect on the perception of variability in social groups. *Personality and Social Psychology Bulletin.*

Stroessner, S.J. and Mackie, D. 1993. Affect and perceived group variability: implications for stereotyping and prejudice. In *Affect, Cognition, and Stereotyping: Interactive Processes in Group Perception,* edited by D.M. Mackie and D.L. Hamilton, pp. 63–86. London: Academic Press.

Tajfel, H. 1969. Cognitive aspects of prejudice. *Journal of Social Issues* 25: 79–97.

Tajfel, H. 1970. Experiments in intergroup discrimination. *Scientific American* 223: 96–102.

Tajfel, H. 1981. Social stereotypes and social groups. In *Intergroup Behaviour,* edited by J.C. Turner and H. Giles, pp. 144–67. Oxford: Blackwell.

Vajsov, I. 1987. Pogrebeniya s idoli ot praistoricheskiya nekropol kraj s. Durankulak, Tolbukhinski okrug. *Dobrudzha* 4: 77–82.

Vajsov, I. 1992a. Anthropomorphe Plastik aus dem prähistorischen Gräberfeld bei Durankulak. *Studia Praehistorica* 11–12: 95–113.

Vajsov, I. 1992b. Antropomorphnata plastika na kulturata Hamandzhiya. *Dobrudzha* 9: 35–71.

Wilder, D.A. 1984. Prediction of belief homogeneity and similarity following social categorization. *British Journal of Social Psychology* 23: 323–33.

3

Changing beliefs in the human body in prehistoric Malta 5000–1500 BC

Simon Stoddart and Caroline Malone

The study of belief and the body requires a comprehensive study of their interaction in a given society. In archaeological case studies, the materialisation of the body is very often restricted to a particular dimension which it can be tempting to study in isolation. In state organised societies, this isolation of focal materialisations – body disposal, figuration, constraints of domestic and ritual architecture – can be dissolved by the use of written sources to create an integrated picture of embodiment, and indeed this has been attempted in some recent studies (Meskell and Joyce 2003). In prehistoric societies, there are very few examples where materialisation of the body occupies sufficient, different dimensions to provide the empirical basis for detailed analysis. There are also few prehistoric examples where both the biological and the social body can be followed in parallel. In the Near and Middle East, the paramount case is that of Çatalhöyük (Hodder 2006). In Europe, the paramount case is that of the Tarxien phase of the island of Malta. Both stand out from their historical sequences, at the very least, in terms of the investment in body related belief that has its traces in patterns of social representation and the biological life cycle.

The Maltese archipelago is found some 80 km south east of Sicily (Figure 3.1). Its prominence in terms of the visibility of monumental remains has been known since the eighteenth century (Houel 1782–87; Pecoraino 1989), but the chronological precision, and thus the precociousness of its inhabitants, have only been firmly established since the 1970s (Renfrew 1973), and the exactitude of many of the details is still being formulated. Nevertheless, it is clear that over the course of the four thousand prehistoric years (5000–1000 BC)

of its occupation, the inhabitants produced varying elements of 1) distinctive representations of the body, 2) distinctive body disposal/display and 3) a distinctive built environment that constrained the directionality of body movement, aided by its setting in the wider physical environment. Extensive movement of the body through specially built structures and the intervening landscape became at some stages, but not at others, a major component of liturgical belief. The body was thus central to prehistoric Maltese belief reaching an enhanced centrality in the Tarxien period. This paper will briefly explore these three dimensions of the body in the understanding of belief. It will concentrate on the one key period, Tarxien (3000–2400 BC), where these three facets of materialisation of body belief (given in short hand as: depiction, disposal/display and direction) converge in a changed social framework,

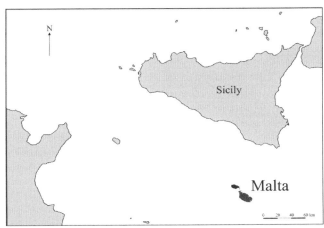

Figure 3.1. Location of Malta

Body representation by size
in Zebbug (not pottery)

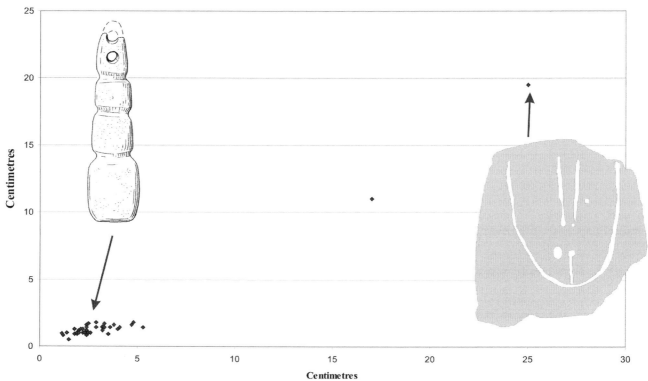

Figure 3.2. The scales of Zebbug depiction

at a radically enhanced level. However, to appreciate this framework, it is essential to contrast this central period with what precedes and follows. Thus we will briefly consider both the entry into this framework (5000–3000 BC) and the radical realignment of belief at about 2400 BC. For *depiction,* we intend all forms of bodily representation (enlarged from the Latin root of this term). For *disposal,* we intend the treatment and display of the body after death. For *direction,* we intend the way in which the built environment impinges on the movement of the body. For the simplicity of a short paper we will divide time into three phases: 5000–3000 BC, 3000–2400 BC and 2400–1500 BC. The complexities of the Maltese archaeological sequence can be pursued in detail elsewhere (Evans 1971), albeit briefly outlined here (Figure 3.10).

First phase (5000–3000 BC)

In the early part of the first phase, evidence for, and thus understanding of, the integration of the body into belief systems are poorly developed. Investigations of Maltese prehistory have concentrated on large scale visible remains, largely neglecting the investigation of earlier agriculturalists, except for some cave deposits.

In the Skorba phase (4400–4100 BC), the product of a small village based society, current evidence suggests that depiction was schematic and small scale. This chronological phase was entirely unknown until excavations at Skorba in the 1960s (Trump 1966) and only a few village sites have been discovered since (mainly in Gozo) and remain unpublished. Depiction was produced by the combination of discrete volumes of clay (wedge shaped heads, almost conical buttock, triangular bodies, pubic triangle motif, tapering sub-cylindrical limbs, linear and circular breasts). The visual implies a clear partition of the body where the individual parts are compartmentalised within the whole. The craftsmanship is additive, building up the body from constituent parts (cf. Farbstein 2006), further implying a very particular belief in the construction of the body. Disposal of the body is unknown. Directional movement of the body in the built environment

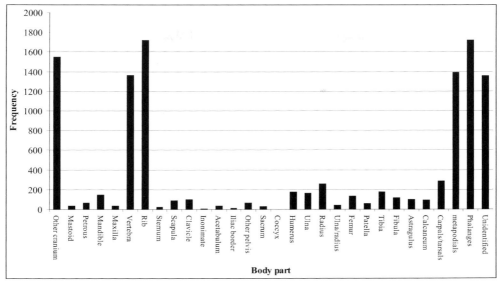

Figure 3.3. Frequency of body parts in the Ggantija period Xemxija tomb

appears to be relatively static in terms of people not moving about the built environment and landscape in an ordered manner. It is, of course problematic to base interpretation on relatively scant evidence, but the excavations at Skorba suggest the presence of small scale rituals embedded in the domestic. A group of figurines, Red Skorba pottery, goat skulls and worked cow tarsals were found inside a small enclosed hut cut into the underlying rock surface. At this stage, the developments in Malta were on a very similar scale to those in neighbouring regions of the Mediterranean.

In the succeeding Zebbug phase (4100–3600 BC) there is distinct change in style or *habitus*, but not in terms of scale. Depiction remains schematic and small scale (Figure 3.2), but takes on a more diverse range of forms and materials, which, in contrast to the previous phase, is uniformly reductive in terms of its approach to the use of materials (cf. Farbstein 2006). Materials are reduced from their original raw form of stone, leather hard clay and bone to create the body form, and in no circumstances produced by additive action. Two schematic stone representations of the human body are known from funerary contexts which focus entirely on the face. Both examples have a sub-circular facial outline, partly bisected by the outline of a nose and, in one case a drilled mouth. Body depictions in clay are not modelled but incised onto poorly fired clay vessels in a form that can only be described as stick figures. Even more schematic are quasi-anthropomorphic pendants carved out of bone, depicting the budding limbs of individuals

emerging from their constituent material. Knowledge of directional movement of the body in the built environment is unknown since the only potential trace of such evidence underlies the larger constructions of later periods, in many cases the temples considered below. The greater richness of this phase is provided by the first detailed information on bodily disposal. The two best known examples of burial, at Zebbug and Xaghra, however, lack any component of display, at least in a form that has survived archaeologically. Family groups appear to have been engaged in a cycle of insertion, and removal, of bodily remains from distinct formalised locations in small hidden underground locations, more precisely rock tombs approached by a central shaft (Malone 2007). For the first time we have evidence of the participation of the dead as individualised participants, which appears to have been restricted to some subadults and largely fully grown adults of both sexes in about equal measure. We thus have a distinct and fresh treatment of the body, albeit still at a restricted scale.

In the final part of the first phase, Ggantija (3600–3000 BC), the disposal of the body appears to continue in much the same pattern as before. The tombs of Xemxija, in so much as they are accurately dated, appear to belong to Ggantija and a related subphase (Saflieni). The lists of bones discovered suggest that the ritual of body disposal was very similar to that of the preceding Zebbug phase (Pike 1971), even though the listings do not permit calculations of the number of individual body insertions within the tomb (Figure 3.3). It is possible that the body may have been shrouded given

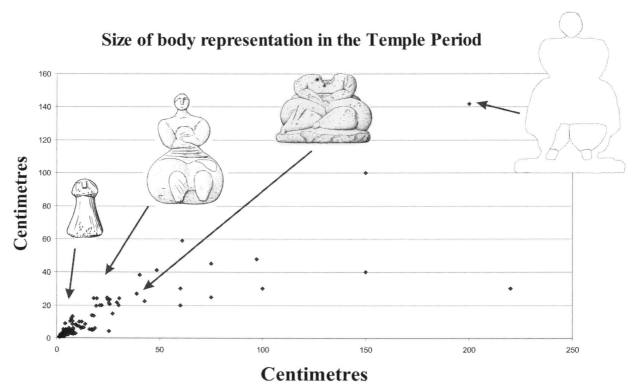

Figure 3.4. The scales of Tarxien body depiction

the large number of V-perforated buttons, mainly of shell, in this and the Zebbug period. The major change is that, above ground, a new community action is added in the form of the impact of the built environment on the directionality of movement. In this phase, the construction of large monuments profoundly affects the liturgical movement of the body. Thus in summary, we have an increasing involvement of the physical movement of the body in belief, reaching a crescendo in the next phase. The study of the Ggantija phase in terms of depiction of the body is more problematic than is normally represented, since, in our opinion, it is very difficult to separate out the Ggantija phase furniture of the great monumental constructions from those of the succeeding Tarxien phase. Only one temple (Skorba), and that a less elaborate temple, has been excavated in relatively modern times and the excavator records that none of the scant terracotta material was of proven Ggantija date (Trump 1966: 40). Of the two burial locations (Xemxija and Brochtorff Circle at Xaghra) also excavated in relatively modern times, neither has produced figurative material that is clearly of Ggantija period. It is our suspicion that most of the elaborate figurative depictions of the human body belong to the final highly elaborate phase of Tarxien which follows, and on which we will now concentrate our attention.

The second phase (3000 BC–2400 BC)

In the second phase, that of Tarxien, the body itself becomes a very substantial focus, indeed locus, of belief, operating theatrically in all three contexts of depiction, disposal/display and direction. These form an interconnected system of materialised belief, where the exclusion of one component would have profoundly affected the whole. Belief systems in the temples are balanced by belief systems in burials and linked by movement through the built environment set deliberately in specific locations in the natural ordered landscape.

In the context of depiction, a multi-scalar operation (Figure 3.4) is introduced indicating the full-scale participation of individuals in the belief systems, from the small scale (private) to the large scale (public). Some bodily depictions are in the order of millimetres (in the context of body disposal). These include minute animal phalanges with human heads carved on their extremities. Others are in the order of metres (in the context of public belief). The most famous is the immovable (and now truncated) statue on the right of the entrance into Tarxien temple. In the scale in between, there are many examples of bodily depiction which could have been re-arranged to provide different combinatory sets in ritual performances, both in above ground temples and in below ground funerary complexes. The body was central to the exposition of structured liturgies of performance.

The crafting of the body (*sensu* Farbstein) was for the first time both reductive and additive. Reduction operated across the full range of scales outlined above from the small bone phalange to the large stone statue. There were ready materials for the full range of scales of production, most especially the globigerina limestone which was fully exploited for all its intrinsic qualities of colour and easy carving during this phase. Additive modelling was applied principally to fired clay, and because of the properties of the material and low level of firing, restricted to the small to medium scale of representation. It is notable that local materials provided the medium for these bodily creations.

The body is generally *depicted* in the form of genderless, idealised individuals, where the face is important but unidentified, where the body is enlarged but ungendered. When clothed, there is a repetitive style of Tarxien dress, focused on the plaited skirt and the gathered cropped hair. These forms subscribe to a common ancestral style, or more broadly *habitus*, that alludes to the persistence of the descent group in successive cycles of life through the medium of changing individuals.

This belief in the submission of the individual person to the ancestral body is made clear by the practice of body disposal and display from the recently studied evidence from the Brochtorff Circle at Xaghra. In some sense, there appears to be a belief in the *survival strategy* (Shilling 2003: 166) of the body by the full participation of the population in an ancestral continuity. Individuals of all ages, from the foetal to the fully adult, were brought into the burial complex, showing a very full participation of all ages and sexes in the funerary action. The age and sex representation in the burial ritual conforms much more closely to the expected life table of a developed agricultural population than in the preceding phase. This population was subject to the infectious diseases that leave little osteological trace, and carry off relatively high proportions of the young. The relatively high numbers of the young in the funerary action also gives a profound sense of the fragility of the physical body in Tarxien life. Furthermore, this fragility was not a product of social action, since evidence for trauma is rare and focused on broken metatarsals, the casual accident of a rocky environment. The fragility of the living body was subject to external forces, unknown and unpredictable to the living population, which must have cut off the lives of many the young before the life cycle was complete and their bodies 'finished'. This circumstance must have had a strong effect on the

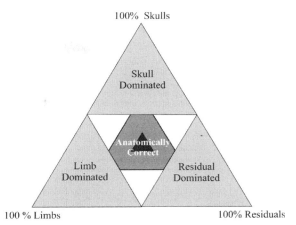

Figure 3.5. The packaging of Tarxien bones

associated belief systems where ancestral continuity became ever more important.

In the funerary action, anatomically conserved bodies are a rarity. When they occur they are placed in significant hidden locations deep within the stratigraphy. Even allowing for the practical effects of a protective stratigraphy, and less marked post depositional effects on adult bodies, this is the deliberate intentional deposition and retention of selected intact, adult and often male, bodily forms. These males may have been the physical projection of that ancestry outlined above (in an intriguing contrast to the mother goddess emphasis of previous interpretations of Maltese cosmology).

In the zones of public display (higher in the stratigraphy), human remains were relocated in the form of three major presentational packages (Figures 3.5 and 3.6): 1) Skull rich, 2) Limb rich and 3) Residual rich (defined as rich in phalanges, (meta) tarsals/carpals, patellae, etc, caused by the offering of skulls and limbs to other locations.). Three examples are outlined here to illustrate the process. 1) At a location to the left of the probable entrance to the burial complex, skulls were gathered in a very visible location. The area concerned has been subject to some considerable collapse, so it is highly probable that this was also originally a zone of stone shelves on which the skulls were placed in the full view of the participants in the body rituals. This skull zone also adjoins a screened off area (identified as the shrine in published literature [Stoddart, *et al.* 1993]) which contained a cache of figurative representations and a static, but moveable, seated pair of figurines. Both of these instruments of ritual action appear to be closely related to the enactment of the individual idealised life cycle. The individual components of the cache of figurative representations are in different stages of

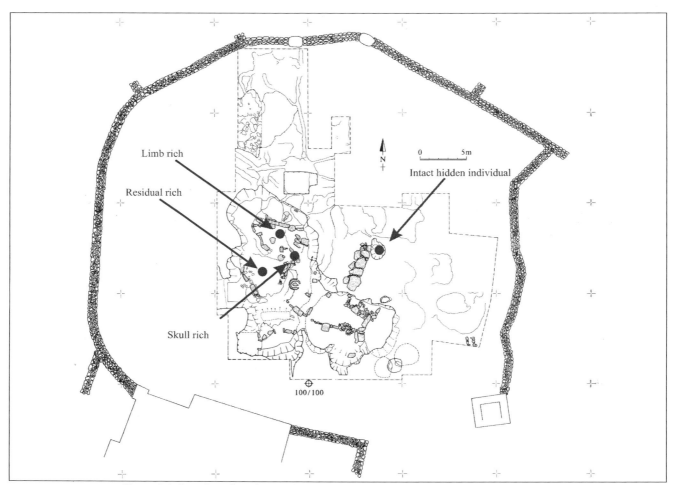

Limb rich

Residual rich

Intact hidden individual

Skull rich

100/100

Figure 3.6. Location of cited examples of bone packages in the Brochtorff Circle at Xaghra

craft production from the rough-out to the finished, damaged, 'adult'. One of the seated pair of figures holds a small child and the other a small pot which most probably contained, and the whole was certainly daubed with, the red ochre to anoint the bodies of the finished life cycle. 2) One of the most prominent limb rich locations is at the physically lowest part of the site. In an area bounded by upright megaliths, a succession of deposits contained these selected parts of the full physical body. 3) The main display area in the centre of the mortuary complex appears to have been subjected to the greatest degree of 'depredation' of skull and limb removal leaving no complete intact individuals in the most prominent central location within the mortuary enclosure. In essence, the community entered the burial area as individuals, but in the course of time lost that individuality as they became displayed clusters of skulls, limb bones and the residue of their repackaging, undifferentiated from the community of which they were originally part.

All these displays of the body were constrained within clearly defined built and natural environments, in both death and life rituals. A similar symbolic structure of open and closed spaces, of symbolism of left and right, was mapped on both burial enclosures and temple precincts. The visibility of the body and the access of the body were constrained, and revealed, in a liturgy of active theatre (Figure 3.7) (Anderson and Stoddart 2005, 2007; Grima 2005; Hayden 1990; Stoddart *et al.* 1993; Tilley and Bennett 2004). Barrier holes on narrowed entrances of temples show how visibility could be revealed in stages, permitting the eye and, under certain circumstances, the body to enter the temple. In the built environment above ground this process of body revelation is fairly easy to orchestrate, by the construction of new architectural features. Below ground, the natural cave system of the Brochtorff Circle at Xaghra was reworked as best as was possible to permit progress of the eye and the body into new enclosed spaces. The architectural orchestration is

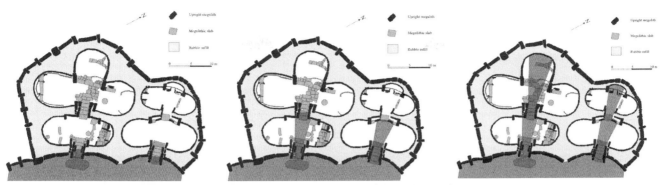

Figure 3.7. The revelation stages of Ggantija temple

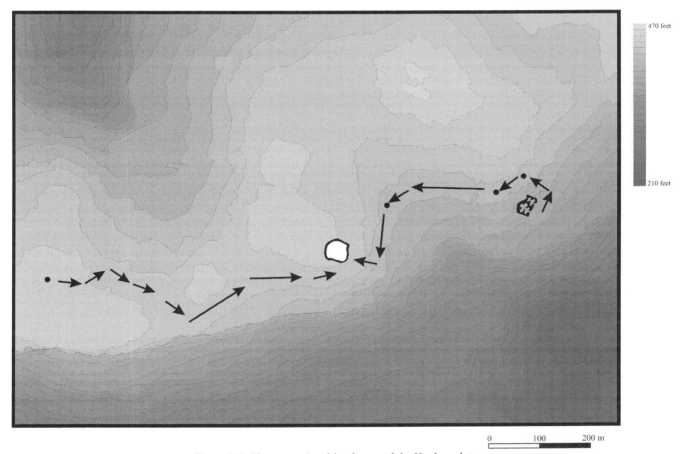

Figure 3.8. The processional landscape of the Xaghra plateau

easier to envisage in the Hal Saflieni monument where the local rock was a softer globigerina and more readily modified to reflect the intentions of the ritual specialists. In Hal Saflieni, the central zone of performance has been preserved, standing as an enclosed space decorated in temple styles, surrounded by smaller niches for the disposal of bodies.

Between these nodal points of ritual activity, individuals must have been engaged in processions across the intervening landscape (Figure 3.8). On the Xaghra plateau we can reconstruct the potential interconnected route ways through the landscape, from the location of three substantial excavated/cleared monuments (Brochtorff Circle at Xaghra, Ggantija and Santa

Verna temples) and three less well known broadly contemporary partly monumental locations. A similar pattern probably existed in the Tarxien – Kordin – Hal Saflieni landscape, but this is now completely masked by urban development. On the Xaghra plateau, the lie of the land suggests that Ggantija was deliberately viewable from the valley below, the access point from the sea. Once the participants exited from the monument they could climb from the artificially extended terrace (still visible in early drawings)

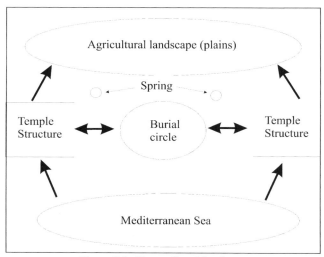

Figure 3.9. The mediated landscape

slightly upslope and follow the natural processional route along the contour following monuments along the edge of the plateau before turning once more upslope to enter the main entrance of the burial monument of the Circle. The entrance of the Circle in turn gave access to another natural processional route along the contour, to the west towards the smaller temple of Santa Verna which was itself accessed by a final climb upslope to one of the highest locations on the plateau. In practical terms, flat processional routes, visible from the agricultural valley below, linked monuments on distinct focal heights in the landscape. Thus central burial grounds (Figure 3.9), the locus of one metaphorical passage of time and space at the human bodily scale, acted as mediation points between temples, the location of another metaphorical transition at most probably a supra-corporeal cosmological scale (Grima *et al.* in press). The burial ground formed a parallel existence to the temples which, as has been recently suggested (Grima 2004), themselves could have acted as mediation points between the Mediterranean world and the agricultural plains that supported the living communities. The body formed a central focus in these belief systems, with superimposed forests (or stone trunks!) of symbols of the cycles of life reinforcing one other: in the disposal of the body, in the manufacture of body representations, in the movement through built spaces and between nodal structures.

Phase	Date	Depiction	Disposal/display	Direction	Digest (social)
Skorba	4400–4100	Schematic Small scale	Unknown	Static	Village based
Zebbug	4100–3600	Schematic Small scale	Unicyclical	Unknown	Family focused
Ggantija	3600–3000	Unclear	Unicyclical	Constrained	Community focused
Saflieni Tarxien	3000–2400	Ancestral Dominant; gender ambiguity; Corpulence; Facial emphasis; multi-scalar	Elaborate Cycles of integration of individual with ancestral; recapitulation of life	Multiple lines of bodily constraint and control	Warm-blooded – humanistic – closer to reality, thus (re-Gell) "the more materially realistic the image, the more spiritually it is seen. " Larger-scale Community focused
Transformation of belief system					
Tarxien Cemetery	2400–1500	Schematic; non facial; Small scale	Individualistic; cremation	Unclear	Individual focus

Figure 3.10. Summary table

This was, however, a belief structure that had inbuilt finality. At least two nodes of the built environment show evidence of the deliberate destruction of bodily representation and the concurrent cessation of the belief system. This is stratigraphically most clear in the Brochtorff Circle at Xaghra, where the destruction of a relatively large (approximately 60 cm high) body image appears to be incorporated in the final Tarxien layers of the site, leaving open the possibility that this action was a final act of the belief system itself rather than an opposing iconoclasm. At the second site of Tas Silg the evidence is more ambiguous since the site not only has immediately succeeding Bronze Age occupation but also the imposition of a substantial Punic Sanctuary above that (Vella 1999).

The constraints of the built environment within the temple spaces may have facilitated a 'panoptical' control of the movement of both live and dead bodies through ritual space by the ritual specialists within the temples and mortuary enclosures. In turn this may have permitted a corresponding exclusion of other members of society. To what extent were the whole population admitted to the temples? To what extent were all the population buried in the great mortuary enclosures? It seems unlikely that even 800+ individuals interred in the Brochtorff Circle at Xaghra could have accommodated the death rate of even a modest population over the 600 years of its Tarxien occupation. Greater and greater investment could have been made in the elaborations of body representation and display of both the living and dead in their respective enclosures above and below ground. The freely granted visual revelation and body passage of the Ggantija phase ritual could easily have been replaced by limited access of body and sight in the Tarxien phase.

Ggantija and Tarxien society show no evidence of differential access to economic resources. Investment in the body may have provided an alternative strategy for the differentiation of a ritual elite from the remainder of the population that did not affect, at least initially, the overriding democratic *habitus* of prehistoric Maltese society. Control of the body space could, over time, have been subverted and manipulated, a state of affairs that was acceptable under stable social conditions. However the transmission of this control of the body from one generation to another would have been problematic. The individuals of each new generation would have been required to re-assert their personal authority, in succession to the personal authority of their predecessors. To put this more theoretically, the *physical capital* accumulated by the ritual specialists in their unfinished bodies could not be transmitted directly from one generation to another (Shilling 2003: 124–126) since their life cycle was of limited length and each individual would have a varying and limited capacity for accumulation (Bourdieu 1986: 245). The capital was increasingly knowledge based and individuals, even if genetically related, would have varying abilities of learning, retention, elaboration and projection of that knowledge. This situation would have been particularly problematic if there was a saturation of the body image, leading to difficulties of continuing classification. Under these conditions of transmission, a range of circumstances could have brought an apparently long lasting and stable system to a close. If a pre-ordained ritual cycle was terminated (Sahlins 1981), if the fragile island ecosystem received a slight shock, if the majority began to understand the manipulation of their bodies by the minority, the response could have been a closure of the belief system, and the adoption of a radically new format.

The final phase (2400–1500 BC). Tarxien Cemetery

Whatever the cause of the closure of the earlier belief system, what followed was a radical reinterpretation of body based belief. Depiction became (with some minor exceptions) once more schematic and small scale. Body disposal and display became individualistic, and took on the changed rite of cremation which broke down the body, with the surviving charred bodily remains wrapped individually in cloth and accompanied by bronze weapons. The pre-existing built environment, although still visibly present, was abandoned or re-deployed, and small-scale monuments (generally described as dolmen) erected in distinct parts of the landscape, most probably for the temporary display of the dead. The body was still part of this belief system, but unlike the preceding Tarxien phase was not integrated with, or reinforced by, the body at every level of action. Transformations in body belief are very visible in historical times. In cases of rich availability of data, major transformations can also be identified in prehistory. Although it would be anachronistic to press the analogy, a transformation had taken place in Malta that was as radical in the changed attitude to the body as that described by Elias in the transformation of the ideologically violent early medieval society into the courtly society of the late Medieval to High Renaissance (Elias 1983). Theorists should also search prehistory to enlarge their scope of these transformations to the full range of human development.

Conclusion

The Maltese case study allows us to examine an explosion of body related belief as part of a longer, less unusual, trajectory (Figure 3.10). Three dimensions of embodiment coincided in the Tarxien phase to provide a mutual reinforcement of belief in the subjugation of the individual body and its life cycle to a longer ancestral course and its prolongation beyond individual memory. At a certain moment in the middle of the third millennium BC, this belief system imploded and there was a reversion to the more 'normal' belief history. We do not have to wait for high modernity for the body to become central to belief systems (Shilling 1993), but in early societies such as those of Malta, the concept of the body is strongly constrained by communal ceremonies that prevent the appearance of individuality. In fact, we could go further to state that during the Tarxien period the subjugation of the individual body to the communal ancestral body had much to do with the construction of the identity of Maltese society at that time.

Acknowledgements

We would like our sponsors, Leverhulme and Templeton, for offering the bodily access to time. The drawings were prepared by Ben Plumridge, Steven Ashley, Jason Gibbon and Simon Stoddart. We would like to thank Robin Skeates for commenting on an earlier draft of this paper.

Bibliography

Anderson, M. and Stoddart, S.K.F. 2005. *Access, visibility and control of power in the Maltese temple.* Unpublished conference paper.

Anderson, M. and Stoddart, S. K. F. 2007. Mapping Cult Context: GIS applications in Maltese temples. In *Cult in Context*, edited by D. Barrowclough and C.A.T Malone, pp. 41–44. Oxford: Oxbow.

Bourdieu, P. 1986. The forms of capital. In *Handbook for Theory and Research for the Sociology of Education*, edited by J.G. Richardson, pp. 241–258. Westport, CT: Greenwood Press.

Elias, N. 1983. *The Court Society.* Oxford: Basil Blackwell.

Evans, J.D. 1971. *The Prehistoric Antiquities of the Maltese Islands: A Survey.* London: Athlone Press.

Farbstein, R. 2006. Rethinking constructions of the body in Pavlovian portable art: a material-based approach. *Archaeological Review from Cambridge* 21(2): 78–95.

Grima, R. 2004. The landscape context of megalithic architecture. In *Malta Before History*, edited by D. Cilia, pp. 327–345. Malta: Miranda.

Grima, R. 2005. *Monuments in Search of a Landscape. The Landscape Context of Monumentality in Late Neolithic Malta*, Unpublished PhD Dissertation, University of London.

Grima, R., Malone, C.A.T. and Stoddart, S.K.F. in press. The ritual landscape. In *Mortuary Ritual in Prehistoric Malta. The Brochtorff Circle Excavations (1987–1994)*, edited by C.A.T. Malone, S.K.F. Stoddart, D. Trump, A. Bonanno and A. Pace. Cambridge: McDonald Institute.

Hayden, C. 1990. *The social Organisation of Space in Buildings of the Temple Period of the Maltese Islands.* BSc thesis, University College, London.

Hodder, I. 2006. *The Leopard's Tale: Revealing the Mysteries of Çatalhöyük.* London : Thames and Hudson

Houel, J.p.L.L. 1782–87. *Voyage Pittoresque des Isles de Sicile: de Malte et de Lipari, où l'on Traite des Antiquités qui s'y Trouvent Encore; des Principaux Phénomènes que la Nature y Offre; du Costume des Habitans, & de quelques Usages.* Paris : Imprimerie de Monsieur.

Malone, C.A.T. 2007. Access and Visibility in Prehistoric Malta. In *Recent Developments in the Research and Management at World Heritage Sites*, edited by M. Pomeroy-Kellinger and I. Scott, Oxford Archaeology Ocassional Paper 16. Oxford: Oxford University Committee for Archaeology,

Meskell, L.M. and Joyce, R.A. 2003. *Embodied Lives: Figuring Ancient Maya and Egyptian Experience.* London: Routledge.

Pecoraino, M. (ed.) 1989. *La Sicilia di Jean Houel all'Ermitage.* Palermo: Sicilcassa.

Pike, G. 1971. The human bones from the Xemxija tombs. In *The Prehistoric Antiquities of the Maltese Islands: A Survey*, edited by J. Evans, pp. 236–238. London: Athlone Press.

Renfrew, A.C. 1973. *Before Civilisation.* London: Jonathan Cape.

Sahlins, M. 1981. *Historical Metaphors and Mythical Realities: Structure in the Early History of the Sandwich Islands Kingdom.* Ann Arbor: University of Michigan Press.

Shilling, C. 1993. *The Body and Social Theory.* London: Sage.

Stoddart, S.K.F., Bonanno, A., Gouder, T., Malone, C.A.T. and Trump, D. 1993. Cult in an Island Society: Prehistoric Malta in the Tarxien period. *Cambridge Archaeological Journal* 3(1): 3–19.

Tilley, C.Y. and Bennett, W. 2004. *The Materiality of Stone: Explorations in Landscape Phenomenology.* Oxford: Berg.

Trump, D.H. 1966. *Skorba. Excavations Carried out on Behalf of the National Museum of Malta. 1961–3.* Research Reports of the Society of Antiquaries of London 22. London: Society of Antiquaries.

Vella, N.C. 1999. 'Trunkess legs of stone': debating ritual continuity at Tas-Silg, Malta. In *Facets of Maltese Prehistory*, edited by A. Mifsud and C. Savona-Ventura, pp. 225–239. Malta: The Prehistoric Society of Malta.

4

Idealism, the body and the beard in classical Greek art

Robin Osborne

All work on past bodies ends up, in one way or another, being concerned with reality and its representation. But there is some truth to the caricature of current academic endeavor which holds that those who think of themselves as working on 'reality' (and who frequently call themselves 'archaeologists' or 'historians') are strongly resistant to the idea that they can *only* ever deal with representation, while those who regard themselves as working on 'representation' (who frequently call themselves 'art historians' or 'literary critics') are equally resistant to the idea that understanding representation requires *any* understanding of reality (I deliberately leave those terms not further defined). No project on changing beliefs about the body is going to get anywhere until those who reckon themselves to work on reality can find a way of talking to those who think they work on representation, and vice versa. This paper takes one of the most famous moments in the history of the representation of the body and tries to show how this moment can be understood only if it is also seen as a moment in the history of the 'real' body.

That there was a marked break in the way in which the human body was represented in Greek sculpture in the early fifth century became apparent with the discovery of archaic sculpture and early classical sculpture in the excavations of the late nineteenth century (compare Figure 4.1, the Anavyssos kouros, and Figure 4.2, the Kritios boy). By the time Humfry Payne published the archaic marble sculpture from the Acropolis in the 1930s it seemed simply obvious that one treated archaic sculpture as a class apart (Payne and Young 1936). But the classic description of the change between archaic and classical sculpture

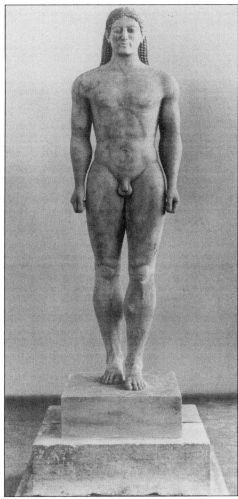

Figure 4.1. The Anavyssos kouros. Courtesy of Hirmer Fotoarchiv, Munich

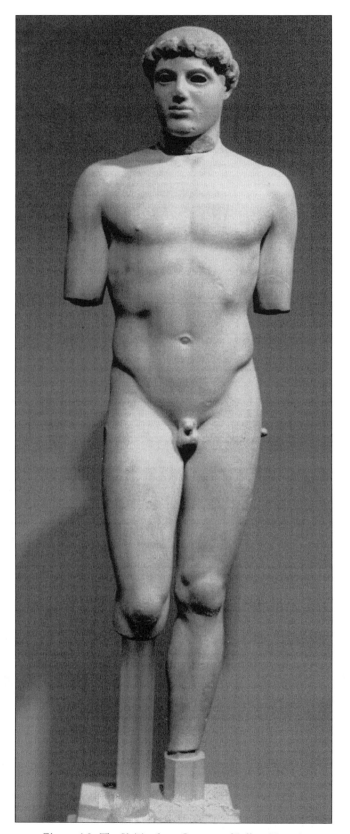

Figure 4.2. The Kritios boy. Couresy of Jeffrey Hurwit

was provided not by a classical archaeologist but by a western art historian specialist in much later art, Ernst Gombrich, in 'Reflections on the Greek Revolution', perhaps the most famous chapter of his classic work *Art and Illusion*, which started off as Mellon Lectures in Washington 50 years ago (1956) and was published in 1960 (Gombrich 1960).

A few quotations give the flavor of the revolution which Gombrich believed to lie behind the changes visible in sculpture. 'There are few more exciting spectacles in the whole history of art than the great awakening of Greek sculpture and painting between the sixth century and the time of Plato's youth toward the end of the fifth century B.C.' (Gombrich 1960: 99). 'What is normal to man and child all over the globe is the reliance on schemata, on what is called "conceptual art". What needs explanation is the sudden departure from this habit that spread from Greece to other parts of the world' (Gombrich 1960: 101). 'Taken all in all it is not too fanciful, therefore, to compare the Greek "conquest of space" with the invention of flying. The pull of gravitation that the Greek inventors had to overcome was the psychological pull toward the distinctive "conceptual" image that had dominated representation heretofore and that we all have to counteract when we learn the skills of mimesis' (Gombrich 1960: 119). 'It may sound paradoxical to say that the Greeks invented art, but from this point of view, it is a mere sober statement of fact. We rarely realize how much this concept owes to the heroic spirit of those discoverers who were active between 550 and 350 B.C.' (Gombrich 1960: 120).

Gombrich did not invent the Greek revolution. Repeatedly in this chapter he simply restates the views of earlier scholars, concerned not to refute them but to exploit their observations by putting them in a new framework – his framework of 'making' and 'matching', in which it is the Greeks who invent 'matching', *mimesis* ('matching' involves copying the appearance, 'making' need only involve creating an equivalent, without any intent to copy the appearance).[1] Since 1960 Gombrich's views have repeatedly been the focus for discussion, both by those centrally concerned with the history of Greek art (Beard 1985; Elsner 2006) and by those more interested in his general framework (Bryson 1983). I revisit Gombrich again here since the question of whether a revolution in the representation of the appearance of the human body has implications for beliefs of the body is central to the possibility of an archaeology of the body.

Although Gombrich variously details the technical advances that marked the Greek revolution – in painting, foreshortening, representation of space, modeling in light and shade, the ability to make hard and inert marble look soft and alive – what marks the revolution is not these features, some, at least, of which can he admits be paralleled in e.g., Egyptian art, but a fundamental change in the questions which the artist is trying to answer, no longer questions about what, but now questions about how. He suggests that what brought about the revolution was the attempt to re-create a specific situation in order to tell a story: narrative demands not simply that we identify the characters but that we have convincing evidence for how they are acting. 'It was the Greeks who taught us to ask "*How* does he stand?" or even "Why does he stand like that?" Applied to a pre-Greek work of art, it may be senseless to ask this question' (Gombrich 1960: 114).

Applied to the body, I take Gombrich's view to imply the following: that until the Greek revolution the body was merely a carrier of identity. By his particular form of body an Egyptian was identified as belonging to a particular class; the pictorial body was little more than another hieroglyphic sign. So Gombrich writes: 'Perhaps only Ikhnaton demanded that his personal, distinctive features should be entered on the map of history, but even these became a stereotype that was applied to the whole royal family' (Gombrich 1960: 103). By contrast, the body in classical Greece conveyed not merely a label, but a manner and/or a motive. We come to see not merely an old man, but an old man moved by anxiety (e.g., the seer from the Olympia west pediment).[2] We see not just a youth, but a youth whose every movement reflects the onset of adolescence (e.g., the Kritian boy, Figure 4.2).[3] Or, in Gombrich's own example of Makron's scene of the Judgement of Paris on a cup, 'Now we can see much better how it was when the god hailed the princely shepherd, how Athene beckoned, how Hera maintained a dignified reserve becoming her character, and how Aphrodite, surrounded and adorned by winged cupids, had her victory assured.' (Gombrich 1960: 111). This is actually a highly implausible way of reading this particular scene, as Gombrich himself more or less admits when he notes that this scene remains highly conceptual, and proceeds to look to Pompeian wall painting to find 'the shepherd dreaming idly by the rural shrine before the quarrel of the goddesses shattered the peace of the scene for ever' (Gombrich 1960: 112). But it is not the plausibility or not of Gombrich's particular readings of particular works which I am interested in here, but the implications which his frame of analysis has for the relationship between representation and bodily belief.

I want to offer two criticisms of this account. The first is theoretical. If we ask what is being 'matched' in classical Greek art, according to Gombrich, that is

not being 'matched' in e.g., Egyptian art, the answer has nothing to do with physical appearance. What is being matched is the idea of the angry/anxious/carefree man/woman/youth. This is just as 'conceptual' as the appearance of a prince/soldier/hunter. While the selection of features known from life that are represented in the Kritian boy are certainly different from the selection of features known from life that are represented in the case of the Egyptian statue, the process involved in moving from observation of features in life, to imaginative projection of those features into a narrative, and on to their representation in painting or sculpture, seem to be identical. Whether the narrative is historical or mythological seems beside the point. Gombrich attempts to draw a line between 'effective' and 'lucid' images, on the one hand, and 'convincing' images on the other (Gombrich 1960: 113), just as he tries to attach significance to 'the gradual emancipation of conscious fiction from myth and moral parable' (Gombrich 1960: 109), but despite his attempt to link the latter to 'the emancipation of the visual image from the near-Pygmalion phase of "making"' (Gombrich 1960: 109) it is hard to see that either distinction can be sustained as requiring from the artist a significantly different set of aims or practices.

My second criticism is that Gombrich's claims fail to fit the history of Greek art. Gombrich is himself far from consistent in his chronology for the Greek revolution. His opening formulation, which I quoted at the beginning, talks of the period from the sixth century to the end of the fifth, though the sculptures he uses to illustrate the change date from the mid sixth-century (Tenea kouros) to 480 B.C. (Kritian boy) (compare my contrasting Figures 4.1 and 4.2). On p. 108 he says that 'If we place the beginning of the revolution somewhere in the middle of the sixth century' 'it took some two hundred years' for it to be complete, with the first illusionist images coming only in Plato's lifetime. His discussion of images of the Judgement of Paris finds Makron, painting around 480, still 'conceptual', but he proceeds to use a late sixth-century representation of Herakles and Busiris to show that Greek artists interpreted 'conceptual' Egyptian art as the representation of reality (taking differences in scale for differences in physical size), although he uses the Alexander mosaic, copying a late fourth-century Greek work, to show the 'new continents of human experience' which representing imagined reality could explore.

This equivocation over the timetable of the revolution Gombrich himself in part acknowledges, remarking in defense that 'No revolution in art can ever be quite abrupt without sinking into chaos' (Gombrich 1960:

114), but the truth is that Gombrich never comes to terms with the relative independence of his revolutions in sculpture and painting. The revolution in sculpture has always been primarily observed and exemplified in the history of *kouroi*, free standing statues of youths, and that revolution began seriously only in the last quarter of the sixth century and was complete by the end of the first quarter of the fifth. The revolution in painting, however, is another matter. The first signs of foreshortening do indeed appear in the late sixth century, and serious exploration of the body in space is clear in the second quarter of the fifth century, but many vase painters show minimal interest in these developments. More importantly, the features central to showing the 'how' in sculpture – in particular the use of facial expression, arguably never become a tool in the vase painter's armoury (this is part of what makes Gombrich's reading of the Makron Judgement of Paris so implausible). It is not arbitrary that, having said that the history of Greek painting can be followed in painted pottery (Gombrich 1960: 109), to illustrate his claims about illusionism Gombrich has to resort to wall paintings and mosaics of the Roman period – albeit wall paintings and mosaics which reproduce, more or less accurately, fourth-century Greek originals. Gombrich draws back from claiming 'that the existence of Homeric poetry alone can suffice to explain the rise of Greek art' (Gombrich 1960: 113), but does make the lesser claim that 'Homeric freedom of narration was as necessary as was the acquired skill of craftsmanship to open the way for the Greek revolution' (Gombrich 1960: 113). But sculptors display little interest in Homeric stories, strikingly little by comparison with tragedians, with neither isolated relief sculptures nor architectural sculpture picking up Homeric stories in either the archaic or the classical period. And the vase painters who do, in some sense at least, respond to the Homeric epics, do so in works which, with few exceptions, continue to emphasize the 'what' over the 'how', with scenes that respond to epic declining sharply in number in the fifth century, not increasing.

Where does this leave the history of the body? On the one hand, we are not in a position to deny that the classical body could, and sometimes did, serve as more than merely a marker of identity. The Kritian boy alone, arguably, serves to guarantee that. On the other hand, not only do many vase painters continue throughout the fifth century to show little interest in the body as other than a marker of identity, but modern discussions also often treat the classical sculpted body as merely a mark of identity. This applies, for instance, to much discussion of the sculptures of the Parthenon which, observing that e.g., the south metopes of the Parthenon show lapiths and centaurs proceeds to

Figure 4.3. South metope 29 of the Parthenon. Courtesy of Hirmer Fotoarchiv, Munich

interpret this as mythical civilisation versus barbarism offered as a celebration of the historical struggle of civilisation versus barbarism that was the Persian Wars, without any reference to the particular form that the represented body here takes.[4]

The last argument is adventitious, of course, but it can be bolstered by consideration of what happens to free-standing sculpture in the fifth century. Gombrich himself noted that 'Greek art of the classical period concentrated on the image of man almost to the exclusion of other motifs, and even in the portrayal of man it remained wedded to types' (Gombrich 1960: 122). And he went on immediately (Gombrich 1960: 122) to emphasise that this applied not simply to 'the idealized type of physique' but also to a limited repertoire in the rendering of movement and drapery. When we compare the Kritian boy or the Riace bronzes (see below) from the years 480 to 460 with the Polyclitan Doryphoros of c. 440 our comparison is obscured by the fact that we know the Doryphoros only from Roman copies, but if we look instead at the portrayal of the male body in the pediments, metopes, or frieze of the Parthenon, sculpted in the 440s and 430s, or on early classical grave stelae, dating to the 420s, we see, if in

Figure 4.4. South metope 30 of the Parthenon. Courtesy of Hirmer Fotoarchiv, Munich

Figure 4.5. South metope 31 of the Parthenon. Courtesy of Hirmer Fotoarchiv, Munich

less extreme form, the same phenomenon: the highly specific bodies of the Kritian boy or of the two Riace warriors, are succeeded by the generalised bodies of the later figures, whose mature beardlessness comes close, notwithstanding the later age of maturation in antiquity, to replicating the impossible body of the *kouros*.

What is happening here can be further illuminated by comparison between the bodies of lapiths and the bodies of centaurs on the south metopes of the Parthenon (Figures 4.3, 4.4 and 4.5). Here we are treated, more or less, to a single lapith body. It is true that some metopes manage softer flesh than others, but the variation in lapith bodies pales into insignificance by comparison to the bodies of the centaurs. Here we are treated to a full range of physical types and conditions, where the condition of the flesh and the physical development of the body seems designed to match the mood, almost the moral presence (or absence), of the beast. In Gombrichian terms this leaves us with a remarkable paradox: the mythical centaurs seem to be 'matched', the observable lapiths to be 'made'.

If one conclusion that I draw is that 'making' and 'matching' are not proving very helpful terms of analysis, I must nevertheless admit that they prove of considerable heuristic value in helping us to see what question we do need to ask about the classical body. And that question has to concern what is 'wrong' with 'matching' the human body. If 'matching' is a good way of conceiving centaurs, why is it not a good way of conceiving ordinary Greek men? Gombrich would have us believe that 'matching' leads to convincing portrayal: does the artist here not want to convince?

The answer, arguably, depends on what one takes him to want to convince of? For Gombrich what the matched body was convincing about was a story. Matched bodies offered a conviction to narrative, indeed demanded a narrative, in the way that made bodies did not – all stories concern particular men, not 'man'. But that power of representation of the body to provoke questions about the story of that body is a power that is not limited to any particular sort of story. The 'matched' heads of the centaurs on the Parthenon metopes invite stories about their attitudes to violence and to women. We variously identify these centaurs as callously brutal, violently lustful, or sympathetic. The matched body invites the viewer to apply to art the skills which she has developed in order to manage

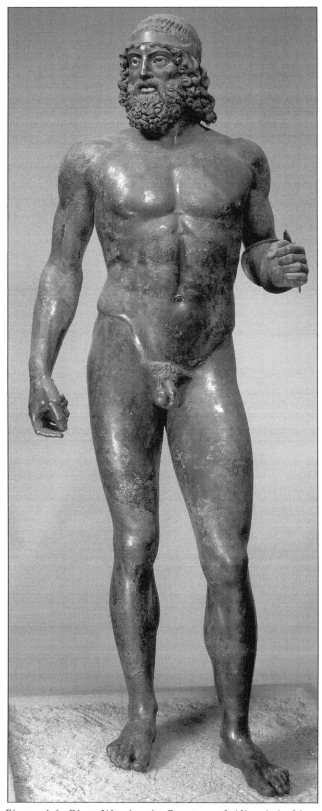

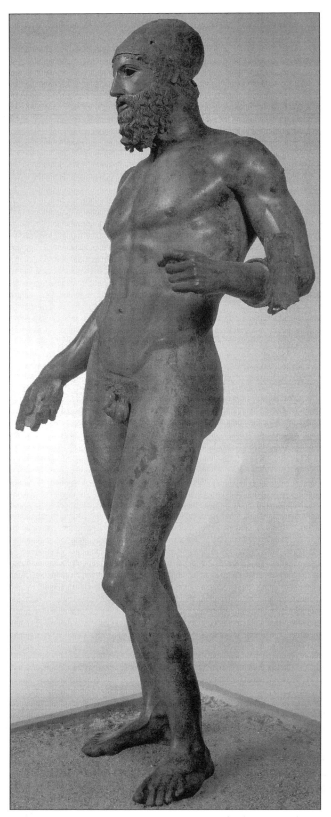

Figure 4.6. Riace Warrior A. Courtesy of Alinari Archives, Florence

Figure 4.7. Riace Warrior B. Courtesy of Alinari Archives, Florence

and survive real life encounters with real bodies. Those skills attempt to determine on the basis of appearance the potential behaviour of the body in question, and in doing so they pay not least attention to sexuality. The way in which viewers react to the 'matched' bodies of early classical sculpture – of sculpture made between the Kritian boy and the Parthenon metopes, is nicely revealed by the reactions of Italian viewers, according to one survey, to the bronze sculptures recovered from the sea off Riace Marina in the 1970s (Figures 4.6 and 4.7).[5] What the bodies of the two Riace warriors convinced Italian visitors to the museum at Reggio in Calabria (and also comic strip artists), was that Riace B was gay and Riace A straight.

The reaction of these Italian viewers reveals the problem with matching. The matched body invites all sorts of stories, but not all sorts of stories may be appropriate to what the sculptures are trying to achieve. How much of a personal history can the sculptures of a temple bear? It is not simply that the sexual history of a matched figure might raise distracting questions. If Plutarch's *Life of Perikles* (ch. 31) is to be trusted, fifth-century viewers were very ready to see particular likenesses in the figures of Greeks fighting against Amazons on the shield of Athena Parthenos. 'Matching' of that sort, too, could only stand in the way of the telling of mythological narrative (much as, for those who perceive them, the allusions to Pericles on stage of the sort detected by Michael Vickers, stand in the way of comic and tragic plots [Vickers 1997]).

There are virtually no bearded naked humans represented in classical sculpture after the Riace Warriors (Osborne 1997). Instead we get the impossible mature beardless man. If there was a Gombrichian moment when it seemed good to Greek sculptors to 'match' rather than 'make', that moment is precisely the moment of early classical sculpture, and is limited in medium as well as in time. That moment soon passed and without appreciably deflecting the course of vase painting. Greeks went on being clothed in conceptual 'made' bodies, deprived of their personal stories along with their facial hair, not in matched bodies. But manner and motive, which, like 'art' itself, Gombrich implausibly associated with the replacement of 'making' by 'matching', were not thereby excluded from what was conceivable. If figures went on being labels, they were not condemned to be 'mere' labels. The range of questions it is appropriate for the viewer to ask of classical sculpture is indeed vastly expanded over the range of questions it is appropriate to ask of archaic Greek, or Egyptian art: but that range is still artificially constricted. And, arguably, it is indeed in that that the art lies.[6]

This constriction on the range of reference of representations is not for want of skill or for failure to realise that anything different was possible, but because not everything that one believes about the body can be included in every communication through the body. In daily intercourse our ability to perceive bodies over a sequence of actions privileges some of our beliefs about the body over other of our beliefs about the body. Sculpture offers all dimensions of the body except time, and in order to recreate in the still frame the privileging which goes on through the relationship between 'frames' sculpture must select. The art of different periods chooses different sets of features from which to make up its bodies, and those sets are always negotiated against the framework of contemporary beliefs about the body. Beliefs about the body are manifested as much in those bodily features not represented as they are in those bodily features which are represented, but no history of art can afford simply to ignore the negotiation with beliefs of the body which has gone into its creation. Gombrich's attempt to understand the history of representation of the body without references to the body's own history is necessarily doomed. Art's history is one product of the mill of the history of the body, but the history of the body provides the stones on which the ingredients of art's history are ground.

Notes

1. 'Reflections on the Greek Revolution' begins 'If I had to reduce the last chapter to a brief formula it would be "making comes before matching". Before the artist ever wanted to match the sights of the visible world he wanted to create things in their own right' (Gombrich 1960: 99).
2. The classic discussion of the Olympia sculptures is provided by Ashmole 1972: chs. 1–3.
3. On the Kritian boy see the analysis by Carpenter 1960 and Hurwit 1989.
4. Castriota 1992: chs. 4–5 for a classic exposition; Osborne 1994a, 1994b for counter-arguments.
5. On the Riace Warriors see Borelli and Pelagatti 1984 and Harrison 1985. On the Italian viewers and comic strip artists' reactions to them see Taplin 1989: 87–9. For further discussion see Osborne 1997: 512, 1998: 32–5.
6. One might go on, in Gombrichian vein, to think about Plato and what Plato objected to in art – the necessary constriction of possible questions, or rather the way in which the artist controls the questions, but that is substance for a further paper.

Bibliography

Ashmole, B. 1972. *Architect and Sculptor in Classical Greece.* London: Phaidon

Beard, M. 1985. Reflections on 'Reflections on the Greek Revolution'. *Archaeological Review from Cambridge* 4 (2): 207–14.

Borelli L. and Pelegatti P. (eds) 1984. *Due Bronzi di Riace* Bolletino d'Arte Serie Speciale 3. Rome: Istituto poligrafico e zecca dello stato.

Bryson, N. 1983. *Vision and Painting: The Logic of the Gaze.* London: Macmillan.

Carpenter, R. 1960. *Greek Sculpture: A Critical Review.* Chicago: University of Chicago Press.

Castriota, D. 1992. *Myth, Ethos, and Actuality. Official Art in Fifth-century Athens.* Madison: University of Wisconsin Press.

Elsner, J. 2006. Reflections on the 'Greek Revolution' in Art: from changes in viewing to the transformation of subjectivity. In *Rethinking Revolutions through Classical Greece*, edited by S. Goldhill and R. Osborne, pp. 68–95. Cambridge: Cambridge University Press.

Gombrich, E. 1960. *Art and Illusion.* London: Phaidon

Harrison, E. 1985. Early classical sculpture: the bold style. In *Greek Art, Archaic into Classical*, edited by C. Boulter, pp. 40–65. Leiden: E.J. Brill.

Hurwit, J. 1989. The Kritios boy: discovery, reconstruction, and date. *American Journal of Archaeology* 93: 41–80.

Osborne, R. 1994a. Democracy and imperialism in the Panathenaic procession: the Parthenon frieze in its context. In *The Archaeology of Athens and Attica under Democracy*, edited by W. Coulson *et al.*, pp. 143–50. Oxford: Oxbow Books.

Osborne, R. 1994b. Framing the centaur. In *Art and Text in Ancient Greek Culture*, edited by S. Goldhill and R. Osborne, pp. 52–84. Cambridge: Cambridge University Press.

Osborne, R. 1997. Men without clothes: heroic nakedness and Greek art. *Gender and History* 9(3) 504–28.

Osborne R. 1998. Sculpted men of Athens: masculinity and power in the field of vision. In *Thinking Men: Masculinity and its Self-expression in the Classical Tradition*, edited by L. Foxhall and J. Salmon, pp. 23–42. London: Routledge.

Payne, H. and Young, G.M. 1936. *Archaic Marble Sculpture from the Acropolis.* London: Cresset Press.

Taplin, O. 1989. *Greek Fire.* London: Jonathan Cape.

Vickers, M. 1997. *Pericles on Stage: Political Comedy in Aristophanes' Early Plays.* Austin: University of Texas Press.

When the flesh is solid but the person is hollow inside: formal variation in hand-modelled figurines from Formative Mesoamerica

Rosemary Joyce

Introduction

In previous work on early Mesoamerican figurines, I have argued that we need to understand such objects as part of the apparatus through which human beings explored and indeed created their understandings of embodiment. Rather than treat figurines strictly as 'representations' of a reality on which they have no influence, or even as models for/models of experience (in the Geertzian sense), I want to approach them as *instruments* of experience.

There are clear warrants for doing so in the fact that the creation of such three-dimensional shaped clay sculptures engages the body physically, as the muscular movements through which clay was shaped are transferred as visible gestural traces to the plastic medium. The embodied movements that repeatedly resulted in the series of objects that today we recognise as 'stylistically' similar also engaged the thinking body, the mind-in-the-body that reflected on the emerging form and its relations to the shaping body and the phantasmic body intended to be materialised. I would go so far as to suggest that figurines might be thought of as bodily extensions, prosthetics, and as such occupy a space bridging the bodily being of the maker and that of the person – human or non-human, living or dead, natural or supernatural – of whom the completed figural sculpture is an image.

Beginning with this set of understandings, I consequently want to think about the technologies of production of figurines not simply as evidence of technical choices structured by the plasticity of clay and the capacities of firing technology. Instead, I want to consider that there were many different ways that any past crafter could have produced an adequate image. The choices made were not simply about the best means to represent a given reality. They were also explorations of what a body was, and what had to be included to have an adequate representation. Representation here should be understood as referring to more than the iconic details that let us 'see' a face, a hand, a thigh, or the curl of a hank of hair as it moves through space. It also involves the decisions to miniaturise the human form, the selection of a relative scale of clay body to flesh body, and – my main concern today – the question of whether to shape a body as simply a skin around a hollow core, or a solid mass of materials of different textures and structures.

The setting: villages on the early Honduran landscape

In order to explore these issues, I will draw on materials from systematic excavations in Honduras that produced stylistically similar figurines in what is known as the Playa de los Muertos style. Our evidence of early inhabitation in Honduras is spotty, as most villages were buried beneath later towns and cities, or under the soil deposited by active alluvial rivers (Joyce 1992, 1996; Joyce, Hendon and Sheptak 2004). Chance circumstances have given archaeologists access to seven sites that produced and/or consumed stylistically comparable fired clay figurines between about 1100 BC and AD 100 (Figure 5.1).

The earliest explored site, Playa de los Muertos, became the type-site for solid figurines with specific stylistic characteristics that I have summarised elsewhere (Joyce 2003; see also Agurcia Fasquelle 1977,

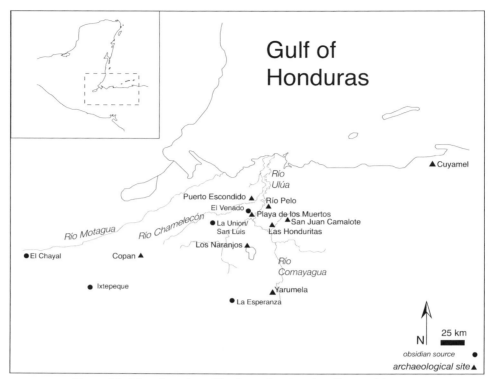

Figure 5.1. Map of northern Honduras showing sites discussed in text

1978). Located on an isolated segment of an ancient levee of the largest river in northern Honduras, the Rio Ulua, Playa de los Muertos is made up of several metres of deposits exposed initially by erosion by the river. Excavations at Playa de los Muertos by four groups of archaeologists between the 1890s and 1970s documented the remains of multiple superimposed houses at one location, and about sixteen human burials whose specific location with respect to the houses is not entirely clear (Gordon 1898b; Kennedy 1978, 1981, 1986; Popenoe 1934; Strong, Kidder and Paul 1938; Vaillant 1934). One of the archaeologically documented burials included two complete Playa de los Muertos figurines. Three radiocarbon dates suggest the main occupation here dated from about 700 BC or later, with a weighted average for the latest house floors of 320–280 BC.

Looting of similar figurines has produced hundreds of examples in museum collections in Honduras and the US, often also attributed to this site. But other archaeological excavations in Honduras have sampled different village sites with figurines of the same style, making it clear that the production of these figurines was not limited to the single village at Playa de los Muertos itself. The largest excavated assemblage from another site comes from the excavations I have co-directed with John Henderson of Cornell University

at Puerto Escondido (Henderson and Joyce 1998; Joyce and Henderson 2001, 2002).

Located 30 km from the Playa de los Muertos site on a tributary stream that ultimately reaches the Ulua down river from Playa itself, occupation of Puerto Escondido began much earlier than can be substantiated for the Playa site. The occupation layers that produced Playa de los Muertos figurines at Puerto Escondido span the likely period of occupation at Playa itself, with earlier levels associated with radiocarbon dates with a weighted average of 800–740 BC, and the later dating to 320–280 BC, contemporary with the latest house floors sampled at Playa de los Muertos. The main contexts for figurines at Puerto Escondido are refuse deposits in one area of the site, where a series of superimposed houses remodelled throughout the earlier part of this period were replaced ultimately by larger architecture including a large formal stone firebox, a stepped platform with stone facing, and a series of stone cists of a size and shape to suggest use in burials. The only one of these cists excavated had been filled in with stones, including a fragment of a life-size stone sculpture of a seated person that presumably was displayed earlier in this area. This cist also incorporated a single small Playa de los Muertos figurine. While no human remains were recovered in this area, in another zone of the site, remains of two badly decayed extended burials associated with the construction of monumental terraces dating to ca. 940–810 BC were recorded. Neither burial incorporated any artefacts, and traces of pigment adhered to the bones.

Contemporary with the Puerto Escondido site, occupants of Las Honduritas, located in a small upland valley to the east, also created and disposed of Playa de los Muertos style figurines. Las Honduritas, upriver on the Rio Cuyamapa, a tributary feeding into one of the main rivers that combined to form the Rio Ulua, produced figurines identifiable in the Playa de los Muertos style; other aspects of the material culture at this site also match those of the Ulua river valley sites of the period. Excavations at Las Honduritas delineated an ancient surface under much later deposits associated with monumental architecture (Joyce, Hendon and Sheptak 2004). On this surface was a dense, clustered deposit composed of reconstructable vessels, many with complex decoration, smashed in place within a 6 x 8 metre area. Radiocarbon dates from this deposit span the interval from 800 to 740 BC. Included with these vessels were a few other artefacts, including seven fragments of Playa figurines shaped from a redder clay than those from Playa de los Muertos or Puerto Escondido. No burials were encountered at this site.

A fourth site, Rio Pelo, was excavated by several groups of researchers affiliated with the Honduran Institute of Anthropology and History in the 1980s (Wonderley 1991; Wonderley and Caputi 1993). Rio Pelo was located far upstream on a tributary of the Ulua that entered downstream of the Playa site. Its location on a colluvial terrace gave the residents of the site access to clays redder in colour and coarser in texture than at Playa or Puerto Escondido. The Rio Pelo site was originally identified because of the presence of large earthen mounds, the remains of buildings constructed during the Formative period (Robinson 1987, 1989). While none of the other three sites have surface-visible remains of such early architecture today, the monumental architecture buried at Puerto Escondido was similar in construction and form before it was buried by river deposits and later remodelling, and it is possible that similar structures were buried in the later architecture at Las Honduritas. The architecture of Rio Pelo was apparently used somewhat later, with a weighted average of eight radiocarbon dates indicating occupation between AD 0–60 (Joyce, Hendon and Sheptak 2004). The sample of figurines from this site was distinguished by a regular small size, and certain other iconographic features. Based on his analysis of contextual information from excavations here, Anthony Wonderley (1991; Wonderley and Caputi 1993) suggested the deposits stemmed from

ceremonial events, possibly marked by feasts. No burials were reported from this site.

San Juan Camalote is the location most distant from the Playa de los Muertos site to have produced similar figurines. Located in a second upland valley to the east, on a tributary of the Rio Cuyamapa upstream from Las Honduritas, San Juan Camalote was a site of construction of an early ballcourt, whose use was investigated by John G. Fox (1994, 1996), as part of a project directed by Julia Hendon and myself (Joyce and Hendon 2000). Here a deposit much like those from Rio Pelo, composed of bottles and bowls of unusual forms and complexity of crafting, yielded three Playa style figurines. While the clay used was distinctively coloured and finer in texture, the imagery and size matched the contemporary figurines at Rio Pelo. Radiocarbon dates give a weighted average date of AD 0–60 for this deposit, identical to the span for Rio Pelo. A stratigraphically earlier deposit with vessels comparable to those at the Playa de los Muertos site itself was dated ca. 380–230 BC. Again, there were no burials documented.

I have argued that the practices of shaping the body in which I am interested recursively engaged figurine production, modification of the body for body ornaments, and processing of the body in death. Two other contemporary sites are thus relevant for this discussion. Even farther east than San Juan Camalote, the Cuyamel caves in the mountains above the valley of the Rio Aguan produced a unique collection of ceramic vessels associated with human skeletal remains. While originally reported by cavers, the site was documented by archaeologists Vito Veliz and Paul Healy (Healy 1974). Included among the vessels, recognisable as comparable to well-dated forms from 1100–900 BC at Puerto Escondido, were examples of larger, hollow figurines. The comparable deposits at Puerto Escondido also produced fragments from what must have been similar hollow effigies or figural vessels representing humans and animals.

Finally, in the mountains bordering the lower Ulua River Valley to the south, reached by following a tributary of the Ulua river upstream from Playa de los Muertos, inhabitants using pottery like that from ca. 900 BC Puerto Escondido began construction of monumental platforms on the northwest shore of Lake Yojoa. These construction projects culminated by 400–100 BC in the currently visible 20 metre tall, 100 metre on the base pyramids of Los Naranjos (Baudez and Becquelin 1973). Incorporated in one of the three large pyramids of this date, Structure IV, was a single, central burial of a person wearing jade costume. Other human skeletal elements were recovered from the same stage of the pyramid (Joyce 1996). Not in direct association, but in deposits probably assignable to ca. 650–400 BC, examples of Playa de los Muertos-style figurines were recovered. At the same time, the inhabitants of Los Naranjos produced a series of close-to-life size stone sculptures of human figures.

The evidence with which I am working, then, consists of heterogeneous human images in fired clay and stone, and worked human bodies and instruments for shaping them. The earliest examples are hollow ceramic figurines and vessels with figural modelling, dating from before 900 BC, from refuse associated with houses at Puerto Escondido and secondary burial of human skeletal elements at the caves of Cuyamel. Solid figurines and figural vessels dating ca. 900–400 come from specialised refuse associated with the construction of major platforms and one refilled cist at Puerto Escondido; from refuse of ceremonies, perhaps also associated with larger architecture, at Las Honduritas; from refuse of the village that built Structure IV at Los Naranjos and interred the main individual buried there, and from household contexts and at least one burial at Playa de los Muertos itself. Finally, feasting contexts associated with monumental architecture at Rio Pelo and San Juan Camalote, dating to ca. 200 BC–100 AD, represent a final set of historically related materials.

Living bodies and crafted bodies in formative Honduras

My argument is that the interplay of processes of modifying the living bodies of humans, and the corpses of the deceased, at times and places that included both the relatively mundane and the specially distinguished, must be considered in any attempt to think through the decision to use clay to make a thin skin enclosing a hollow interior, or to shape layers of specific detail around a solid core. From this perspective, the formal characteristics of figurines are not simply iconic, but indexical of the experiences and understandings of the living bodies of figurine makers.

Living bodies, crafted bodies

If the body is seen as a product of flows of substances, then the living bodies of formative villagers in Honduras must be understood at least in part as made of the thick fermented and unfermented liquids that formed the main foods served in the pottery bowls, bottles, and small jars found in these early sites. The flesh that was formed by the flows of these moist substances was malleable, and subject to bodily disciplines of routinised postures, routines of labour,

and surface inscriptions. Our main evidence of these facts of life comes from the artefacts that were used to modify and extend the body's surface and flesh.

The early villagers of northern Honduras were cultivators of plants, including maize, from which pollen dating to before 2000 BC has been recovered in cores near Los Naranjos (Rue 1989). By 1100–900 BC, the people of Puerto Escondido were processing cacao and, we believe, fermenting it to form a mild beer, with traces of cacao recovered from distinctive narrow-necked bottles (Henderson and Joyce 2006). The use of maize may have been for fermented beverages as well, or for thick stews or gruels like the later *atole*, since the vessels known from before 1100 BC are small incurved rim bowls and open bowls, and small neckless jars. Larger jars added after 1100 BC may have contained water or facilitated transport of larger quantities of brewed beverages. Until 900 BC there is no evidence of pots with exteriors carbonised, suggesting that as in other contemporary sites in Mesoamerica, indirect heat (stone boiling) methods of cooking were predominant (Clark and Gosser 1995). After that date, some pottery plates with carbon encrusted lower faces resulting from direct exposure to fires, possible evidence of a shift in cooking methods, are found.

At Puerto Escondido, working of shell ornaments started before 1100 BC, and similar forms were executed in jade after 900 BC. Belts of pierced shell pendants, shell disks and carved spires that likely formed parts of complex ear ornaments, were produced in the early period at the site. Fired ceramic ear plugs, very thin rings of the finest clay, and others of shell, bone, and (after about 900 BC) jade, were the most common ornaments at Puerto Escondido, Playa de los Muertos, and Los Naranjos. Individual beads of shell, bone, and stone formed sets marking wrists, neck, and ankles in the burials from Playa de los Muertos (Table 5.1). The habitual use of any of these ornaments engaged the person with an extension of their flesh and simultaneously shaped the way they differentially experienced the bodily sites provided with these harder exterior prosthetics. There are suggestions in the distributions of body ornaments in burials that different bodily sites were emphasised at different ages: ankles and wrists more commonly in younger individuals, neck and ears in adults. At least at Playa de los Muertos, shell was incorporated exclusively with the bodies of juveniles.

The malleability of the flesh was also marked, literally, through the use of ceramic stamps and seals, transferring painted designs across the flesh or, possibly, additional garments of bark cloth or other textiles (inferred from representations of small pubic aprons and more rarely enveloping cloaks in figurines).

Burial ID	
Burial A (child)	shell bead wristlet
Burial B	greenstone bead necklace with 3 'duckbill' pendants
Burial 1	greenstone bead necklace
Burial 2	greenstone napkin ring ear spools
Burial 4	clamshell pendant
	2 ceramic stamps
Burial 5	greenstone bead wristlet
	clay napkin ring ear spools
Burial 7	greenstone pendant
Burial 8 (child)	shell and greenstone necklace with skull and duckbill pendants
	greenstone bead belt
	2 Playa de los Muertos style figurines
Burial 11	incised clay ear spools
Burial 14 (child)	greenstone bead necklace
	greenstone and white shell bead wristlet
Descriptions based on review of material curated at the Peabody Museum	

Table 5.1. Personal ornaments and related artefacts in burials at Playa de los Muertos

The stamps recovered at Puerto Escondido and Playa de los Muertos are technologically, morphologically, and stylistically closely related, and include both roller seals and handled stamps with unit designs (Holly Bachand, personal communication). The late deposits at Rio Pelo, in contrast, produced a large sample of unit stamps with handles unrelated to other samples in the region.

Even the abundant obsidian flakes and blades that make up a large part of the material collections from these sites were technologies for the manipulation of the body's labile matter. The figurines that depict human subjects wearing ear, neck, wrist, and ankle ornaments like those found in burials, also show complex treatments of the living, growing hair, with geometric designs shaved in, and beads threaded on long locks hanging down from the head.

Complementing these malleable substances, bodies also demonstrably contained a solid framework of bone whose nature and contribution to embodiment was known to early Honduran villagers from their manipulations of the bodies of the dead. Our earliest evidence for mortuary disposal comes from the cave sanctuaries at sites like the Cuyamel caves, or the Gordon caves near Copan (Gordon 1898a; Joyce 1996; Rue, Freter and Ballinger 1989). Here, vessels identifiable with types dating to 1100–900 BC at excavated villages were associated with human bone that likely were secondary deposits. Defleshing or allowing the flesh of the dead to decompose before reclaiming the bones and disposing of them was a form

of body practice through which living people came to understand their own bodies as composed of a shell of perishable flesh surrounding more durable internal elements that could be separated and re-collected in groups. It is intriguing that the osteologist's report on the two very fragmentary burials from early Middle Formative Puerto Escondido noted pigment adhering to the bones, possibly from painting of already defleshed elements. Disarticulated human remains were also recorded in a context scattered with red pigment in the slightly later deposits at Los Naranjos.

Crafted bodies, living bodies?

If we now turn to a consideration of the more obviously crafted bodies in these early villages, the hand-modelled figurines that are my central topic in this paper, we might begin by exploring how the techniques of production and the intended and actual uses of these crafted bodies related to the composition of the embodied persons whose products, and thus bodily extensions, they were.

Our earliest examples from well-excavated sites are fragments of hollow figurines or figural vessels, thin skins of clay finished in the same manner as contemporary jars and bowls. Some likely were features from containers used for the same kinds of liquid or semi-liquid foods that circulated through other vessels lacking such markings. Here, we might draw on Mary Weismantel's (2004) analyses of Moche figural jars to think of these ceramic shells as facilitating flows of bodily substances, in the same manner as such substances flowed through networks of living persons. While Weismantel's subject materials emphasise flows through sexual acts, the early Honduran hollow figural vessels emphasise the movement of liquids through bodies that may be more centrally concerned with the cycling of foods into the body's interiority through the open mouths depicted on these figures.

If at least some of the liquids contained in such early jars were *chichas*, indigenous alcoholic drinks, it is possible that there were literal flows of pre-chewed maize or manioc that connected living human bodies to crafted ceramic bodies. Such masticated carbohydrates would act as starters for fermentation, as they do in contemporary traditional lowland tropical American societies. Even without this consubstantial relationship between the contents of living and crafted bodies, as containers of liquids that flowed into human bodies, the crafted figures were indexical of the presence of such foodstuffs within the bodies of persons.

The channelling of flows of liquids out of effigy vessels to be consumed by living persons is consequently extremely interesting; the potters in fact chose, apparently systematically, to avoid the identification of apertures of figural vessels or hollow figurines with bodily orifices. In a stirrup spout vessel modelled as a Playa de los Muertos style person lying face down with head up and legs raised, the feet of the figure occupy the opening of the bottle. There is no obvious connection between orifices that would have allowed liquids to flow from living bodies, and those through which liquids move in these crafted bodies. Hollow figurines similarly place necessary openings not where the anatomy of living persons might have suggested (in the mouth, eyes, nose or ears, for example), but at sites that were solid on living bodies, such as the back of the head. What figurines, as models of living bodies, emphasise is a relationship between an enfolding skin and its mobile contents, not between apertures and orifices.

Unlike living bodies, these hollow selves were shells with no internal framework. The production of solid figurines, first present in Honduran deposits slightly later than the hollow effigies, maintains the division of outer skin/inner contents, but replaces the hollow, liquid- or vapour- filled void with a solid armature of clay. Roughly shaped in the form of a body with arms, legs, and a peg for the neck, this inner skeleton is covered by thin layers of finer clay, sometimes mixed with crushed limestone (Agurcia Fasquelle 1977, 1978), built up in layers and capped by a fine layer of modelled features. This layered composition is very obvious in the redder pastes of the figurines from Rio Pelo and Las Honduritas, where the final layer is a whiter cap that produces the same uniform beige surface colour of other Playa figurines. It is also evident when such figurines shatter in superimposed layers.

The interior armature on solid Playa-style figurines recalls the skeletal structure shown emerging out of the fleshed body of a life-size stone sculpture from Los Naranjos, probably created between 700 and 500 BC (Joyce and Henderson 2002). In the case of this sculpture, and the much smaller figurines, the flesh of the living body is transubstantiated into an apparently permanent, durable form. But it is worth asking whether this solid flesh was understood as so different from the less enduring human flesh it mimicked.

While we today emphasise the solid state achieved by firing the Playa de los Muertos figurines, privileging the end product over the process, we should not assume the same stance for the makers of these objects. In the process of production, these craft workers modelled a thick moist mass of clay and water, not unlike that produced when hard corn kernels are soaked and ground for maize foods, or hard, fermented, sun-dried cacao seeds are ground to make cacao foods. A regular cycling of dry to wet to dry, plant to food to flesh to bone, was part of the experience of embodied being for the makers and users of Playa de los Muertos figurines. The actual shaping of the miniature bodies of Playa figurines took place while the clay was wet, just as the shaping of the larger, living bodies of Playa figurine makers did while the flesh was wet.

What firing Playa de los Muertos figurines did was put an end to the malleability of these crafted bodies, as the death of humans ended the period when living flesh and hair could be manipulated. Unlike the living persons who made, used, and may have understood themselves to be represented by them, Playa figurines ended their lives fully fleshed, transfixed by fire at one point in what in the living flesh was an ongoing flow. But they were not removed from time. Instead, like the hard skeletal cores of living bodies, from which the less substantial plant-fed flesh disappeared, Playa de los Muertos figurines (and indeed, the rare larger stone sculptures made at the same time at Los Naranjos and Puerto Escondido) were broken into pieces and disposed of in ordered fashions. As with the bodies of living persons, the disposal of the bodies of crafted persons was structured by the ways that ancient Hondurans experienced their embodied selves.

The crafted dead, the permanently young, and the spirits within

My arguments above are intended to suggest that it is

artificial for us to separate human beings from figurines and consider the latter solely as 'representations' of the former. Instead, both are crafted persons; and both may have been understood as living persons or parts of persons.

In both kinds of bodies, interior substances were distinct from those forming the outer surface visible to the world. The external appearance of living bodies and crafting bodies was made similar by the reproduction in small scale of the ornaments worn by the human subjects. Three dimensionality, with depiction of anatomical features on all surfaces (including the underside of seated figures, and the front, sides, and back of standing figures) was a necessary concommitant of making crafted bodies that indexed the whole living body.

The interplay between hollow figurines (enclosing flows of moving air), hollow figural vessels (enclosing liquid foods), and solid figurines (enclosing hard skeletons) exemplifies a range of substances that likely were understood as also contained within the human skin. Beneath a surface appearance of similarity, the contents of even the effigy vessels were likely varied, and perhaps the concealment of what the skin covered and its cloaking in a socially coordinated surface was important in the experiences of early Honduran persons. While unlike other contemporary Mesoamerican societies, no fired clay masks or images of people wearing masks are reported from any site with Playa de los Muertos style figurines, a repeated image in the style is a person wearing a cloak, pulled over the top of the head so that only the face is visible. A unique figurine shows a person with the face completely obscured by bands of textured material, perhaps textiles.

The disarticulation and disposal of crafted persons, fired clay or flesh and bone, was a complex focus of cultural production in these early villages and sanctuaries. We can propose the circulation of human remains through primary interment near house sites or within monumental architecture, through secondary sites of disposal like the mountain caves of Copan and Cuyamel, or incorporated in later burials. We can also propose the circulation of ceramic remains through similar contexts.

Based on the common attribution of whole figurines in museum collections to human burials, and the presence in one professionally excavated burial at Playa de los Muertos of two complete figurines, it has been common to consider these likely intended for burial. Certainly, one of the earliest hollow figurines was recovered from the caves of Cuyamel, providing a possible genealogy for this practice. But this is not where the vast majority of such figurines have been recovered in documented excavations, nor even where known whole figurines were found.

The early deposits from Puerto Escondido provide one suite of systematically buried Playa de los Muertos figurines. Most are broken in such a way that the heads were separated from the bodies, and a large number of the fragments recovered were from seated bodies. A single miniature figurine, also of a seated person, was included in this location. It may not be a coincidence that this was also the site where a cist appropriately sized for human burial contained a fragment of a large stone sculpture of a seated human figure. One complete miniature Playa style figurine was set in the fill of this cist. It represents long linear marks that recall the representations of long bones on the contemporary human torso with skeleton emerging through flesh from Los Naranjos.

Overlapping chronologically with Puerto Escondido, at least three fragments from Las Honduritas were from torsos of seated figures, and two are from upper bodies of standing figures. Two of the fragments represent portions of figurine heads, with the punctated pattern used for the closely cropped hair on elderly figures. At a minimum, four distinct figurines were disposed of as part of the event that produced this deposit. One of these likely depicted a seated, older figure, and at least one other seated figurine was deposited. Standing postures are most commonly attributes of Playa de los Muertos figurines depicting youthful life stages, particularly points in ceremonies of transition when new hair styles and ear ornaments were adopted (Joyce 2003). While the fragmented condition of the figurines from Las Honduritas makes it impossible to be certain, the dimensions of preserved torsos closely match intact figurines depicting this marked stage in the lifecycle. The deposit apparently resulted from actions that involved the use and disposal of figurines representing both elders and youths.

At Playa de los Muertos itself, one burial excavated in the 1920s contained two figurines. The individual in this burial was recorded as a child. In addition to a greenstone bead belt, this child was buried wearing a shell and greenstone bead necklace with pendants in a characteristic duckbill shape seen on figurines, and others in the shape of defleshed skulls.

The later deposits from Rio Pelo, described as from refuse from feasting, contained a distinctive assemblage of figurines of standing and seated subjects, many with heads broken from bodies. The same deposits yielded a very large number of stamps used for body ornamentation. A similar feline pelt apron was present on many examples. The similar contemporary deposit from San Juan Camalote yielded a standing body of the same type, wearing the same distinctive pelt, along with a small animal figurine, missing its head (Fox 1994: fig. 45b). The rounded base and small size are consistent with the interpretation of this as a pendant, like most documented miniature Playa de los Muertos figurines (Joyce 2003). A cross-hatched pattern on the body of this figurine is characteristic of other Playa de los Muertos animal miniatures, representing monkeys or some other animal with a curling tail.

The Puerto Escondido and Playa de los Muertos contexts arguably resulted from social ceremonies related to the death of human persons. Here, seated figures, images of adult persons, were dismantled and buried as were the living bodies. The reuse of the cist grave at Puerto Escondido for the fragment of the body of a stone sculpture may have accompanied the removal from the same location of defleshed human skeletal elements for disposal elsewhere. In their place, a Playa figurine depicting a skeletalised body was left. The Playa de los Muertos burial, apparently completely articulated when encountered, was accompanied by a full-size seated figurine of an adult person, and a small-scale replica of the same subject. The somewhat earlier and stylistically distinct, ancestral figurine recovered from the Cuyamel Cave, similarly, was complete, although in association with disarticulated human remains.

The contrast between these mortuary contexts, with their structured disposal of seated adult and elderly figurines, and the more complete destruction of the figurines recovered at Las Honduritas is striking. Deposited in a context where complete or almost complete vessels were left articulated in place, these figurines, representing both youthful and elderly persons, were fragmented so badly they were not recognised initially as figural, but were collected as presumed construction materials. The layers of clay used to form the final shape around the core were peeled away from each other. In the lack of a directly associated burial, this context itself contrasts markedly with those at the other two sites and may represent a different kind of event in the life of the ceramic persons and any fleshed persons with which they were connected.

The deposits from Rio Pelo and San Juan Camalote offer yet another form of treatment of crafted bodies. Here, the scale of excavations makes the lack of evidence for any burials much more secure. At both sites, the deposits recovered are related to moments in the construction histories of buildings of monumental scale. At both sites, the range of vessels included numbers of bottles and relatively fewer bowls. San Juan Camalote definitely, and Rio Pelo possibly, also yielded specialised vessels for burning plant resins, a common

ritual act in later Honduran societies. While many of the figurines from these sites are headless, some are complete, so it would be hard to argue that breaking the figurines and disposing of their heads and bodies separately was of any concern here. The crafted bodies embedded in these settings are of young women, standing or seated, with exaggerated narrow waists and wide hips and thighs. No identifiable examples of the elderly seated figurines with their distinctive punctated hairstyle were included. If figurines like these were used, as I have previously suggested, in rites of passage, then we may be dealing with at these two sites with the refuse from rites held at an earlier point in the lives of human persons.

Permanently commemorated as youthful, the living humans who were indexed by these figurines continued their own life trajectories elsewhere, while these crafted parts of their selves remained in places that were newly marked as sites of special interest by the construction of new aggregate architectural bodies, of which the crafted bodies of figurines formed a part.

Bibliography

Agurcia Fasquelle, R. 1977. *The Playa de los Muertos Figurines*. MA thesis, Department of Anthropology. New Orleans: Tulane University.

Argucia Fasquelle, R. 1978. Las figurillas de Playa de los Muertos, Honduras. *Yaxkin* 2: 221–240.

Baudez, C. and Becquelin, P. 1973. *Archéologie de los Naranjos, Honduras*. Etudes mesoaméricaines 2. Mexico, D.F.: Mission Archeologique et Ethnologique Française au Mexique.

Clark, J.E. and Gosser, D. 1995. Reinventing Mesoamerica's first pottery. In *The Emergence of Pottery*, edited by W.K. Barnett and J.W. Hoopes, pp. 209–222. Washington, DC: Smithsonian Institution Press.

Fox, J.G. 1994. *Putting the Heart Back in the Court: Ballcourts and Ritual Action in Mesoamerica*. Doctoral dissertation, Harvard University. Ann Arbor: UMI.

Fox, J.G. 1996. Playing with power: ballcourts and political ritual in southern Mesoamerica. *Current Anthropology* 37: 483–509.

Gordon, G.B. 1898a. *Caverns of Copan, Honduras*. Harvard University, Peabody Museum of Archaeology and Ethnology Memoirs 1(5). Cambridge, MA: Harvard University.

Gordon, G.B. 1898b. *Researches in the Uloa Valley, Honduras*. Harvard University, Peabody Museum of Archaeology and Ethnology *Memoirs* 1(4). Cambridge, MA: Harvard University.

Healy, P. 1974. The Cuyamel caves: Preclassic sites in Northeast Honduras. *American Antiquity* 39: 433–437.

Henderson, J.S. and Joyce, R.A. 1998. Investigaciones arqueológicas en Puerto Escondido: Definición del FormativoTemprano en el Valle Inferior del Río Ulúa. *Yaxkin* XVII: 5–35. Tegucigalpa.

Henderson, J.S. and Joyce, R.A. 2006. Brewing distinction: The development of cacao beverages in Formative Mesoamerica. In *A Cultural History of Cacao in the Americas*, edited by C. McNeill, pp. 140–153. Gainesville: University Press of Florida.

Joyce, R. 1992. Innovation, communication and the archaeological record: A reassessment of Middle Formative Honduras. *Journal of the Steward Anthropological Society* 20 (1 and 2): 235–256.

Joyce, R. 1996. Social dynamics of exchange: changing patterns in the Honduran archaeological record. In *Chieftains, Power and Trade: Regional Interaction in the Intermediate Area of the Americas*, edited by C. Henrik Langebaek and F. Cardenas-Arroyo, pp. 31–46. Bogota: Departamento de Antropología, Universidad de los Andes.

Joyce, R. 1999. Social dimensions of Pre-Classic burials. In *Social Patterns in Pre-Classic Mesoamerica*, edited by D.C. Grove and R.A. Joyce, pp. 15–47. Washington DC: Dumbarton Oaks.

Joyce, R. 2003. Making something of herself: Embodiment in life and death at Playa de los Muertos, Honduras. *Cambridge Archaeological Journal* 13: 248–261.

2001. Beginnings of village life in Eastern Mesoamerica. *Latin American Antiquity* 12: 5–24.

Joyce, R.A. and Henderson, J.S. 2002. La arqueología del periodo Formativo en Honduras: nuevos datos sobre el <<estilo olmeca>> en la zona maya. *Mayab* 15: 5–18

Joyce, R.A. and Hendon, J.A. 2000. Heterarchy, history, and material reality: 'communities' in Late Classic Honduras. In *The Archaeology of Communities: A New World Perspective*, edited by M.-A. Canuto and J. Yaeger, pp. 143–159. London: Routledge Press.

Joyce, R.A., Hendon, J.A. and Sheptak, R.N. 2004. Rethinking Playa de los Muertos: exploring the Middle Formative Period in Honduras. Unpublished ms. under review for a volume edited by A. Cyphers and K. Hirth.

Kennedy, N. 1978. Acerca de la frontera en Playa de los Muertos, Honduras. *Yaxkin* II (3): 203–215. Tegucigalpa.

Kennedy, N. 1981. *The Formative Period Ceramic Sequence from Playa de los Muertos, Honduras*. Doctoral dissertation, Department of Anthropology, University of Illinois, Urbana-Champaign.

Kennedy, N. 1986. The periphery problem and Playa de los Muertos: a test case. In *The Southeast Maya Periphery*, edited by P. Urban and E. Schortman, pp. 179–193. Austin: University of Texas Press.

Popenoe, D.H. 1934. Some excavations at Playa de los Muertos, Ulua River, Honduras. *Maya Research* 1: 62–86.

Robinson, E. 1987. Sula Valley diachronic regional and interregional interaction: A view from the east side alluvial fans. In *Interaction on the Southeast Mesoamerican Frontier: Prehistoric and Historic Honduras and El Salvador*, edited by E.J. Robinson, pp. 154–195. BAR International Series 327 (i). Oxford: BAR.

Robinson, E. 1989. *Prehistoric Settlement of the Sula Valley, Honduras: Spatial Analysis and Social Interpretation*. PhD dissertation, Department of Anthropology, Tulane University, New Orleans.

Rue, D.J. 1989. Archaic Middle American agriculture and settlement: recent pollen data from Honduras. *Journal of Field Archaeology* 16: 177–184.

Rue, D.J., Freter, A. and Ballinger, D.A. 1989. The caverns of Copan revisited: Preclassic sites in the Sesesmil River valley, Copan, Honduras. *Journal of Field Archaeology* 16 (4): 395–404.

Strong, W.D., Kidder II, A.V. and Drexel Paul, Jr., A.J. 1938. *Preliminary Report on the Smithsonian Institution-Harvard University Archaeological Expedition to Northwestern Honduras, 1936*. Smithsonian Miscellaneous Collections 97 (1).

Vaillant, G. 1934. The archaeological setting of the Playa de los Muertos culture. *Maya Research* 1: 87–100.

Weismantel, M. 2004. Moche sex pots: Reproduction and temporality in ancient South America. *American Anthropologist* 106: 495–505.

Wonderley, A. 1991. Late Preclassic Sula plain, Honduras: regional antecedents to social complexity and interregional convergence in ceramic style. In *Formation of Complex Society in Southeastern Mesoamerica*, edited by W. Fowler, pp. 143–169. Boca Raton, FL: CRC Publications.

Wonderley, A. and Caputi, P. 1993. Pelo II Complex. In *Pottery of Prehistoric Honduras: Regional Classification and Analysis*, edited by J.S. Henderson and M. Beaudry-Corbett, pp. 67–76. Monograph 35. Los Angeles: UCLA Institute of Archaeology.

6

Fractal bodies in the past and present

Chris Fowler

'...What you have brought us is the body...' [Canaques informant to anthropologist Maurice Leenhardt, cited in Csordas 1999: 143]

Introduction

The body has been subject to an array of approaches in the last twenty years. A number of these have questioned the degree to which identities should be understood as fixed within the body. Through ethnography and analysis, anthropologists such as Marilyn Strathern have stressed the way that bodies in other cultures may be understood in relational ways that accentuate the composite and contextually changeable character of the person (e.g., Strathern 1988). At the same time, despite the dominant modern narrative of bodily identities as being innately fixed within the body's biology, sociologists and cultural theorists, such as Judith Butler, have illustrated how bodies are produced through social and cultural practices. Butler's work on performativity (Butler 1990, 1993) suggests that bodily identities are enacted in relation to both previous acts, and 'fictions' or ideals of bodily conduct which no individual is able to achieve. As a result, each of us struggles with numerous referent actions and images as we negotiate our identities through bodily conduct. This work focuses on bodies in the modern West, while many anthropological studies have focussed on non-industrialised societies – we could suggest that the tension between the relational and the fixed aspects of bodily identity occurs in many if not all cultural contexts (see LiPuma 1998). To me this indicates the need to understand patterns in how relational features of identity are negotiated with reference to the body and how certain aspects of identity are naturalised as fixed in the body – patterns which may be present whichever period or place we are studying.

While a body is the locus of the individuated person inhabiting it, that body is also a social locale open to outside influence. Personhood may extend outside a body through personal relationships and through personal objects. It is now conceivable that the brain is not the sole locus where personal experience is realised and archived, and further attention must be given to features like 'muscle memory' and the embeddedness of human lives within place and landscape. There have even been recent claims that organ transplants can carry memories from the donor to the recipient ('cellular memory'). Whatever we make of these ideas, our understandings of the relationship between the body and the person are clearly diverse, complex and continually changing,[1] yet a dominant discourse exists in Western culture. I would suggest that one aspect of personhood – individuality – has been raised to the status of a dominant mode of personhood in the west through that discourse. In secular understanding, the body is the property of the autonomous individual owning it. Bodily differences, including gendered differences, are secondary to a neutral citizenship protected by human rights accorded to the inhabitant of each human body, as Cecilia Busby (2000: 221), among others, has argued. Each individual is morally and legally responsible for their own actions. Individuals own as well as belong, and it is their right of ownership over their bodies which define those bodies in the West. The argument warning against thinking about present and past bodies and persons as individuated indivisible units will not be rehearsed here. Instead, I will work from the point of view that there are relational features of personal identity in all communities, whether or not these are brought to the fore in common practice and discourse. I will focus on cases where this relational feature *is* emphasised, and attend to some mechanisms through which relations are traced.

The emphasis on relational identities adopted here is not a denial of the body's materiality. While some scholars emphasise the perceptual apparatus and affordances of the body, positing the body's peculiarities as the basis for human understandings of the world at large (e.g., Merleau-Ponty 1962), others have focussed on bodily practices, techniques and comportment, stressing culturally distinct ways that bodies are shaped and experienced through these techniques (e.g., Mauss 1979a and b, Csordas 1999). The body is a sensual, physical yet plastic medium of social and cultural action, action carried out by the inhabitant of the body and by others in an interactive way. A body is active, it is living and lived, but it is also a material thing. As such, bodies are understood in terms of the material worlds they inhabit. I will focus here on one core mechanism through which understandings of the relationships between body and world are conveyed – fractal relations.

Fractal patterning is a common and powerful core mechanism in conceptualising the human body. Some suggest that fractal relations may have been appreciated by past communities as part of how they made sense of the world (e.g., Chapman 1996, 2000; Fowler 2004a). Others have examined relationships between things and bodies (for instance) and described patterns which seem to fit this term, but have not adopted it. There have been two main routes towards appreciating fractal relations in archaeology – one is through examining how metaphors are drawn between different material media (e.g., Tilley 1999 – who does not use the term), and the other has been through examining fragmentation (e.g., Chapman 2000). By examining material metaphors, for instance, Tilley has drawn together a series of examples illustrating how the human body is thought about through other media – the form and substance of the Batammaliba house, for example, which also cite the arrangement of the cosmos as a whole (Tilley 1999: 41–9). Yet, as I will explain, fractal thinking ultimately extends beyond metaphor in that the patterns that are shared by different buildings, objects and bodies are manifestations of a single scheme of relations. In other words, these things do not stand for each other, they are produced *out of each other* through a single logic to relationships. Furthermore, fractals do not only

operate by fragmenting things and, as I will argue, articulating parts and wholes is only aspect of fractal relations. However, to date, interpretations of bodies in fractal relations have frequently focused on the fragmentation of the body (and objects) into parts. To that extent they have only discussed one node of fractal relations, and one dimension along which past bodies were treated, understood and experienced. Not only has this emphasis on whole forms and parts ignored other aspects of fractal relations, but it has tended to gloss over the messy, substantial, growing and decaying matter of the body. Here I suggest that it is necessary to consider other aspects to fractal relations, any of which may become elevated to the key principle through which bodies may be perceived. This will allow us to grasp further ways that relational identities in the past could have been generated, and past bodies understood.

Fractal thinking: fragment, flow and form

The fractal

> *…any of various extremely irregular curves or shapes for which any suitably chosen part is similar in shape to a given larger or smaller part when magnified or reduced to the same size.* (Merriam-Webster On-line dictionary, definition of 'fractal')

There are different ways to conceive of bodies, to shape them, and to deconstitute them but these commonly revolve around the substantial composition of the body. Many of these schemes involve an equivalence in the matter and form of the human body and the rest of the world. In many cultural spheres the body is understood as made of several different aspects – for instance, different understandings of 'humours' in the ancient world, medieval and early modern Europe. These humours exhibited certain qualities, and were equivalents of elements outside of the body. The body and the universe were presented as reflections of each other. Differentiated bodily substances that encapsulate qualities which have a broader worldly circulation are also well-attested through ethnographic studies in, for instance, Africa and Melanesia. The human body does not emerge as something entirely distinct from the rest of the world, but as composed out of the same essences as other bodies – the bodies of humans, animals, plants and the landscape itself – often too of spiritual beings.

Figure 6.1 depicts a schematic of a fractal person. The body is that of a human being, containing within him or herself the bodily substances of his or her

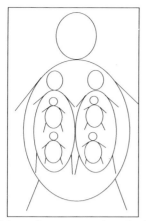

Figure 6.1. Schematic representation of a fractal person

parents, then, through their bodies, those of their grandparents and so on. Some of these influences are male, some are female – these are complementary aspects of the body. The body is also that of a clan, containing within it the moieties and families that compose it. The body is also that of a gift object which, in passing repeatedly from donor to recipient, donor to recipient, comes to contain the names of each of those who have shaped its biography, and so grow in fame to encompass a growing society of exchange partners. The size of the gift object is small, but in moving, it can encompass relations from a large geographical area, and therefore grow in scale. This is a very sketchy description of a fractal person, based on studies of Melanesian personhood (for a more detailed discussion see Fowler 2004a: 25–31 and 48–51, for anthropologists' analyses see Gell 1999; Mosko 1992; Strathern 1988; Wagner 1991). It illustrates how the same patterns appear at different scales, and compose different bodies through a variety of media. Roy Wagner (1991) coined the term the 'fractal person' to convey this translation across scales and consider socio-political differences in how 'big men' and 'great men' stood with respect to such acts of translation. The use of this concept is itself a metaphorical translation of a term from mathematics (Mandelbrot 1982), and I consider it to be of heuristic value in comparing how different cultural understandings of the body and person operate through social relations and material media.

The idea of a fractal body and person can be applied more broadly, and encapsulates relationships considered by earlier anthropologists. For example, the features of sympathetic magic (Frazer 1923, Chapter 3) or the operation of an *imago mundi* (Eliade 1957) can be understood as articulated in fractal patterns. Without referring to fractals specifically, but referencing earlier work on sympathetic magic, Schwarz (1997: 4) describes Navajo understandings of the body and person in terms of a combination of homology, complementarity and synecdoche:

> These concepts structure the complex relationship of parts to the whole world constructed according to paradigms set forth in the Navajo origin story. Parts share similar structure (homology). Wholes are made up of dual integrated components (complementarity). And every part is equivalent to the whole, so anything done to, or by means of, a part is held to take effect upon, or to have the effect of, the whole (synecdoche).

This conceptual framework is arguably not unique to the Navajo (though precise Navajo configurations of it in terms of material things, social relations, practices and cultural understandings of the world may be distinctly Navajo), and it employs a fractal patterning to relationships. It provides one example of a fractal logic – in another case perhaps complementarity within a whole might be supplanted with multiple compositions of components rather than two, for instance. Fractal patterning is common in many different cultural contexts (consider for example, Hindu concepts of the person and world discussed by Parry 1994 and Oestigaard 2004, or Polynesian artworks or European medieval relics and religious art discussed by Gell 1998: 137–43). Distinctive concepts of the body are themselves displayed through this mechanism, through this guiding principle in organising relations. For instance, Strathern describes how horticultural activity provides the metaphor for Melanesian fractal relations which grow and produce buds of potential which are then cut off and transplanted as a gift to a new garden. There they will continue to grow until they bud again. By comparison, Southern Indian metaphors revolve around the body as being a kind of vessel, through which different essences must be channelled in appropriate and auspicious ways. But in each case, the fractal body is open to transformation – for instance, by removing and replacing its parts, by altering the ratio of substances within it, by pursuing one relationship over another, and by changing its form. To focus on fractal relations is not to remove the distinctiveness of different contexts, but to recognise a recurring technique in how relationships between body and world are understood.

Of course, fractal thinking like this does not apply only to human bodies – by its very nature it must encompass all other features of the world too (see Chapman 1996, 2000; Fowler 2004a, 2004b, 2008). This – a shared logic of composition for the body and the world – allows archaeologists to understand concepts of the body and the person by examining the treatment of media other than human bodies alongside the treatment of those bodies. But, differences in how bodies (and things) are treated still need to be thought about with reference to a wide range of ways that fractal relations can operate. This is important both in developing how we understand relational identities and because of the challenge this presents to how we interpret patterns in material remains from the past. To date, only the fractal as a fragment has received the necessary attention.

Fragments

A number of archaeologists have come to this conception of bodies, persons and the world through identifying patterns in the material residues of the past: in particular, the deliberate fragmentation of human bodies and objects, where certain parts were removed from the rest. Some recent interpretations of these fragmented bodies and objects have been influenced by understandings of fractal bodies based on reading ethnographic studies of Melanesian communities carried out by Marilyn Strathern, Roy Wagner, Debbora Battaglia, Mark Mosko and others. Marilyn Strathern suggests Melanesian persons have been characterised as dividual – composed out of the relations between others, such as the two parents responsible for a person's conception, and also inalienable from relations with others. Each body is owed to others for the food that sustains it, the bloodlines that produced it and so on. Debts like these are repaid by producing gift objects from bodily labour. These gifts are parts of the composite body which are extracted like cuttings from a plant, and given to others who absorb them and consequently grow. A Melanesian person is therefore potentially *partible*. This means that personal essence can be transferred between bodies through media like objects or pigs or taro which are externalised parts – or fragments – of the body. The Melanesian body is also *inseparable* from the life force that animates it so that state of the body and the person are mutually affective – e.g., poor moral conduct is reflected in poor skin, poor health, poor products. Gifts therefore equally reflect the character of the person – they are *pars pro toto*. Features of a person are distributed throughout the material world in the things they give and receive, such as 'fame' or 'image' in certain prestigious exchange goods.

Through his study of Neolithic and Copper Age of southeast Europe, *Fragmentation in Archaeology: People, Places and Broken Objects in the Prehistory of South-Eastern Europe*, John Chapman (2000) characterises Neolithic relations as revolving around the creation of parts from wholes, and distribution of those parts.

In the Balkan Neolithic people lived in tells, villages that grew higher generation after generation as mud built houses were levelled and built over. The living reduced the remains of the dead to fragments through mortuary rites, and made clay figurines and vessels which were frequently broken. While some parts of these broken objects, many of which were anthropomorphic, were deposited in pits in the ground or at dwellings to be abandoned and destroyed, other parts were removed. Chapman interprets this fragmentation as part of a strategy in social relations. By the Copper Age, the dead were buried in single burials sometimes with collections of metalwork and other intact objects. This, Chapman argues, signalled new claims for personal wealth and status based on the accumulation of goods which were increasingly valued for their intrinsic properties, and heralded the demise of strategies that used objects to trace chains of intimate relations between people. His long-term narrative, then, is one of the loss of fractal identities over time. Chapman's interpretation of Neolithic enchained relations draws directly on an analogy with how people in Melanesia use objects in relating to one another and producing personal identity, but, as I have argued elsewhere (Fowler 2004a: 66–8), it is almost always intact bodies and objects which are shown as parts of larger wholes in Melanesian ethnographies – persons may be composite, but their parts are not fragmented objects, rather whole things which are simultaneously fragments of their person. If taking a sherd from a vessel smashed at the end of a feast acknowledges a debt to be repaid in the future, it is a different sort of debt to that owed by the single recipient of a *kula* shell to its donor. The sherd cannot materialise the feast in a way that can be passed on, while the *kula* shells do manifest the relations that compose them and carry those forward. Through the sherd, one temporary relationship of membership in an event is commemorated.

While investigating the distinctiveness of how these prehistoric relations articulated parts and wholes (and thereby, I think, usefully showing different kinds of partible relations to those postulated for Melanesia), Chapman's book identifies only the very narrowest end of a cone of possibilities for how past people thought about their bodies and their relationships in fractal ways. In particular a simple tension between fractal and 'representational' forms of relations oversimplifies things. I would suggest that the analogy with Melanesian prestigious goods exchange is more appropriate to the Copper Age material, suggesting not that there was decline in fractal thinking, but that the emphasis in how it operated had shifted. Indeed, fractal frameworks for understanding persons, bodies

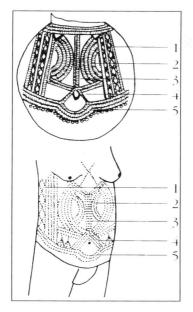

Figure 6.2. a) top: Parallel decoration on hlefenda vessel and hleeta scarification on woman's body; b) middle: Ngum-Ngumi spirit vessel; c) bottom: woman's (left) and man's (right) granaries.

and the world at large do not need to rely on the literal relationship between parts and wholes suggested by Chapman. Schwarz (1997: 5) follows Frazer's and Mauss' studies of magical contagion in pointing out that a 'part' can be left as any kind of trace from a footprint to a personal object. Physical partition of the body, or fragmentation of objects is not needed to distribute parts of the person throughout the world or for parts of the world to influence the person. However, fractal thinking is likely to result in physical manifestation of the same relations through bodies, objects, and architecture equally and there should be a sense of shared form or essence or patterning to each. Chapman does not fully explore what this patterning might be since he says less about form and substance than part and whole in his book. Chapman has identified one role that fragmentation may play in fractal relations – but fragmentation may also play a role in other forms of fractal relations than those stressing partibility.

Flows

There are other fractal mechanisms in arranging relations not traced by Chapman, perhaps because of the limited range of analogies explored in his book. Until relatively recently the Ga'anda of Nigeria designed the bodies of granaries and *hlefenda* ceramics to accentuate fertile round bellies, and decorated them with designs like *hleeta* scarification welts that were used to mark women's bodies accumulatively in rites of passage as they advanced towards adulthood (Berns 1988; see Figure 6.2). In participating in rites of passage women's bodies were filled with spiritual energy and their scars were daubed red to illustrate this. Granaries were filled with fertile grain. And the *hlefenda* vessels held the potent spirit of the dead person – one aspect of their composite self – for a year after death, when it was then smashed releasing that aspect. Other vessels take the shape of the diety spirit *Ngum-Ngumi* decorated with some of the patterning of *hleeta*, human bodily features and representations of objects (see Figure 6.2b). Here I would suggest bodies are like vessels, permeated by flows of potent essences, and their boundaries and forms are carefully monitored in the direction of such flows throughout society and the cosmos in beneficial or auspicious ways. These objects are manifestations of the same social relations that are made material in human bodies – they are therefore fractal. And since each form manifests the same principles, we can see that the idea of the vessel becomes vital to life at all scales, and could turn our attention to flows of energies or substances between these decoratively delineated containers.

McKim Marriott's studies in Southern India demonstrate that here *substances* have fixed values, so that alcohol is hot and grain is cold, in that context (Marriott 1976). The Indian person is, Cecilia Busby (1997) argues, permeable to the movement of these substances, like a vessel, and the person is made hot or cold, for instance, by absorbing these essences. Parts and wholes are not important, she argues, but flows of substances that are never extracted from but extend out of the person influentially. In India the qualities that are fixed in substances give value to things, bodies, relations and identities – making identity substantial. Exchanges alter the ratio of substances contained by each permeable person, and this change is felt through the body. Hindu cremation serves to break that vessel, refine the essences of the body, and relocate those refined essences. This should not be read as an indication that all communities attending to flows between bodies are the same. Strathern (1988: 245) indicates that there are flows of substances outside the ceremonial exchange sphere between Melanesian bodies – which can also be seen as vessels – but she suggests these can only be released as parts which then grow (in) the bodies to whom they are released. Flows are therefore mediated as 'cuttings' from the body in this case.

The body may be seen as a vessel through which essences flow. In cases where flows are usually stressed over partibility the vessel of the body may be fragmented, but usually only after the death of the person in order to allow absolute dispersal of personal essences. While fragmentation occurs somewhere in the mortuary process in many communities – of Melanesian persons through bringing together and re-dispersing the media of their lives in mortuary exchanges, of Ga'anda *hlefenda* vessels by smashing them, of Hindu bodies by cremation – it does not always indicate the *same* understanding of fractal relations as enchainment via objects or fragments with specific biographies. Fragmentation may play a different role in the holistic scheme of relations here.

Considering the significance of vessels as a cultural technology, vitally embedded in Neolithic life, we could offer a slightly different angle on the patterns Chapman (2000) identifies at Balkan tells. Pots were made from clay, as were the tells on which people lived, and clay is frequently analogous to flesh, citing a tie between flesh, land, and kin. Not only were figurines made from clay but some pots – which facilitated the transmission of flows of substances between bodies – were anthropomorphic, depicting human bodies as vessels. We see the body and the house and even the tell modelled in ceramic miniatures and can imagine equivalent substances moving equally through each

of these containers at various scales. Where figurines were fragmented and parts removed and deposited at other households perhaps what we can see is the conceptual mixing of substance between different kin groups, and an intimate connection between personhood, substance and place (cf. Jones 2005). At the same time, links were drawn between the human body, the social body of the household, vessels as conduits for relations, and the physical matter of the land on which the community lived.

The homologous fractal

So far we have seen examples that attend to whether a body is presented whole or in parts, and as a vessel or reduced to substance. Homology refers to the replication of the same form, at whatever scale, lending the potential to trace the presence of each shape at different scales and through different material media. Here I will take homology to refer to form or structure equally.

Discussing luck charms in contemporary Japan, Inge Marie Daniels (2003) argues that it is the form of the object that makes it effective here – for example, a rice scoop takes the form that distributes luck. While rice scoops in the past were made from the wood of sacred trees, this is no longer the case (*ibid*: 624). The shape, 'rice scoop' is a word, character and form that distributes luck, so all rice scoops are *engimono* – good luck charms. Relations rely on the effects of the material form in this Japanese example, and forms and symbols may be effective simply in terms of their shape and what that shape 'achieves' (e.g., arrows shoot, seeds grow [*ibid*: 625]). As archaeologists we can also think of examples where certain forms have practical and social effects through the activities that those forms participate in repeating – for instance, architecture. Colin Richards' analysis of the layouts of houses, tombs and henges in Neolithic Orkney, (and ultimately the shape that henges lend to the landscape) plays on homology of form at different scales (Richards 1996a and b). Each place is effective in conveying a message to those experiencing it because it shapes that experience in a comparable way. Richards is able to show how – at slightly different times and places in the later Neolithic of mainland Orkney – the social body is constituted according to the same logic. The household, potentially composed of male and female inhabitants and different lineages, gathers around the central hearth, consuming food transformed by fire. Villagers congregated at the open fire in the centre of Barnhouse where they transformed clay, rock and shell into ceramic vessels and stone tools (see Jones 2002: 122–31). Late in the inhabitation of the village, some members of the community (perhaps heads of lineages or households?) met at a large hall, shaped like a house but rather larger, again with a central fire, the architecture allowing a translation of the grammar of who sat where around the household fire into this larger scale. Finally, the henge at Stenness replicated that spatial arrangement again at a scale large enough to bring together representatives of all of the communities on the island. Such fractal thinking may have been brought to bear on the human body, perhaps through considering the commingling of elements in bodies, vessels and buildings, though this requires further consideration. Indeed, it is notable that Richards also considers how the elements are arranged by this architecture so that, for instance, fire is always at the centre of the world – within the house, the henge and the island landscape. Fire is missing from the tomb of the dead, lit only at midwinter sunrise. And when bodies were transformed to dry bones some time after death, they were placed in these transformed houses – bodies without flesh in houses without fire. Fractal relations may have been a key force among the cosmological principles at play here.

Summary

Fractal logics seemingly operate through a combination in patterns of form, substance and parts/wholes (and probably other mechanisms not covered here), and it should be clear that I have used these categories for heuristic clarity rather than to suggest any essential difference between them. Different fractal schemes may place different emphases on form and matter as well as partiality or intactness in different ways, so some of these features may come to the fore in certain events, and some trends in this emphasis may be mobilised by some interest groups in social and political ways. As already noted, flows in Melanesia are characterised as flows of parts, according to Strathern – while both are clearly present (as are referents of form) one plays a more dominant role in cultural understanding. Any attempt at a holistic understanding of past relations must consider these different factors alongside one another, and think about the local tropic schemes and socio-political institutions that articulate them.

Fractal bodies and earlier Neolithic mortuary structures

During the earlier Neolithic in much of the geographical British Isles people were probably relatively mobile, pursued mixed subsistence patterns, made ceramic vessels which were used in conveying the stuff of plants and animals into the human body, used stone tools and sometimes exchanged goods like stone axes over long distances. The dead were often disposed of through methods of exposure to the elements we cannot fully observe. Some bodies were lodged at chambered cairns, mounds with stone chambers, or wooden mortuary structures, and some of these were broken up and their bones sorted over time. Many of these mortuary sites probably contained bodies while they passed through phases of decay, transferring them in seclusion from being the corpses of the recently deceased to dry bones. Such bones were seemingly valued in a new way, perhaps as relics of the ancestral dead, and some were removed from the mortuary structures.

To date, consideration of bodies in the earlier Neolithic has largely focussed on the fragmentation of the dead body as a statement of reduction from a whole into parts. This has led to many useful interpretations – until recently none of these explicitly referred to fractals, but either the beginning or implication of fractal thinking was sometimes there in arguments regarding homology or the equivalence of human bodies and other media. For example, Julian Thomas reflected on the relationship between bodies and vessels at West Kennet chambered long barrow:

> The bodies had been brought into the chambers whole, and had been broken down into their constituent parts, which were then spatially disaggregated. In the same way, the pottery vessels in the secondary deposits had been broken, and the parts scattered. Like human bodies, the integrity of the pots had been compromised by this 'breaking', as had their facility as containers of liquids. (Thomas 1999: 206)

Here Thomas views pots and bodies as equivalents (see also Thomas 2002: 40–1), but does not follow up on this equivalence beyond suggesting styles of ceramic decoration became associated with commemorating certain categories of person. Lucas (1996) sees vessels, the most common artefact entering tombs with bodies, as standing for that body throughout the mortuary process, before being finally broken:

> … it is worth noting the large size and open form of these vessels – their suitability for communal eating or feasting has been pointed out before and it is this aspect of them which makes them such apt funerary gifts too. They re-affirm the communality which the living share with the deceased, they act to re-affirm that persons membership of the group. The significance of this is then played upon to its fullest when the body is disarticulated and kinship is annulled: the vessel is smashed, underlining the severance of ties which bound them together and marking the transition to ancestor. (Lucas 1996: 104).

Going further, he suggests one style of vessel was presented as gifts commemorating the new status of the ancestor (whose bones were seemingly sometimes then removed). Lucas' study traces the rite of passage from the affirmation of life, to liminal deconstition, to formation of new status, and illustrates the role of vessels alongside bodies in this process. Alongside the disintegration of flesh from the bones Lucas (1996: 103) stresses the importance of points of articulation – joints – and the segmentation of the body. When bodies were initially laid out in the mortuary chambers he suggests that 'Goods are deliberately placed at certain locations around the body, most commonly the head, but also at points of articulation, i.e. the hips or knees and the placing of goods here might be referencing this segmentation.' (*ibid.*). Lucas sees these acts as statements about the articulation of 'kinship or affiliation with others' (Lucas 1996: 104). This suggests a fractal comparison of the human body with the community that composed it. We could say that kin relations were specifically demarcated by placing objects next to points of bodily articulation, then broken down first by bodily disarticulation, and second by smashing the carinated vessels which had stood alongside those bodies. Later, plain vessels were offered to anonymous and disembodied ancestors in return for 'plain' bones (i.e., not articulated and, as Lucas points out, no longer identifiable kin), removed, perhaps as a sacred substance, from the site.

Lucas' narrative offers an inspiring reflection on how social relations are traced through and transformed alongside bodies. This is arguably an effect of fractal relations. Other studies focus on contextualising the making and breaking of bodies and pots within broader patterns, embed them in a wider materiality. Working on the Neolithic in southern Scandinavia, Tilley (1996: 315–24) suggests equivalence of human bodies with the forms of objects and architecture (e.g. skulls, pots and chambers), and considers the qualities of substances in this relationship. He also recognises equivalent transformations applied to human bodies and to objects as part of a holistic field of social reproduction in which people, things and places were all embedded. I have developed a similar perspective by considering fractal patterning at Manx Neolithic chambered cairns.[2] Manx chambered tombs were located on low hills between the rocky highlands and the sea. The architecture of these monuments varied, but always included stone chambers, the access to which was usually restricted by portal stones. The walls of these chambers were composed from local stone, but not all of it shared the same point of origin. For instance some stones composing Ballaharra chambered tomb were of wave-washed sandstone and some of

slatey Manx group rock. Quartz was used to temper much contemporary pottery while stones with quartz veins were used to form the entrances to chambers, including a large quartz nodule which juts from one of the portal stones to stand above the entrance to Cashtal Yn Ard. Quartz pebbles were brought, probably from the beach, on journeys to Cashtal Yn Ard. Bone was stored in at least some of these chambers, and at one site, Mull Hill, some chambers were filled with quartz rubble. Anthropologically, luminous white materials like milk, fat, semen, and bone are commonly seen as important ancestral essences – a quality they share with luminous things like shells in Melanesian contexts. I have suggested that in the Neolithic around the Irish Sea substances like quartz, bone and shells had a shared value (Fowler 2002, 2004b; Fowler and Cummings 2003). Quartz was presented as a substance associated with transformations from the wet and fluid body to the dry and enduring bones of the ancestral dead. The location of chambered tombs near running white water and between the sea and the rocky uplands meant the living were likely to experience flows of white, sacred energies in moving through the landscape to the monuments, and white sparkling quartz when entering into the antechambers of the sites during rites of passage in their lifetime which also gave them access to ancestral materials and transformed their personal identities.

Arguably, then, visitors to such sites were presented with a component of the dead body alongside equivalent components of ceramic vessels, chambered cairns, and the landscape. Their own, living bodies may have been understood as composed of different materials, as permeable to flows of essences, as susceptible to influence through contact with such substances, and ultimately as something that had to be fragmented in order to be fully transformed. I would suggest the living body was a conceptual vessel which was gradually broken upon death and reduced to substance (see Figure 6.3). Pottery was also fragmented – exposing the quartz flecks in the fabric of the vessel – during ritual practices at locales like chambered tombs. The chambers themselves were the ultimate vessel, one which was not itself fragmented. I would suggest this form was presented as the person at the scale of the whole community, a person composed of the elements of the landscape, and of sacred substance from the past including bone, stone, and pottery. The *form* of the chamber was also the conduit of a *substantial* connection to the past, to which bodies and objects or their parts could be added and from which substance could be removed or essences transferred. *Fragmentation* was one key episode in allowing new forms to be attained: making

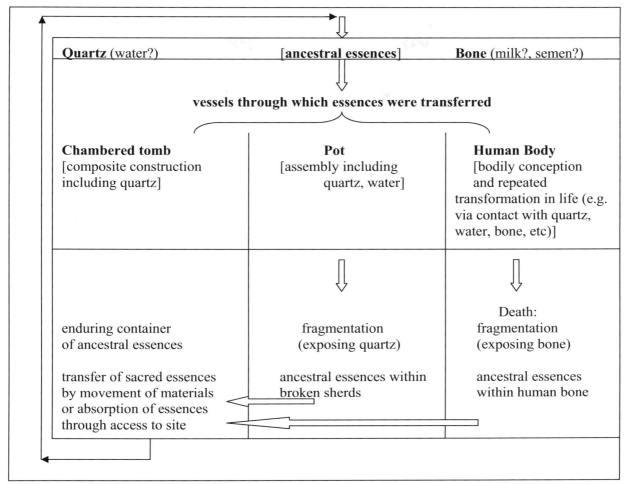

Figure 6.3. Postulated path for the parallel movement of ancestral essences contained in quartz and bone through human bodies, ceramic vessels and chambered tombs in the Manx earlier Neolithic.

monuments from the landscape, pots from clay and quartz, and turning pots and human bodies back into substances which could then be absorbed into the body at a communal scale.

Conclusion

I have focused here on how fractal patterns in relationships may give shape to bodies and people's experiences of them in culturally specific ways, and illustrated that such shapes can be observed in patterns in many kinds of media at multiple scales. It remains a challenge for us to decide whether or when, for instance, bodies might be valued more in terms of their form, as substance, as relative to an event in which they participate, as emblems of desirable social relations, as the group (or even world) scaled down, or as an expression of individuality. Such cultural

schemes may have been contested and struggled with continually through contrasting strategies in the use of substances, objects, architecture and bodies. Different interest groups take up certain strategies to greater or lesser effect, pulling on certain scales of action or certain metaphors over others. As I have argued, fragmenting things is undoubtedly a key part of many of these strategies but fragmentation does not stand alone as a technique in mediating fractal relations, and we should not consider partible relations as the only fractal mechanism and only explanation for fragmented bodies. Neither should we allow the bodies we find in single burials to stand as representations for indivisible persons, or see intact objects as wealth or resources, and as a result fail to consider their place in fractal schemes or relational identities.

By focussing on European and British prehistory in my archaeological examples I am being highly selective. Fractal relations are clearly not to be attributed only to non-literate societies. For prehistorians such materially-focussed interpretations are particularly tempting precisely because we can only recover the material media through which people lived their lives, and not written presentations of their words and discourses. There are implications here for historical archaeologists as well as prehistorians, and there are clear implications for those who would study past bodies – most significantly that we cannot abstract bodies from the rest of the material world. The body is both a material thing and a conceptual media. In interpreting the body it is important to attend to the practical media of the day – whether it be horticulture, ceramic technologies, weaving, hunting, cooking, and so on. These were all vital activities in which bodies were involved, and through which sense was made both of bodies and of the world. Isolating bodies as things of and in themselves risks – as seems to have been made clear to Leenhardt – bringing our view of 'the body' to communities who never had it.

Acknowledgements

Thanks to Kevin Greene, Sam Turner, Jane Webster and Nick Winder for discussing the use of the fractal concept.

Notes

1   For instance, there are various forms of western literature on personhood and religion, on holistic and other alternative understandings of bodies and medicine, and on personal development and 'self-help'.
2   For fuller details synthesising the key features of these sites in terms of the materials used to construct them and activities at them, and for primary reference sources see Fowler (2004b), and for full details on landscape location see Cummings and Fowler (2004).

Bibliography

Barraud, C., de Coppet, D., Iteanu, A. and Jamous, R. 1994. *Of Relations and the Dead: Four Societies Viewed from the Angle of their Exchanges*. Oxford: Berg.
Battaglia, D. 1990. *On the Bones of the Serpent: Person, Memory and Mortality in Sabarl Society*. Chicago: Chicago University Press.
Berns, M. 1998. Ga'anda scarification: a model for art and identity. In *Marks of Civilization: Artistic Transformations of the Human Body*, edited by A. Rubin, pp. 57–76. Los Angeles: Museum of Cultural History, UCLA.
Busby, C. 1997. Permeable and partible persons: a comparative analysis of gender and the body in South India and Melanesia. *Journal of the Royal Anthropological Institute* 3(2): 261–278.

Busby, C. 2000. *The Performance of Gender: An Anthropology of Everyday Life in a South Indian Fishing Village*. London: Athlone Press.
Butler, J. 1990. *Gender Trouble: Feminism and the Subversion of Identity*. New York: Routledge.
Butler, J. 1993. *Bodies that Matter: On the Discursive Limits of 'Sex'*. New York: Routledge.
Chapman, J. 1996. Enchainment, commodification, and gender in the Balkan Copper Age. *Journal of European Archaeology* 4: 203–242.
Chapman, J. 2000. *Fragmentation in Archaeology: People, Places and Broken Objects in the Prehistory of South-Eastern Europe*. London: Routledge.
Csordas, T. 1999. Embodiment and cultural phenomenology. In *Perspectives on Embodiment: The Intersections of Nature and Culture*, edited by G. Weiss and H. Faber, pp. 143–162. London: Routledge.
Cummings, V. and Fowler, C. 2004. The form and setting of Manx chambered cairns: cultural comparisons and social interpretations. In *The Neolithic of the Irish Sea: Materiality and Traditions of Practice*, edited by V. Cummings and C. Fowler, pp. 113–122. Oxford: Oxbow Books.
Daniels, I.M. 2003. Scooping, raking, beckoning luck: luck, agency and the interdependence of people and things in Japan. *Journal of the Royal Anthropological Institute* 9: 619–38.
Eliade, M. 1957. [trans. W. Trask] *The Sacred and the Profane: The Nature of Religion*. London: Harvest/Harcourt Brace Jovanovich.
Fowler, C. 2001. Personhood and social relations in the British Neolithic, with a study from the Isle of Man. *Journal of Material Culture* 6(2): 137–163.
Fowler, C. 2002. Body parts: Personhood and materiality in the Manx Neolithic. In *Thinking Through the Body: Archaeologies of Corporeality*, edited by Y. Hamilakis, M. Pluciennik and S. Tarlow, pp. 47–69. London: Kluwer/Academic Press.
Fowler, C. 2004a. *The Archaeology of Personhood: An Anthropological Approach*. London: Routledge.
Fowler, C. 2004b. In touch with the past? Bodies, monuments and the sacred in the Manx Neolithic. In *The Neolithic of the Irish Sea: Materiality and Traditions of Practice*, edited by V. Cummings and C. Fowler, pp. 91–102. Oxford: Oxbow Books.
Fowler, C. 2008. Landscape and Personhood. In *Handbook of Landscape Archaeology*, edited by B. David and J. Thomas. Walnut Creek, pp. 291–299. CA: Left Coast Press.
Fowler, C. and Cummings, V. 2003. Places of transformation: building monuments from water and stone in the Neolithic of the Irish Sea. *Journal of the Royal Anthropological Institute* 9: 1–20.
Frazer, J. 1923. *The Golden Bough: A Study in Magic and Religion*. Abridged version. New York: MacMillan.
Gell, A. 1998. *Art and Agency: An Anthropological Theory*. Oxford: Clarendon.
Gell, A. 1999. Strathernograms, or the semiotics of mixed metaphors. In *The Art of Anthropology: Essays and Diagrams*, edited by E. Hirsch, pp. 29–75. London: Athlone.
Jones, A. 2005. Lives in fragments? Personhood and the European Neolithic. *Journal of Social Archaeology* 5: 193–224.
LiPuma, E. 1998. Modernity and forms of personhood in Melanesia. In *Bodies and Persons: Comparative Views from Africa*

and Melanesia, edited by M. Lambek and A. Strathern, pp. 53–79. Cambridge: Cambridge University Press.

Lucas, G. 1996. Of death and debt: a history of the body in Neolithic and Early Bronze Age Yorkshire. *Journal of European Archaeology* 4: 99–118.

Mandelbrot, B. 1982. *The Fractal Geometry of Nature*. San Fran_ cisco: W.H. Freeman.

Marriott, M. 1976. Hindu transactions: diversity without dualism. In *Transaction and Meaning: Directions in the Anthropology of Exchange and Symbolic Behaviour*, edited by B. Kapferer, pp. 109–137. Philadelphia: Institute for the Study of Human Issues.

Mauss, M. 1979a. [trans]. The notion of body techniques. In *Sociology and Psychology: Essays. M. Mauss*, edited and translated by B. Brewster, pp. 97–105. London: Routledge Keegan Paul.

Mauss, M. 1979b. [trans]. Principles in the classification of body techniques. In *Sociology and Psychology: Essays. M. Mauss*, edited and translated by B. Brewster, pp. 106–109. London: Routledge Kegan Paul.

Mosko, M. 1992. Motherless sons: 'divine kings' and 'partible persons' in Melanesia and Polynesia. *Man* 27: 697–717.

Oestigaard, T . 2004. Kings and cremations: royal funerals and sacrifices in Nepal. In *Belief in the Past. The Proceedings of the Manchester Conference on Archaeology and Religion*, edited by T. Insoll, pp. 115–124. Oxford: BAR International Series 1212.

Parry, J. 1994. *Death in Banaras*. Cambridge: Cambridge University Press.

Richards, C. 1996a. Monuments as landscape: creating the centre of the world in late Neolithic Orkney. *World Archaeology* 28(2): 190–208.

Richards, C. 1996b. Henges and water: towards an elemental understanding of monumentality and landscape in late Neolithic Britain. *Journal of Material Culture* 1: 313–36.

Schwarz, M.T. 1997. *Moulded in the Image of Changing Woman: Navajo Views on the Human Body and Personhood*. Tucson: University of Arizona Press.

Strathern, M. 1988. *The Gender of the Gift: Problems with Women and Problems with Society in Melanesia*. Berkeley: University of California Press.

Thomas, J. 1999. *Understanding the Neolithic*. London: Routledge.

Thomas, J. 2002. Archaeology's humanism and the materiality of the body. In *Thinking Through the Body: Archaeologies of Corporeality*, edited by Y. Hamilakis, M. Pluciennik and S. Tarlow, pp. 29–46. London: Kluwer/Academic Press.

Tilley, C. 1996. *An Ethnography of the Neolithic: Early Prehistoric Societies in Southern Scandinavia*. Cambridge: Cambridge University Press.

Tilley, C. 1999. *Metaphor and Material Culture*. Oxford: Blackwell.

Wagner, R. 1991. The fractal person. In *Big Men and Great Men: Personifications of Power in Melanesia*, edited by M. Strathern and M. Godelier, pp. 159–173. Cambridge: Cambridge University Press.

From substantial bodies to the substance of bodies: analysis of the transition from inhumation to cremation during the Middle Bronze Age in Central Europe

Marie Louise Stig Sørensen and Katharina C. Rebay

Introduction

One of the examples investigated within the Leverhulme Research Programme *Changing Beliefs of the Human Body* is the attitudes to the body being expressed through the spread of cremation during the so-called 'Urnfield culture'. The Urnfield culture, approximately 1300–800 BC, is generally seen to represent a period during which a radical change of mortuary practices, from inhumations to cremations, spread over large parts of Europe. This phenomenon has been extensively discussed, and it remains seminal to our understanding of prehistoric Europe. The spread of an apparently radically different burial rite can in some ways be seen as one of the earliest instances in European prehistory of 'mass conversion', and this has often been the assumption underwriting the interpretations. Many explanations have accordingly presented external factors, such as migration, as the reason and mechanisms for the change (Kimmig 1964). The archaeological data have, however, increasingly begun to suggest greater complexity in terms of variation and transitional stages, and a return to the question of the spread of cremation is indeed timely. The focus of renewed research should, however, be both the mechanism through which the new practices were emulated and adapted within local settings and whether and to what extent these changes in burial practices imply alterations in beliefs.

Explanations for the assumed change in beliefs have most often been sought in ethnographic parallels, in particular Hindu cremation practices, or historical sources such as descriptions of cremation burials in classical Greece. With regard to beliefs, it has been accordingly been proposed that the spread of cremation during the Middle Bronze Age indicates the development of a concept of a soul separate from the physical body; this has been based on the presumption that cremation was used, indeed needed, to release the soul upon death. This view can be found already in the seventheenth century; Sir Thomas Browne's (1605–1682) essay on urn burials provides, for instance, an extensive reflection upon various historical version of cremation burials stating that 'Many have taken voluminous pains to determine the state of the soul upon disunion; but men have been most phantasticall in the singular contrivances of their corporall dissolution; whilest the sobrest Nations have rested in two wayes, of simple inhumation and burning' (Browne 2005: 2). This argument is still favoured by many scholars (e.g., Gräslund 1994; Oestigaard 2004). Such interpretations do not, however, link the question of how this transition was realised to observations of how communities changed their ways of practicing burials; and they usually pay little attention to the variations in the actual responses to the body, that can be seen within the cemeteries. The project *Changing Social Practices of Death in Bronze Age Europe* therefore aims to focus upon variations in the performance and ritualisation of cremation and the specific changes observed in the shift from the use of inhumation burials to the use of cremations in urns will be seen as the means of dissection what this change was about and how it became articulated. It is our explicit goal to investigate the beliefs associated with this shift in burial practice in a manner that can explore cremation beyond a presumed soul – body duality and that will engage with variations that are expressed at different scales of social action and interaction. We need, therefore, to develop a comparative perspective as it is only through the variations that we will detect the different ways that one set of practices and associated believes could be transformed into another. The project will accordingly explore the archaeological data with regard to how burials were performed and the extent to which they were the results of decisions informed by the merger of different ideas and understandings. It also aims to explore how the practices emerging combined innovations and tradition concerns and technologies. In other worlds, the project aims to produce an embedded explorative 'reading' of these changes in terms of the agency of both community and individuals.

In response to these needs the project has been designed around a comparative investigation of selected 'burial landscapes' from Hungary, Southern Germany/ Austria, the Netherlands and Denmark. The aim of this paper is to reflect upon the discursive framework within which such a project can take place rather than providing a detailed study. The results of the first extensive case study, the Pitten cemetery in the Lower Austria (Sørensen and Rebay 2008) will be outlined in order to provide examples of the kind of practices that need to be included in further analyses.

Inhumation versus cremation

Archaeology has for more than a decade with apparently increasing sophistication been discussing how death, and in particularly burials, must be understood as significant social moments. Strong arguments have been put forward for burials being social events and staged performances that provide an opportunity for communities to reconstruct themselves after the disruption of death (Barrett 1990; Mizoguchi 1993; Parker Pearson 1999). Despite these arguments we are still rather ill-equipped to analyse change in burial practices, and while we have become better at investigating the single grave, as a particular construction with its own distinct choreography (e.g., Sørensen 2004), we have somewhat lost sight of the challenging observation that the form burials take may change and that they may change rapidly and drastically and that such changes may affect large geographical areas. We do not presently have a developed theoretical language to

use for such observations. Such changes do, however, provide us with powerful insight into the nature of society and they should inspire us to resituate burials as significant expressions of social understandings and beliefs. The spread of cremation during the end of the Middle Bronze Age in central Europe and neighbouring regions is an important example of beliefs and practices being shaped locally and simultaneously being part of a wider cultural development.

In order to appreciate the magnitude of the change to cremation and the longer term bodily ontology this emerged from we need briefly to outline the trends in burial practices in continental temperate Europe during the late third and early second millennia BC as they set the background to the changes that occur later. By the end of the third millennium BC, burial practices became explicitly focused upon the construction of mortuary settings in which the individual takes centre-stage. Burial constructions became increasingly elaborate and were consuming considerable resources and time. Large areas were stripped of fertile topsoil for barrow building, which took months to construct, and objects, including bronze and textiles, were placed within the graves. During this time burials must have been considerable social investments. The presentation of the deceased was a dominant concern with objects and structures used to characterise the individual in terms of age, gender, status, and regional identities. It seems that this emphasis was shared over large areas and that a normative view about what constituted a grave had developed. By the Middle Bronze Age, approximately 1500–1300 BC, the deceased was typically lying in a life-size or bigger container such as a tree coffin or a stone chamber. He or she was placed extended on the back, fully dressed, wearing ornaments, with other objects, such as weapons, placed on or around the body. The body was at times covered by additional layers of textile, hides or furs and the container for the body was usually closed with a lid, using wooden planks or stone slaps. The graves were placed under mounds of earth and/or stones, and they were often clustered in small barrow cemeteries.

In these burials, the body was architecturally (and probably also in other ways) the central point. Other elements, i.e., ornaments and structures, were typically either placed in particular positions on or in relationship to the body or they were part of the construction made to present and 'house' the body. In this burial tradition, the dead body continued to appear like a living body, it was presented as still possessing the same physical and social characteristics. These burials emphasised the deceased as a substantial body, and this was a body that was recognisable, corporeal and familiar.

While cremation is occasionally found in earlier

periods, from around 1200 BC it began to become the dominant burial practice in most areas of Central Europe and by 1100 BC cremation was either very common or the absolute dominant form within a very large area stretching from France to Hungary and from southern Sweden to northern Italy. It is this phenomenon that has been labelled the Urnfield period or culture. With the typical Urnfield cremation rite the deceased was burnt on a pyre, and the burnt remains were collected and contained within an urn. The latter was most commonly buried in a pit with no other or only modest features associated with it such as a few stones set around the urn or used as its lid. The urns were often placed within large cemeteries, the so-called urnfields, or they may be placed as secondary burials in the fill of older barrows. At the time when fully formed cremation burial had become dominant, many aspects of the earlier inhumation burial practices had changed or were substantially transformed. In particular, the emphasis upon the similarity to the living body in terms of size and appearance had disappeared, and the use of objects and structures to 'annotate' and decorate the deceased had almost ceased.

As was the case in inhumation graves, the body was also central to the cremation burial; but through the cremation it became a much more ambiguous substance. As physical matter, the cremated body had lost its resemblance to the living body; it had lost its exterior existence and it was being turned inside out with only the hard bits remaining. The familiar surface and appearance of the body had gone, and even the hard bits were fragmented, discoloured and disarticulated. The cremated body existed only as substance or as a condensed or token body. In addition, with the introduction of cremation the traditional relationships created or explored during burial between the body and objects shifted. The relationship between the body and its objects broke or ceased to be relevant as objects could not anymore be placed in specific pre-described positions in relationship to the body and its different parts. In this change, it seems that the use of objects in social negotiation of identities and positions changed from taking the form of a somewhat prescriptive part of the laying out of the deceased to becoming a more informal aspect of the final treatment of the body and one that often appears 'invented' as a response to the specific situation. It seems that some of the explicit significances, which were formerly associated with the placing of objects within the setting provided by the burial, ceased to be relevant. The cremated body is still housed; but while the body placed in an inhumation burial was laid out and things organised around it, for the cremation it became a matter of gathering the remains and load or fill them into a container (Figure

Figure 7.1. Urn burial (Grave 56, Pitten; Hampel, Kerchler and Benkovsky-Pivovarová 1981: Taf. 124)

7.1). These changes seem to reveal the formation of a new 'tradition' and the formulation of new beliefs in the widest sense of that word. The large scale at which this took place as well as the local variations upon the general themes makes this both a very challenging and an important example of change in the machination of beliefs about death and the dead body.

Approaching the investigation, or how do we study change in beliefs?

These differences in the treatment of the body discussed above emerged, however, over some time. The investigation of how the change came about must therefore take a temporal approach and trace and dissect the in-between stages rather than simply focussing upon the contrasting understandings of the body signalled by these different burial practices. For the rest of this paper we will therefore engage with the question of how changes in beliefs may be investigated.

At this point our primary concern and interest are not, therefore, to try to explain why beliefs change in terms of what cremation meant or represented to the Bronze Age communities, rather we aim to investigate how they changed. This meant tackling the overarching question differently from many traditional discussions and developing alterative approaches to the data. We therefore found it necessary, at least as an initial strategy, to react against the long tradition of identifying the explanation of *the* introduction of cremation as *the* research question. This has been an approach that aimed to 'understand what the changes meant' without there being an explicit and data informed parallel discussion of what it is that is changing! Furthermore, we wanted to avoid becoming sidetracked by assuming the explanation can be found in some historical or ethnographic analogy. In its stead we aimed to utilise the actual practices and decisions made by the prehistoric community to further refine and guide the research questions.

We propose that the analysis of burial practices should be formulated around questions that are phrased in a manner that makes it what particular practices, i.e., a set of routine and decisions, we aim to investigate. This may sound too simplistic or even banal, but in reality there is often a substantial epistemological gap between questions asked of the data and the social reality they are assumed to inform about. The importance of stressing this point is therefore that previous approaches in their focus upon explaining 'the introduction of cremation' have approached cremation as a coherent totalising phenomenon. As a consequence, cremation – in its entirety and almost as if it is a thing – is contrasted with inhumation as a similarly robust entity. This, furthermore, pushes explanations towards external or foreign agencies since in their total difference it becomes inconceivable that inhumation can 'develop' into cremation. Even more significantly, this absolutism is not supported by evidence. There has been a strong tendency in the study of the spread of the Urnfield cremation rite to formulate the research questions in a manner that lacks clear resonance with the details and variation of the data. The explanations offered for the introduction of the Urnfield culture and the spread of cremation have therefore often existed in tension with the accounts emerging from the analyses of individual cemeteries.

We therefore suggest that a more constructive approach to this question must focus upon particular contexts of decision making and practices in order to trace how specific stages within the construction of burials may become differently formulated in respond to new ideas and emerging understandings of death and of the proper form of burials.

Case study: the Middle Bronze Age cemetery of Pitten

Taking this approach to a specific case study has made it possible to further refine these questions in a manner that was sensitive towards the specific practices shaping and forming the cemetery. It was particularly striking to find that the change of burial practices did not take place quite as radically as normally presumed, rather it was a process that took

place over several hundred years. The case study also revealed a number of unexpected details that are important for the comparative investigation of other cemeteries as they suggest distinct features of the emerging understanding of the cremated body.

As the first case study we selected Pitten, a Middle Bronze Age cemetery situated in Lower Austria, south of the Danube, in a hilly, fertile landscape between the Austrian Alps and the Hungarian plain. The cemetery, which was repeatedly covered by layers of silt due to flooding, has been very well preserved and shows wide ranging variations in how individuals were treated after death. The cemetery contains both inhumation and cremation graves; this makes it a particularly interesting case study as it allows a detailed contextual investigation of the simultaneous use of apparently radically different burial practices by a local community and thus providing insight into how a community was weaving different practices together through a range of mergers and innovations. The striking variations in the treatment of the body make it difficult to summarize the common characteristics of the cemetery. Of the 221 graves excavated, 75 individuals were inhumed and 154 were cremated; these are found in a variety of grave constructions and the different practices are interspersed throughout the cemetery. Most of the cremated bodies were buried at the place of their pyre, with a minority being relocated or deposited in an urn. The form of grave construction also varies and includes shaft graves, flat graves, burial mounds made both of soil and stones, ditches and 'mortuary houses'. The graves themselves were designed for an individual, but the burial mounds were used and at time designed for multiple burials, sometime contemporaneous and at other times with graves added later (Teschler 1985: 128).

One of the important observations made through the analysis of this cemetery is that many of the inhumations and cremations share common characteristics in terms of grave architecture, post-funerary rituals and the treatment of the body, and both burial forms may be found within a single burial mound. There seems to be no radical shift or revolution in the performance of the funerary rites despite the essential difference between inhumation and cremation. On the contrary, change seems to have been gradual, and the introduction of new elements does not follow a strict chronological or evolutionary trend. Through the variations and details an impression of experimentation with the dead body and the proper form of its grave emerges. 'Innovative' forms of burials are built using established knowledge and experience resulting in some traits being continued and others relinquished. Through experimentation and tacit understandings of what a

Figure 7.2. Cremated bones (Grave 28, Pitten; Hampel, Kerchler and Benkovsky-Pivovarová 1981: Taf. 118)

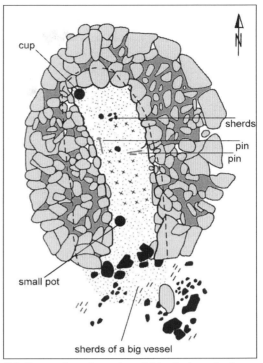

Figure 7.3. Bronze dress elements matching body parts of a cremation (Grave 189, Pitten; Hampel, Kerchler and Benkovsky-Pivovarová 1981: 96)

grave is, the local community responds to and gives local form to external influences.

Another important observation was that the data suggests that cremation was not seen as a total destruction of the body. While the cremation must be seen as a transformation of the body into another substance, and thus a deliberate destruction of the intactness of the corpse, the case study shows that the cremated remains are still perceived as representing a body and that this was emphasised and articulated in a number of explicit ways. This seems to contrast with the assumptions underlying interpretations of cremation as the release of the soul from the empty shell of the body. It is therefore worth stressing that the cremated bones would often have been recognisable as such and visually distinct. The larger pieces of the skull, the vertebral column, the teeth, and the long bones were probably all identifiable to the Bronze Age community, and the remains after the cremations were clearly subject to 'bodily-treatments'. It is therefore also important to stress that most of the cremation burials were left at the place of the pyre; in some cases whole body parts remained intact, and in one grave the cremated feet still rested parallel to one another (Hampel, Kerchler and Benkovsky-Pivovarová 1981: Taf. 118) (Figure 7.2). The pyre would therefore automatically represent a potential link to the body, and there is much evidence to suggest that the body was placed on the funerary pyre in the same way as the body would be laid out in an inhumation grave. The dead body was in both cases extended on its back and was dressed in what we presume was everyday attire. Bronze dress elements include pins, usually one for males and two for females, rings and ornaments were attached to the body. After the cremation itself, the remains of the body, and thus its continuous presence, might just need reaffirmation. This is done, for example, through the erection of a protective

structure, a grave, and through some rearrangement of the bones and the placing of objects in a manner that confirms 'the body'. Dress elements have, for instance, in a number of graves been found in exactly the place where they would be on the living body, suggesting they were deliberately rearranged after the cremation to match the correct body parts. One grave, for example, contained two pins placed at the shoulder region, a finger ring in the middle body region where the hands would rest, and pottery towards the head and at the side of the body (Figure 7.3).

Based on such examples, we propose that the cremated body continued to be perceived and treated as a corporeal entity as long as it was not moved away and separated from the rest of the pyre. It seems to have been very clear which burnt bones represented which body part, and therefore also where the grave goods should be placed. Next, one may ask whether this is merely a generic marking of the remains as a body or whether more specific comments upon whom the deceased were are also maintained in these early cremations. Or in other words, which variables were recognised and taken into consideration when making up the category 'body' or 'person' on the basis of cremated remains? To answer this, we analysed whether age and gender distinctions were emphasised

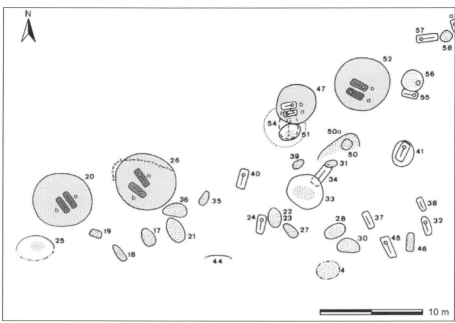

Figure 7.4. Burial mounds with parallel grave chambers for inhumations in Pitten (after Hampel, Kerchler and Benkovsky-Pivovarová 1981: Cemetery Plan)

in the same way in cremations as in the inhumation graves within the cemetery.

Some of the inhumations in the cemetery are double burials deposited together in one burial mound; the grave architecture of at least seven burial mounds was clearly designed to contain more than one body (Figure 7.4). In these cases, the grave chambers were usually built parallel to one another but the orientation of the bodies themselves varies. It is interesting to note, that in the cases where the bodies were similar in terms of sex and age, they were oriented in the same way, while in the cases where age and sex differ they were opposing each other. This implies that the sex of the deceased played an important role for the display and orientation of the corpse. Burial mound 5 shows that this pattern is continued even if inhumation and cremation burials occur together. Amongst the well-preserved remains of a funeral pyre pieces of the skull were recorded and suggest a body orientation from the northwest to the southeast. The biological evidence and a pair of pins suggest this was a female. Another, non-cremated body was buried in close connection with this cremation as it was lying parallel to the remains of the pyre but its head was placed in the opposite direction. This body was classified as a mature male, hence respecting the traditional gender based orientation used in this cemetery (Figure 7.5). This may suggest that the specific individuality of the body or at least its social identities survive the cremation.

The stone grave constructions, which were very common within the cemetery, also help to clarify how the cremated remains were seen and classified by the local community. The stone constructions were usually placed on top of the remains of the funerary pyre and range in forms from simple soil and stone covers, to mounds with elaborate stone constructions. Some of these constructions are built to create a body sized grave chamber, suitable to house a body and at the same time covering and delineating part of the pyre. Through this practice a part of the pyre became *de facto* defined as the body. These constructions thus give physicality to the cremated bones, and they reconstitute the life-size of the fragmented remains.

Finally, interaction, social engagement and communication with the dead at Pitten did not end with interment and abandonment for both, inhumation and cremation. There is a variety of evidence for post-funerary activities in Pitten that might shed some light on connected beliefs about bodies, grave goods and the afterlife. If cremation was about releasing the soul, an ongoing interaction with bodily remains would not make very much sense. Clusters of sherds were, however, frequently found outside but close to grave structures, especially near the entrances and close to the head of the deceased. This can be interpreted as offerings or remains of feasting at the burial site. Since traces of these actions were found in different layers, it is likely graves were repeatedly visited.

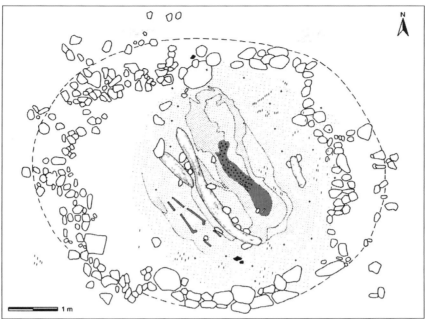

Figure 7.5. Burial mound 5 in Pitten (after Hampel, Kerchler and Benkovsky-Pivovarová 1981: Taf. 13)

Figure 7.6. Grave 121 with door opening in Pitten (Windl 1983: Abb. 9)

Another clear evidence of extended interaction is suggested by graves with door openings or other entrances (Figure 7.6). Stratigraphic evidence suggests that the door opening was left open long enough for sand layers to accumulate inside and outside the graves (Hampel, Kerchler and Benkovsky-Pivovarová 1981: 64), and pottery clusters are found in front of such doors suggesting activities took place near to the opening into the grave. These graves seem to stress the need for physical access to the deceased. Moreover, the architecture of the graves with door openings does not only mimic the architecture of the living, it also enables the living to engage with deceased members

of community. Again, the data suggests that in the earlier phases of cremation the remains of the body retain a meaningful relationship to both the social and individual identity of the deceased and to the living group.

The evidence of so-called 'grave robbing' is one further aspect that confirms the continued presence of a meaningful body despite its transformed status. Systematic removal of grave goods is widespread during the Early and Middle Bronze Age and known from cemeteries such as Gemeinlebarn or Franzhausen (Neugebauer 1991; Neugebauer and Neugebauer 1997) and the early phases of Pitten (Hampel, Kerchler and Benkovsky-Pivovarová 1981). The predominant interpretations for this practice have been materialistic, considering bronze to be such a valuable material that the sacrilege of disturbing a grave would be accepted despite fear of the ancestors. The phenomenon of reopening graves and removing objects is, however, too wide spread to be meaningless. It should therefore be rethought as a repeated and accepted social practice – a ritual (see also Rittershofer 1987). The objects associated with the dead body were probably not meant to be in the earth forever; they were not necessary designed to accompany the deceased beyond a certain stage. After that stage, presumably associated with the process of decomposition, objects could legitimately be transferred back into the possession of the living. During this time, the person in the grave might not have been perceived of as 'totally dead' or on the transition between life and death. It is usually presumed that grave robbing ended with the introduction of cremation. In Pitten there is, however, evidence that this tradition continued, despite it being more difficult to trace for cremation graves. Good indicators of grave robbing are bones that are disordered after burial as well as green discolouring of the bones despite bronze objects being absent from the graves (Sprenger 1999: 44). It is, therefore, significant that more than half of the cremated bones with no bronze artefacts show green discolouring. This shows that bronze artefacts had been associated with the cremated bones during a particular stage of the burial and then later removed (Teschler-Nicola 1985: 137). As is the case with the inhumation graves, it seems likely that the removal of bronze grave goods took place several years after the interment. Graves might have been reopened, or the cremation pyre was left open and only reassembled and buried at a later stage during which choices were made about how to reconstitute the body and its possessions.

This outline of the observations reached through the first case study can be used to define three 'contexts of action' in which we can discern how ideas influence and shape burial practice. The first of these is the location of cremation burials within exiting 'burial landscapes', the second is the reconstitution of the body through its treatment and through grave structures, and the third is the relationship between objects and the body during and after the cremation.

Placing and linking: spatial variation between cremation and inhumation burials

The first context of action within which we can track how decisions may be made and influence the introduction and development of new beliefs are the decisions about where the cremation should be located. It is common for early cremations to be placed within existing barrow cemeteries or even to be placed as secondary burials in the fill of older barrows. It is also common that inhumation and cremation co-exist for some time. This strongly suggests that while the body itself is treated in a very different manner that results in substantial transformation and erosion of its exteriority, the burial of the cremated body is still perceived of as 'belonging' within the existing cemeteries; presumable as a burial it still has relevant similarities or connections to inhumation burials. This connection may be confirmed through practices that stress its similarities to the other graves. This point is further supported by the not infrequent location of cremation burials next to Early Bronze Age cemeteries (for example Franzhausen, Austria [Neugebauer 1993])

which suggests that this is not merely a question of continued use of the same location, but more explicitly about linking the cremations to existing cemeteries. It seems that the difference in the treatment of the deceased does not mean that the burials in other ways are different and should be separated from each other. In time this connection becomes weaker and urnfields are used without apparent links to earlier cemeteries. An important objective of the project is therefore to investigate this relationship in greater details. In particular, the spatial integration of the two burial rites and the transitional stages between them will be investigated for a number of cemeteries.

Re-constituting the body

Through cremation the body becomes transformed and fragmented, but during the ensuing burial of some or all the remains it seems to become reconstituted in some manner. This is therefore a context of action where beliefs about what the remains are or represent will guide decision-making. The project will therefore analyse whether and how the different remains of the cremation pyre are separated and given attention during subsequent treatment. It seems clear that in some cases the bones are carefully separated from the ash, charcoal and other materials before burials. The cremated bones may even be sorted and placed within a cist or similar construction in a manner that clearly makes references to specific parts or to the shape of the body. The bones may also have been cleaned and subjected to further treatment, such as being wrapped in textile, before burial. In the other extreme, the content is a mix of charcoal, ash, burnt earth, burnt bronze fragments, organic material and bones – all apparently swept from the pyre without any attempt of separating the remains of the body from other things, or the remains of the pyre in itself becomes the grave. Within these differences we can discern a range of attitudes to or understandings of the nature of the body that remains. We therefore need to explore these differences further. The early cremation graves in which the shape of the body is outlined through the cremated bones will be a focus of special attention and the means through which the body is indicated or redefined, such as the shaping of its part, the use of diagnostic bones, or the construction of coffins or grave chambers around it must be investigated with such questions in mind.

The body and its objects

The third theme is the relationship between the body

and objects, in particular dress fittings. In some cases dress fittings were burnt together with the body, while in others it seems that such minor personal objects were 'given to' or included in the burial at a later stage after the cremation. This difference suggests variations in the understanding of the substance being buried, and we therefore want to investigate whether there are other characteristics which overlap with this distinction, and also whether there is discrimination with regard to what types of objects are used as they may represent different relations to the body. At the other extreme, the need for continuous interaction with the body and the architectural forms and practices that developed to make this possible will also be focus for comparative analysis as this suggests a strong link between the living and the dead body.

The three contexts of action and decision making outlined above are merely a way of guiding the analysis towards how changes in beliefs are expressed and made real through bodily practice that involved making decisions, using existing technologies and aiming at specific effects. They are not intended as an exhausting investigation of how the changes came about, but rather as a set of guiding principles that will allow both detailed investigations of individual cemeteries and comparative analysis at different spatial and temporal scales.

Conclusion

Within the history of research, one of the most popular explanations for changing burial practices has always been a change of population. With regard to the Urnfield culture the apparent dramatic change in burial practices meant this was seen as a period of violence and warfare. The detailed investigation of how local community expressed these changes, and thus how they became effective and took form, begins to sketch a very different impression. Rather than rupture and dramatic shift we begin to discern a version of this change in believes and practices that is simultaneously about widespread cultural change, resulting from new beliefs about the ways of treating deceased members of society and the need for these views to be comprehended and translated into particular practices at local levels. The variations and the co-existence of different versions, both extreme opposite and hybrid forms, suggest that the idea of cremation did not come to local community framed within a so specific and detailed understanding of the body and death that divergence was not possible; indeed, in the case of Pitten the impression is rather that the local community had to invent its own

understanding of what this change entailed, and the result was that cremated remains for a long time in many ways were perceived similar to inhumed bodies.

Bibliography

Barrett, J. 1990. The monumentality of death: the character of early Bronze Age mortuary mounds in southern England. *World Archaeology* 22: 179–189.

Blischke, J. 2002. *Gräberfelder als Spiegel der Historischen Entwicklung während der Mittleren Bronzezeit im mittleren Donaugebiet.* Universitätsforschungen zur prähistorischen Archäologie 80. Bonn: Habelt.

Browne, T. 2005. *Urne-Burial.* London: Penguin.

Gramsch, A. 1995. Death and continuity. *Journal of European Archaeology* 3.1: 71–90.

Gräslund, B. 1994. Prehistoric soul beliefs in Northern Europe. *Proceedings of the Prehistoric Society* 60: 15–26.

Hampel, F., Kerchler, H. and Benkovsky-Pivovarová, Z. 1985. *Das Mittelbronzezeitliche Gräberfeld von Pitten in Niederösterreich. Ergebnisse der Ausgrabungen des Niederösterreichischen Landesmuseums in den Jahren 1967 bis 1973 mit Beiträgen über Funde aus anderen Perioden, Band 2: Auswertung.* Mitteilungen der prähistorischen Kommission 21/22, 1982–1985. Wien: Verlag der ÖAW.

Hampel, F., Kerchler, H. and Benkovsky-Pivovarová, Z. 1981. *Das mittelbronzezeitliche Gräberfeld von Pitten in Niederösterreich. Ergebnisse der Ausgrabungen des Niederösterreichischen Landesmuseums in den Jahren 1967 bis 1973 mit Beiträgen über Funde aus anderen Perioden, Band 1: Fundbericht und Tafeln.* Mitteilungen der prähistorischen Kommission 19/20, 1978–1981. Wien: Verlag der ÖAW.

Harding, A.F. 2000. *European Societies in the Bronze Age.* Cambridge: Cambridge University press.

Kimmig, W. 1964. Seevölkerbewegung und Urnenfelderkultur. In *Studien aus Alt-Europa,* edited by R. von Uslar and K.J. Narr, pp. 220–283.

Kristiansen, K. and Larsson, T. 2005. *The Rise of Bronze Age Society: Travels, Transmissions and Transformations.* Cambridge: Cambridge University Press.

Mizoguchi, K. 1993. Time in the reproduction of mortuary practices. *World Archaeology* 25: 223–35.

Neugebauer, C. and Neugebauer, J.W. 1997. *Franzhausen: Das frühbronzezeitliche Gräberfeld I.* Horn: Ferdinand Berger and Sohne.

Neugebauer, J.W. 1991. *Die Nekropole F von Gemeinlebarn, Niederösterreich. Untersuchungen zu den Bestattungssitten und zum Grabraub in der ausgehenden Frühbronzezeit in Niederösterreich südlich der Donau zwischen Enns und Wienerwald,* Römisch Germanische Forschungen 49.

Neugebauer, J.W. 1993. *Archäologie in Niederösterreich – St. Pölten und das Traisental.* St. Pölten: Niederösterreichischer Presseverlag.

Nönnig, K. 2002. *Hinweise archäologischer Quellen auf Gender Rollen in der Mittelbronzezeit.* Wien: Diplomarbeit.

Oestigaard, T. 2004. Death and ambivalent materiality – human flesh as culture and cosmology. In *Combining the Past and the Present: Archaeological Perspectives on Society,* edited by T.

Oestigaard, N. Anfinset and T. Saetersdal, pp. 23–30. BAR International Series 1210. Oxford: BAR.

Parker Pearson, M. 1999. *The Archaeology of Death and Burial.* Stroud: Sutton.

Rittershofer, K.F. 1987. Grabraub in der Bronzezeit. *Berichte der Römisch-Germanischen Kommission* 68: 5–23.

Sørensen, M.L.S. 2004. The Grammar of drama: an analysis of the rich Early Bronze Age grave at Leubingen, Germany. In *Die Dinge als Zeichen: Kulturelles Wissen und Materielle Kultur*, edited by T.L. Kleindin. Universitätsforschungen zur prähistorischen Archäologie 127. Bonn: Habelt.

Sørensen, M.L.S. and Rebay, K. 2008. Interpreting the body: burial practices at the Middle Bronze Age cemetery at Pitten. *Archaeologia Austriaca* 89 (2005): 153–175.

Sprenger, S. 1999. *Zur Bedeutung des Grabraubes für sozio-archäologische Gräberfeldanalysen. Eine Untersuchung am frühbronzezeitlichen Gräberfeld Franzhausen I, Niederösterreich. Fundberichte aus Österreich, Materialheft A 7.* Wien: Berger.

Teschler-Nicola, M. 1985. Die Körper- und Brandbestattungen des mittelbronzezeitlichen Gräberfeldes von Pitten, Niederösterreich. Demographische und anthropologische Analyse. In *Das mittelbronzezeitliche Gräberfeld von Pitten in Niederösterreich. Ergebnisse der Ausgrabungen des Niederösterreichischen Landesmuseums in den Jahren 1967 bis 1973 mit Beiträgen über Funde aus anderen Perioden, Band 2: Auswertung*, edited by F. Hampel, H. Kerchler and Z. Benkovsky, pp. 127–272. Mitteilungen der prähistorischen Kommission 21/22.

Windl, H. 1983. Fürsten der Bronzezeit in Pitten. Sonderausstellung im Museum für Urgeschichte in Asparn an der Zaya vom 1. April bis 31. Oktober 1983. Katalog des Niederösterreichischen Landesmuseums, Neue Folge 135.

8

The extraordinary history of Oliver Cromwell's head

Sarah Tarlow

The point of microhistories is to take something apparently small – an incident, an artefact or a place, for example, and show, through studying the details of one small case, how it exemplifies and relates to much bigger questions of cultural, social and political history. In this chapter the extraordinary history of Oliver Cromwell's head will be used to think about changing understandings of the human body between the seventeenth and the twentieth centuries.

On the 3 September 1658 Oliver Cromwell, Protector of the Commonwealth, regicide and parliamentarian turned autocrat, died at the age of fifty-nine. In the course of his political career he had played a major role in the trial and execution of Charles I, become Lieutenant General of the New Model Army, and Lord General for the Irish and Scottish campaigns, led the rump Parliament and eventually taken a monarchic role himself as Lord Protector of the Commonwealth. He championed religious tolerance and opened up public office and membership of the universities to those of non-Anglican faith to degree that would not be seen again until the nineteenth century. At the same time, his military activities, especially in Ireland, were accomplished with excessive brutality and did damage to the relationship between Britain and Ireland that is still unrepaired. This chapter, however, is not about Oliver Cromwell's life. It is about his head (Figure 8.1) and what happened to it after 1658.

After his death, the body of Oliver Cromwell was examined and then embalmed (Pearson and Morant 1935: 7). In accord with normal surgical practice of the mid to late seventeenth century, as known from written sources, the internal organs were removed, including the brain which was taken out by sawing the cap of

the cranium. The skull cavity was then filled with 'powder and tow', the top of the skull replaced and the scalp sewn together over it all. The post-mortem examination of the bodies of illustrious persons was

Figure 8.1. 'The Wilkinson head', almost certainly the real head of Oliver Cromwell

fairly common at the time, but these were private autopsies, designed to establish the cause of death, and were far removed from the public anatomies of the seventeenth, eighteenth and nineteenth centuries which were carried out on the bodies of executed criminals, and later of the anonymous poor (Richardson 1988; Sawday 1994). Cromwell's brain was noted to weigh an enormous six and a quarter pounds. The average human adult brain weighs about three pounds, so even using Troy measures with twelve ounces to the pound, Cromwell's brain would be quite remarkable (Pearson and Morant 1935: 8). At a time when character was held to depend on physiological make-up, and in particular of the balance in the body between the secretions of the key organs according to the theories of Hippocrates and Galen, the size of those organs was anticipated by the behaviour of the individual in life. At the same time, the brain also had its modern meaning as the place of understanding and therefore a large brain also had its modern association with great intelligence. Thirty-three years earlier, the fact that King James's brain was so large had been taken as 'a marke of his infinite judgement' (Nichols 1828: 1037 cited in Pearson and Morant 1935: 29).

Several seventeenth century accounts of Cromwell's death and the events subsequent to it make great matter of the necessity to embalm his body soon after death and inter it in advance of his state funeral (e.g. Guizot 1887: 451; Gaunt 1996: 204). Although embalming was not normal for the mass of burials in the seventeenth century, it was standard in the case of very powerful individuals whose funerals required extensive preparation. Royalist sympathisers embellished the account of his funeral with the assertion that Cromwell's body needed embalming and early interment because its decomposition was exceptionally rapid and unpleasant. This invokes the idea that the state of the body indexes the state of the soul. A corrupt and filthy body is a reliable proxy for a corrupt and filthy soul. The idea that moral goodness and physical cleanness of the body correlate is both medieval and modern; buttressed on the one side by the incorruptibility of the saintly body and on the other by attempts to reform private and public life by environmental cleanliness.

Interestingly, embalming may also have been seen as a way of keeping the body from being claimed absolutely by death. Christian Friedrich Garmann, a Lutheran doctor living in Dresden from 1640–1708 contends, in a treatise on death that was published posthumously by his son, that there is still some life in a mummy because the embalming substances prevent corruption from setting in and thus death is staved off (Ariès 1981: 354). Ariès cites a Latin tract composed

in the seventeenth century by a German doctor called Christian Garmann which offers many examples of the sensibility of the cadaver. So the embalming of the natural body, as well as the creation of an artificial one, might have acted to challenge an individual death by promoting the continuity of a person's social existence. This social existence was popularly recognised even in cases where embalming and effigy-making did not take place, as is clear from the many examples Garmann gives examples of people taking care not to hurt the bodies of the dead, or minding what they said in front of the newly dead who could still, in some sense, 'hear'. Philippe Ariès also relates to this the belief in the efficacy of dead bodies or parts of bodies as medicine or charm. Charles II reportedly drank a potion containing forty-two drops of extract of human skull during his last illness, although it failed to cure him (Ariès 1981: 358). 'Mummy', made from the bodies of the dead, especially executed criminals, was a widely available medicine throughout the early modern period and into the eighteenth century.

The major threat that death posed to the public body in the early modern period was that ordinary processes of corruption would expose the body's subjection to natural process. In an age of 'self-fashioning' (Greenblatt 1980) the body's boundaries and continence needed special policing. The ingress or egress of substances into or from the body constituted an exchange between the body and the world and increasingly required privacy (in the case of evacuation) or the control of elaborate codes of etiquette (in the case of ingestion). Controlled and mastered bodies should ideally not smell, seep or intrude in any unpleasant way on others, according to contemporary manuals of polite conduct. The dead body, however, was at risk of emitting foul air, liquid or matter and so betraying its corporeality. Jeremy Taylor wrote in 1651 that the processes of decay should not be observed by others:

> It is good that the body be kept veiled and secret, and not exposed to curious eyes, or the dishonours wrought by the changes of death discerned and stared upon by impertinent persons. (Taylor 1651 Section 8)

For Cromwell's body that risk was addressed both by attempting to slow the natural processes of decay through embalming, and by circumventing it altogether through the substitution of an effigy for the human corpse.

After the post-mortem examination and the skilful embalming of Cromwell's body, the corpse was taken by night with some ceremony to Somerset House where the lying in state took place (Firth 1901: 444). What was laid out for public display, however, was not the actual body but an effigy (Figure 8.2); the coffin

Figure 8.2. Cromwell's effigy lying in state

carrying his remains stayed under the table. The effigy had a wax face moulded by an expert artist, Thomas Symond, engraver to the Mint, and a wooden body made by a man called Philips, carver to the House. A number of nineteenth-century historians of Cromwell put forward theories suggesting that Cromwell's actual body was secretly buried in some other location – citing no seventeenth-century evidence, but claiming that the construction of an effigy and the apparent burial of the remains well before the funeral was suspicious. In fact, in cases of the death of great or famous people, it was normal practice to bury an effigy rather than the body itself (Llewellyn 1991: 54): there was nothing particularly unusual about this aspect of Cromwell's obsequies. Nigel Llewellyn (1991: 54) observes:

After death the natural body was accorded a programme of treatment, but even here the objective of the ritual was the survival and re-presentation of the social body rather than the conservation of the natural body *per se*. In order that the burial could effectively mark transition – the points between death and life, horizontal and vertical, above and below the earth – the body could not simply be left to the bacteria. [the body could be embalmed and/ or]… One of the most important aims of the funeral … was the preservation of social cohesion and the denial that any one individual death presented an irreparable threat to continuity.

The construction of an effigy, or at least of a convincing wax mask of the face was necessary so that a life-like version of the actual body could be seen, unmarred, at the funeral. Highly naturalistic effigies were prepared for the funerals of Henry VIII, Elizabeth I and for most royal deaths of the early modern period. Nigel Llewellyn describes an effigy prepared for Henry, Prince of Wales in 1612 which had moving arms and legs (Llewellyn 1992: 55).

The preservation of an idealised 'body' after death, in the form first of the effigy and after of a 'monumental body' (a memorial) challenged the democratic uniformity of death. If the bodily event of death treated rich and poor alike, it reduced the powerful to the same status as the lowest in society. The death of great men and women also left a hole in the fabric of social power which required ideological darning. The social order was threatened by death, writes Llewellyn, and therefore the artificial body was in some ways charged with the task of re-establishing social difference (Llewellyn 1992: 104).

Ernst Kantorowicz developed a theory of medieval political theology which he referred to as 'the king's two bodies': the king has not only his corporeal body, which may sicken and die, but also the body politic – a transcendent royalty which cannot die, as in the acclamation 'The King is dead. Long live the King!' (Kantorowicz 1957). The King is the head of the Body Politic which literally incorporates the other members of the state.

The theory of the Two Bodies held that the loss of a natural body – at death – should not entail the loss of the social body which endures. Given the instability of the dead natural body, the effigial body provided a materialisation of the king's (or in this case the Protector's) Body Politic, which would carry the outward symbols of his political role. In the case of Cromwell, it is interesting to note that the effigy – the social body – was literally made to bear the symbols of head of state – the crown, globe and sceptre, and was clad in robes whose signification of social role was strictly controlled by sumptuary laws. To borrow Binford's phrase in a context he probably never anticipated, the effigy was a 'social persona' (Binford 1972: 225–6).

According to the *Mercurius Politicus* (a public journal):

> the effigies [*sic, passim*] itself apparelled in a rich suit of uncut velvet, being robed first in a kirtle robe of purple velvet, laced with a rich gold lace and furred with ermins, upon the kirtle is the royal large robe of the like purple velvet laced, and furred with ermins, with rich strings, and tassels of gold; his kirtle is girt with a rich embroidered belt, in which is a fair sword richly gilt, and hatched with gold, hanging by the side of the effigies; in the right hand is the golden scepter representing government; in his left hand is held the globe, representing principality; upon his head the cap of regality of purple velvet, furred with

> ermins. Behind the head is a rich chair of estate of cloth of gold tissued; upon the cushion of the chair stands the imperial crown set with stones. The whole effigies lies upon a bed covered with a large pall of black velvet, under which is a fine Holland sheet upon six stools of cloth of gold tissued; by the sides of the bed of state lies a rich suit of compleat armour representing his command as General; at the feet of the effigies stands his crest, as is usual in all ancient monuments. (cited in Pearson and Morant 1935: 31)

Cromwell's highly ornamental effigial body tells us much about attitudes to the self and the body in the late seventeenth century. Manuals of etiquette in the early modern period show that sumptuous dress for the aristocracy was not considered effeminate or suspicious but appropriate to the rank and social position of the person (Scholz 2000: 18). Sumptuary laws in this period, therefore, were aimed at ensuring that clothing corresponded to the status of the body it covered. Scholz (2000: 39) has discussed the way that the body in the sixteenth and seventeenth century needed to be moulded 'as an index of one's social self', a process which could involve 'a high degree of theatricality'. Both the use of the body as a medium for establishing social position, and the theatricality to which Scholz refers are very evident in Cromwell's laying out. When John Donne referred to his body as 'a little world made cunningly/ Of elements and an angelic sprite' (Holy Sonnet V. Cf. George Herbert's line in his poem 'Man' that the body is 'in little, all the sphere') he was invoking a view of the self – and the body – as a microcosm of the universe. This microcosmic view held that the whole world was inside the body, including the presence of God. Thus adorning the body's surface was necessary in order to make visible that which was interior to the self: the body's plastic exterior was in the service of its un-mouldable interior. This is generally considered to be a Renaissance concept of self and body, contrasted with a Protestant self where it is the interior that is mouldable (Scholz 2000: 55–56), an autonomous self talking directly with God in place of the courtly self created through social discourses. But in the case of Cromwell we see a wholly Protestant context employing an understanding of the microcosmic, courtly, exterior body which differed little from that of the early seventeenth-century Catholic Donne.

Cromwell's body was buried quietly at Westminster Abbey, while preparations for the funeral continued. At some point the lying in state was replaced by a standing in state – probably another effigy altogether. He died on 3rd September, but his state funeral did not take place until 23rd November, postponed from 9th November (Guizot 1887: 431). Oliver Cromwell's

Westminster funeral was celebrated 'with a pomp which far exceeded all that had ever yet been displayed in England' (Guizot 1887: 431). The effigy was placed at the centre of an elaborate structure which was processed to the funeral followed by 9000 mourners. Only the effigy, not the body itself which had already been buried, was used at the proper funeral.

After the funeral the effigy was, according to one source, set up above the burial place of the body. What happened to the recumbent effigy for the year and a half after the lying in state is not known, but the destruction of two effigies of Cromwell, one by burning and one by hanging and riot, is recorded in public journals of May and June 1660 at the time of Charles II's restoration to the throne (Pearson and Morant 1935: 37). The capacity of the effigy to signify the person could make it the object of vilification as much as of honour.

Punishment of the body

The Royalists, however, were not content with acting out their revenge upon the effigial body alone. Following the Restoration to the throne of Charles II, an order of parliament commanded that the bodies of Cromwell, along with three other prominent parliamentarians, John Bradshaw, Henry Ireton and Thomas Pride be exhumed, hanged at Tyburn and buried under the gallows. The coffins of Cromwell, Ireton and Bradshaw were exhumed and taken by cart and sledge to Tyburn, where the bodies were pulled from their coffins and hanged all day. Thomas Pride's body was not taken to Tyburn on that occasion; it might have been too decayed to exhume and hang. Although the parliamentary act stipulates that the bodies should be hanged in their coffins, numerous eyewitness accounts of the event tell us that the bodies were taken out of their coffins and then hanged: as one witness put it,

> the odious carcasses of O.C., Major General Ireton, and Bradshaw were drawn in sledges to Tyburn, where they were hanged by the neck from morning till four in the afternoon. C. in a green-seare cloth, very fresh embalmed; Ireton having been buried long, hung like a dried rat, yet corrupted about the fundament. Bradshaw in his winding sheet, the finger of his right hand and nose perished having wet the sheet through; the rest very perfect, in so much that I knew his face, when the hangman, after cutting it off, held it up; of his toes I had five or six in my hand which the prentices had cut off. Their bodies were thrown into an hole under the gallows, in their seare cloth and sheet. … and their heads were set up on the south end of Westminster Hall (Edward or Samuel Sainthill [there is some inconsistency between sources],

in a manuscript of Rev. T.R. Nash, cited by Pearson and Morant 1935: 45)

One of the valuable parts of an exercise in microhistory like this, is that it forces us to examine our own beliefs and taken-for-granteds. One of those is that we – I mean modern, anglophone westerners – have a fairly clear-cut idea of where life stops. When certain indicative functions of the body, like respiration, circulation and brain activity cease to occur the person is dead; the social person as a responsible agent ceases to exist. That does not seem to have been the case in the seventeenth century.

Michel Foucault has famously written about changing attitudes to the body in the post-medieval era, and he gave particular attention to the punishment of the body (Foucault 1977). Foucault's history traces a change from pre-modern punishment which is retributive, violent and acted upon the body by causing it pain, to a modern form of punishment which is rehabilitative, psychological and enacted upon the body through the promotion of new kinds of bodily discipline. It is obvious from the story of Cromwell's head, however, that punishment of the body in a pre-modern sense is not just about causing pain. In keeping with Foucault's observations, though, the punishment inflicted on Cromwell, Ireton and Bradshaw, was public and humiliating. It was an act of social and political censure; that it could be carried out upon corpses suggests that the social identity between someone and their body did not cease at death: that the body continued to act as an index of the person past the point of death. A punishment to the body of Cromwell was a punishment to Cromwell as he was in life – some form of retroactive harm was done to him. Since Cromwell (and Ireton and Bradshaw) could not suffer physical pain at this point, the aim of this bodily punishment must have been to cause harm to his dignity. This was done by violating the cultural norms of bodily privacy and control which would normally be maintained by the living individual and safeguarded after their death. Given the special significance attached to guarding the privacy of the body's orifices by this time, the public display of Ireton corrupted about the fundament was especially degrading.

Did the punishment of the body have an effect on the fate of the soul? Certainly there were popular beliefs in the literal resurrection of the body which persisted into the nineteenth century and explain much of the early resistance to the practice of cremation, for example. However, the frequently stated belief that scattered body parts would come together at the resurrection imply that the treatment of the dead body would not determine the fate of the soul. In Taylor's

Figure 8.3. A possibly fanciful representation of the heads of Cromwell, Bradshaw and Ireton on spikes above Westminster Hall

The Holy Dying, this point is made with reference to the martyrdom of saints:

> And St. Ignatius, who was buried in the bodies of lions, and St. Polycarp, who was burned to ashes, shall have their bones and their flesh again with greater comfort than those violent persons who slept among kings, having usurped their thrones when they were alive, and their sepulchres when they were dead. (Taylor 1651: section 8)

As a prominent Royalist theologian, however, Taylor would probably have imagined that Cromwell's soul was doomed anyway, as this quotation suggests. Thus it seems unlikely that the treatment of Cromwell's body was intended to affect the fate of his soul which was, according to Protestant doctrine, determined by Cromwell's personal relationship with God.

The public display of the head, however, for maybe twenty years or more, must have been for purely this-worldly reasons: it would act, presumably, to reinforce a political ideology by demonstrating the consequences of opposition; and at the same time be part of the personal humiliation of Cromwell and his associates demanded by the returning royalists. Philippe Ariès (1981: 348) describes how, in the second half of the seventeenth century, the piles of bones lying visibly on the surface of graveyards began to be considered

distasteful and an affront to the dignity of the dead. New rules specifying minimum depth of burial and so on were introduced to address this hitherto altogether unremarkable state of things. Routine public display of mortal remains at the time of Cromwell's exhumation, was both exceptional and exceptionable in Protestant contexts.

The headless bodies were buried in a pit at Tyburn, unless you believe one of the many alternative, though mostly nineteenth-century histories that has Cromwell's body secretly removed and buried elsewhere, either after the hanging or at the Red Lion inn in Holborn where the bodies were moved from cart to sledge (Fraser 1973: 692). One of the more outrageous theories is that Cromwell's body was exchanged at that point with that of Charles I (Fraser 1973:695), although how the executioner could fail to notice that he was hanging a man whose head had already been removed is not clear. This idea is almost certainly false: eyewitness accounts of the opening of Charles I's coffin in 1813 report seeing the old king's own decapitated corpse (Halford 1813, cited in Pearson and Morant 1935: 5). Other stories, which are almost certainly untrue and are not supported by much – or indeed any – contemporary evidence have Cromwell's body secretly buried in Yorkshire, Huntingdon, Northborough, Naseby battlefield, Oxford, or sunk to the bottom of the Thames (Firth 1923: 451–2). However, if some of the organs removed at Cromwell's embalming were interred elsewhere that would not be unusual for the period: heart burials in particular were fairly common for high status individuals.

The three heads were fixed on spikes and displayed on wooden poles above the south end of Westminster Hall (Figure 8.3). There they remained for many years, as attested by the letters and journals of many Londoners and visitors. The exhibition of heads of political criminals was already known at this time. In 1770 in central London, according to Grosley, a Frenchman visiting the city, the heads of three traitors executed after the 1745 rebellion were still on poles above Temple Bar (Grosley 1772, Vol 2: 10). I do not know if these heads were routinely embalmed; if not it is unlikely that after twenty-five years of exposure, weather and scavengers, there would be more than crania on the poles. It is possible that heads were dipped in some kind of tar before display (Pearson and Morant 1935: 46n): if this were the case with Cromwell's head that might explain its exceptionally good state of preservation.

The body politic and the early modern body

The metaphorical significance of the head in this context is significant: the fact that Cromwell's head, rather than his foot or his shoulder was displayed on a pole, and in a cabinet of curiosities, is more than incidental. First there is the ironic symmetry that Cromwell's body should eventually suffer the same fate as Charles I; second there is the special significance of the head, as synecdochal of the body and its metaphorical significance in politics. The head of state governs and represents the body politic. The head bears the crown, symbolic of office, and 'the crowned heads of Europe', for example, signifies a ruling elite. Just as Cromwell's body, at his funeral, had been made to stand for the 'body politic' in a metaphor that would have been familiar to all his educated contemporaries, so the head of the head of state was an appropriate metonym in a political context.

We do not know exactly when Cromwell's head came down, or how – the account of another French traveller records it as still on show in 1671; there is an ambiguous reference to it in 1681 which may suggest it had already fallen; another account, albeit one which contains other known inaccuracies, has it still in place in 1684 (Pearson and Morant 1935: 58). So the head remained on a spike for probably about twenty to twenty-five years. There then follows the most obscure part of its history. Most sources agree that the head was blown

down in a storm and picked up by a watchman. It was then either secretly kept by the watchman or passed to a Cromwellian sympathiser. In any case, its location was kept quiet at a time when having possession of the head would probably be considered evidence of treasonous political views.

The Body as Curio

The next mention of the head is in 1710, when a German account records that the head was part of the collection of Claudius DuPuy, a Swiss calico-printer, residing in London, who owned four rooms of 'curiosities', for private view rather than as a money-making venture (Pearson and Morant 1935: 22). Within fifty years of Cromwell's exhumation his head had thus changed its meaning entirely. At the time of its fall from the roof it was a political object whose possession was so dangerous it had to be kept secret. But by 1710, if the German account is reliable, it was part of a gentleman's cabinet of curiosities, the ownership of which afforded cultural capital to its possessor. From the eighteenth to the early twentieth century, Cromwell's head was an object of curiosity and exchange. This phase of the story blurs the distinction between body and artefact, as the body part was collected, exhibited, bought and sold.

DuPuy died intestate in 1738 (Pearson and Morant 1935: 22). Either upon his death, or some time before it, the head came into the possession of the Russell family. An account by John Kirk, a medallist, mentions having seen the head in 1775 when it was in the possession of the Russells, although it is not clear whether it was being exhibited for money or whether the writer was granted private access. In around 1770 the head was offered for sale to the master of Sidney Sussex college, Cambridge by Samuel Russell the elder, described by Pearson and Morant (1935:13) as 'a strolling actor of drunken habits'. Presumably Russell thought that Sidney Sussex College might have an interest in owning a part of their famous alumnus.

The Master of Sidney Sussex was called, in the anonymous narrative source from which this incident comes, Dr Ellison. William Elliston was Master of Sidney from 1760–1807. The narrative claims that Ellison discussed the incident with Dr Powell, Master of St John's College. Dr Powell was Master of St John's between 1765 and 1775, so the interview must have taken place around then. The college, however, did not purchase the head. 'Dr Ellison imagining it might create some prejudice against him to have bought the head declined treating with the man for it.' (Pearson and Morant 1935: 12). Whether this prejudice was due to Cromwell's politics and place in history or to the practice of trading for human body parts in general is not specified.

In 1780 James Cox, a jeweller of the City of London, saw the head exhibited near Claremarket in London when it was still owned by Samuel Russell. Russell's version of the history, recounted through a third party, is that Cox tried many times to buy the head but Russell wouldn't part with it until he was in such debt to Cox that he was forced to sell it to him for £118 in 1787 (Pearson and Morant 1935: 14). Cox soon sold the head on at a considerable profit to three men, perhaps called Hughes, who wanted to exhibit it in Mead Court, Old Bond Street. An advert and a 'narrative' was prepared for this exhibition by John Cranch in 1799.

Cranch's narrative is one of the main sources for the history of the head, but it also contains interesting explanations for the physical form of the relic. He notes, for example, that the ear is missing:

> This is accounted for by another of the (Russell) family traditions which is that when the Protector's relations and admirers were occasionally admitted to see the head, they took those opportunities to pilfer such small parts as could best be come at, or were least likely to be missed. The ear is said to have been taken away by one of the Russells of Fordham. (Pearson and Morant 1935: 15)

The collection of minor body parts as souvenirs is not new, but it is interesting. The removal of Cromwell's ear by a visiting descendant compares with Sainthill's having five or six of Bradshaw's toes after his hanging. Again the body part is synechdocal of the person as a whole.

In 1814 the head was obtained by Josiah Henry Wilkinson, in whose family it remained until the middle of the twentieth century.

As object of terror

The novelist Maria Edgeworth describes being shown the Head by Wilkinson at a private house on 9 March 1822. After breakfast the whole group, of whom Maria Edgeworth was one, were told the story, while Wilkinson's sister and brother in law were made to take turns holding the head up for the hour that the story took. She observed, in an unpublished letter seen by Pearson and Morant (1935: 25–26): 'Mr Wilkinson its present possessor doats upon it – a frightful skull it is…' Her reactions were closer to fear and repugnance than curiosity. While researching this chapter I came across a reference on an unreliable internet site that Cromwell's head has an 'occult' history, although disappointingly this turned out to relate to a 2005 performance piece, constructed around the idea of

Cromwell's head being trapped in the telephone exchange of the Royal Edinburgh Psychiatric Hospital (Mongrel, 'Aroundhead'). But Edgeworth's reaction provokes some academic questions: when did the dead body become scary? When did the disembodied head become an object of terror? We can assume that Edgeworth was, in 1822, familiar with Gothic horror genre novels; did that tradition inform her reaction to the head? This remains at present an unanswered research question. In any case, the Victorians had a taste for the horrific and the ghoulish. Cromwell was a bogey man by then, but outside Ireland, the memory of his crimes was no longer close enough to inspire real anger. Even Maria Edgeworth, as an Irish woman, albeit an Anglo-Irish one living in London, responded to his head as a ghoulish object rather than to its former owner.

The Wilkinson head as an object of scientific inquiry

At the time of the study by Pearson and Morant in 1935, the head was still in the possession of the Wilkinson family. It had been in the family for over a century and was at that time owned by Canon Horace Wilkinson. Canon Wilkinson had refused to allow the BBC to film the head in 1954, although he did permit personal visitors, friends and family to see the head: there is a photograph from about 1950 of Angela Thirkell holding the head in the archive of the writer's papers at Leeds University. Other twentieth century photographs also exist: one of Canon Wilkinson himself with the head was on the Fitzwilliam Museum website at the time of writing this chapter.

In the twentieth century, the debate over the authenticity of the head became intense. Numerous letters in periodicals in the early decades of the century traded anecdotes and folklore about the fate of Cromwell's body and his head and cast doubt upon the status of the Wilkinson head. Thus, first in 1911 and then again in 1935, 'scientists' were allowed to examine the head itself with the aim of making an objective assessment of its provenience and determining whether it was really Cromwell's head. Although he had allowed members of the Royal Archaeological Institute to examine the head in 1911, he did not allow them to publish their observations. However, in the early 1930s Wilkinson did allow Karl Pearson and G.M. Morant access to the head to make a thorough scientific study, taking many photographs and indeed 'skiagrams', which seem to be x-ray images of some kind. Their results were published by *Biometrika* in 1935 as *The Portraiture of Oliver Cromwell with Special Reference to the Wilkinson*

Figure 8.4. Pearson and Morant attempted to fit the measurements of the Wilkinson head to contemporary portraits, masks and busts of Cromwell

Head. It was dedicated to, and acknowledged the assistance of Ramsay Macdonald, the prime minister at the time the research was carried out, and it is a serious product of respectable science. Although the dedication to Ramsay Macdonald describes the work as 'a slight token of gratitude', there is nothing in the least slight about the volume which is an extremely thorough and lengthy study of more than a hundred pages, plus numerous plates. The aim of the study was to determine the authenticity of what had become known as the Wilkinson head. By scientific examination of the head Pearson and Morant move from standard bio-anthropological determinations, like the age and pathologies of the man, to attempts to fit the head to all known portraits, busts and masks of the Protector (Figure 8.4). Their extremely thorough attempts to trace the history of the head constitute the main source for the historical narrative of this chapter. Their conclusion is 'that it is a "moral certainty" drawn from the circumstantial evidence that the Wilkinson Head is the genuine head of Oliver Cromwell' (Pearson and Morant 1935: 109).

In its first centuries, it was not the authenticity of the head that really mattered but its verisimilitude. Indeed,

in the case of the effigy that did duty for Cromwell in the funerary rituals we know, as did everybody at the time, that it was not the actual body at all. Although real bodies and body parts had considerable currency in the eighteenth and nineteenth centuries as curiosities and as objects of pleasurable horror, waxworks were equally popular. Mme Tussaud, whose legacy remains part of the essential tourist itinerary of London, arrived in England in 1803 and spent thirty-three years touring Britain with her collections which included wax models of the heads of guillotined victims of the French Revolution. She set up a permanent exhibition in London in 1835. By the twentieth century, however, mere verisimilitude would not suffice: an object purporting to be Cromwell's head had to really be Cromwell's head. The debate about its authenticity was not directed at any particular end – in other words, it didn't really matter for any greater purpose whether the head was actually Cromwell's, but it was considered important to know, nevertheless (so important, in fact, that the Prime Minister of the day took an interest and made available the art collections held at Chequers, the official country home of the Prime Minister).

As locus of ethical propriety

At the time Pearson and Morant carried out their study in the 1930s they expressed no ethical qualms at all about examining and photographing the head. In 1952 William Kent, the author of *London: Mystery and Mythology* quizzed Canon Wilkinson about whether it was appropriate to keep the head on a mantelpiece, but only on the grounds that the remains of a important national figure surely ought to be on public view. Kent asked Wilkinson whether he felt it right to keep the head privately rather than making it available to the public. His reply:

> Canon Wilkinson demurs to this view on the grounds that they are Christian remains and there are descendants of Cromwell still living. Perhaps he feels it would be dishonouring for the skull to be in a museum, but some will think it would be no more so than having it on a mantelpiece.

Wilkinson's response – that Cromwell was a Christian and that his descendants are still alive and it would therefore not be appropriate to exhibit the head to the general public – manifest ethical concerns (albeit not strong enough for him to actually rebury the head) which became increasingly troubling to many people during the later part of the twentieth century.

If you want to see Cromwell's head today, for example, you cannot. In 1960, a few years after

Wilkinson's death the head was reburied (or re-immured) at an undisclosed location in or adjacent to Sidney Sussex college chapel. Here we intersect with a set of cultural values relating to the dead body that we already recognise as archaeologists – that the display of dead bodies has become unethical. A new sensitivity to the way that the dead are treated is beginning to emerge by the mid century – at first limited to the remains of Christians and concerns for living descendants, but later, and as a result of civil and indigenous rights movements' campaigns in the cultural realm, to include the bodies of other past people.

Conclusion

The relationship between bodies and selves is not always the same. Even what we often refer to as 'the modern body' has different contextual and mutable meanings. We cannot always differentiate clearly between body and artefact. On some occasions Cromwell's body signified Cromwell's social person – as when it was exhumed, hanged and decapitated as a punishment for crimes committed by Cromwell. On other occasions it was an interesting collector's item, conversation piece or family heirloom: functioning like an artefact. On yet other occasions an artefact has taken the social role of Cromwell – as at his funeral where an effigy formed the central focus of ritual. Cromwell's head has consistently represented Cromwell in some way, but its authenticity has not always been a major concern. His several bodies – the natural one, the many artificial and monumental ones (not even considered here) – had social meaning long after he breathed his last. If nothing else, the extraordinary history of Oliver Cromwell's head should make us wary of assuming that dead bodies are inert in terms of social agency.

In the case of Oliver Cromwell, the capacity to be involved with politics, present at major historical moments, inspire strong emotional reactions and even to be involved in commercial transactions, were hardly diminished by the minor matter of decapitation.

Bibliography

Ariès, P. 1981. *The Hour of our Death*. London: Penguin

Binford, L. 1971. Mortuary practices: their study and their potential. *American Antiquity* 36(3:2):6–29. Reprinted in Binford, L. 1972. *An Archaeological Perspective*. New York

Firth, C. 1923 [1901]. *Oliver Cromwell and the Rule of the Puritans in England*. London: G.P. Putnam's Sons

Foucault, M. 1977 (trans Alan Sheridan) *Discipline and Punish: The Birth of the Prison*. Harmondsworth: Penguin (first published as *Surveiller et punir: naissance de la prison* 1975 by Editions Gallimard)

Fraser, A. 1973. *Cromwell: Our Chief of Men*. London: Weidenfeld and Nicolson

Gaunt, P. 1996. *Oliver Cromwell*. Oxford: Blackwell

Greenblatt, S. 1980. *Renaissance Self-fashioning: From More to Shakespeare*. Chicago: Chicago University Press.

Grosley, P.-J. 1772 (trans. T. Nugent). *A Tour to London, or, New Observations on England and its Inhabitants*. London: Lokyer Davis (first published as *Londres* 1771, Lausanne)

Guizot, F. 1887 [1854] *Life of Oliver Cromwell*, 9th edition. London: Richard Bentley and Son

Halford, H. 1813. *An Account of what Appeared on Opening the Coffin of King Charles I*. London:

Kantorowicz, E. 1957. *The King's Two Bodies: A Study in Medieval Political Theology*. Princeton: Princeton University Press

Kent, W. 1952. *London: Mystery and Mythology*. London: Staples Press

Llewellyn, N. 1992. *The Art of Death*. London: Reaktion Books

Moshenska, G. 2006. The archaeological uncanny. *Public Archaeology* 5(2): 91–99

Pearson, K. and G.M. Morant 1935. *The Portraiture of Oliver Cromwell with Special Reference to the Wilkinson Head*. Offprinted from Biometrika vol 26. London: Biometrika

Richardson, R. 1988. *Death, Dissection and the Destitute*. Harmondsworth: Penguin

Sawday, J. 1994. *The Body Emblazoned: Dissection and the Human Body in Renaissance Culture*. London: Routledge

Fresh scars on the body of archaeology: excavating mass-graves at Batajnica, Serbia

Slobodan Mitrović

Introduction

Hundreds of bodies, the suspected victims of violence that had swept the Balkans in 1999, lay in Batajnica near Belgrade. In 2001, forensic experts, including a team of archaeologists, were called upon to examine remains from the site mere kilometers away from the capital of Serbia and Montenegro. It was suspected that the hundreds of bodies from several mass graves originated from different events and from different places in Kosovo and Metohija. Sorting through human debris archaeologists looked for clues to how the people died and to their identities, and also tried to detach the daily life from the clothed bodies in the ground that went together with it. This paper discusses the complex nature of the contemporary mass grave site and the role of the archaeologist in interpreting the data. It also deals with the relationship between the sensual and bodily imprints, and life on site during the process of exhumation.

The text engages in a kind of dialog with Lindsey Weiss' essay *The Role of the Landscape in International Tribunal Proceedings* (forthcoming), which discussed the nature of evidence presented in the Balkan war crime trials in the Hague Tribunal. I begin by discussing the historical background, then the contents of the site, the archaeological techniques used, and conclude with some comments on the social effects of violence, terror, and guilt. Throughout this piece, my own experience in the field as an archaeologist, and as a Serbian, dialogues with the theoretical analysis.[1]

The Belgrade weekly *Vreme* (transl. *Time*; at the time hailed as the most clear-headed, liberal – democratic) was, through both Balkan wars in the 1990s, very involved in uncovering war-crimes and crime-scenes

– a policy that gave the magazine a bad reputation in pro-regime pro-president Slobodan Milošević circles. *Vreme* also published some of the data from the archives from Batajnica mass grave excavations, and especially important were the reports by Skrozza and Ćirić, which contained information on the new discoveries and building of the case against perpetrators. One article from *Institute for War and Peace Reporting*[2] also published a report with a similar set of data. It is this patchy information along with my own recollections and scraps from my journal from that time that I draw on. I have been in contact with the *International Committee on Missing People* (ICMP) for additional data on excavations, but, due to the fact that the institution's relationship with the Hague Tribunal involves supplying of data for trials, only the evidence made public can be used. Especially given the nowadays atmosphere of awaiting the finalization of important war crime cases and the beginning of new ones.

In the last fifteen years we saw incessant conflicts occurring during the fragmentation of the Balkans, following the dissolution of the USSR. In the case of contemporary Balkans and Serbia in particular, one can straightforwardly talk about the counter-globalising process, a specific reaction to decades of the targeted integration of South Slavic and other peoples in Yugoslavia. Presently, almost sympathetically known as 'the blind-spot of Europe', what once used to be called Yugoslavia is still an unstable region with an inherent uncertainty to it. That the country was a conglomerate of Catholic, Orthodox and Muslim populations living peacefully together is an oft-heard description of pre-civil war times (but see Verdery 1999). The communist regime created a cultural model

Figure 9.2. SAJ Firing range before the start of excavation in 2002. (Image property of Belgrade District Court)

Figure 9.1. Map of Serbia and the surrounding countries, with mentioned place names

under the slogans of brotherhood and unity, in which polities were unfortunately not able to experience true multi-culturality and learn tolerance.[3] Nationalism prevailed – exposing the dictated uniformity and a makeshift ideology – which caused such a return of the oppressed chauvinism and nationalistic narcissism – first in the civil war in Croatia, then spreading to Bosnia, and finally in the conflict in Kosovo. The latest one was a grim culmination, and the ethical question for me as a Serbian archaeologist was how to confront and explain – firstly to myself – the war crimes, as well as the delusional politics that permeated the society.[4]

The setting

In mid-summer 2002 I joined the members of Batajnica mass grave site research team (under the auspices of International Committee on Missing People, Belgrade District Court, and the Institute of Forensic Medicine

in Belgrade) that already included three physical anthropologists, two medical anthropologists, two autopsy specialists, two technicians from the Belgrade morgue, and five archaeologists. All members of the team had to sign non-disclosure agreements saying that we would not reveal any kind of information that we came across during the course of our work. The names of the people on the team were being kept secret somewhat, as there were people in Serbia who were unhappy that Batajnica exhumations were taking place (*IWPR* 2002), and certainly the sentiment was similar within the Serbian police forces – and perhaps more so within the complex that belonged to the Special Antiterrorist Unit (Specijalna Antiterostička Jedinica – SAJ) of the Ministry of Internal Affairs (Ministarstvo Unutrašnjih Poslova – MUP). In the meantime, however, a lot of articles came up in the foreign and the Balkan press, and as of 2006 there is a huge amount of data that is being prepared for the Hague Tribunal so that the court can assess the war crime in the light of this crucial evidence.

The Town of Batajnica (effectively a suburb of Belgrade) lies off the road to Novi Sad, some twenty kilometres northwest from Belgrade city center (Figure 9.1). The mass graves were uncovered just a kilometre away from the highway, in the Special Antiterrorist Unit (SAJ) complex in Batajnica just off the right bank of the Danube.[5] All the pits are located at the north end of SAJ firing ranges three hundred meters long (*ICMP* 2001, *IWPR* 2002). This enclosed area was some seventy meters north-south and fifty metres east-west, delimited by a high improvised fence made of planks of wood, packed earth and trees (Figure 9.2).

To get to the firing range one needs to go through the military barracks and pass by training grounds. Only those who carried a special court order could

Figure 9.3. SAJ Firing range and the excavation site after removal of top-soil, autopsies performed under the tents on the left, the tent on the right was over pit 3. (Image property of Belgrade District Court)

pass through (*IWPR* 2002). The excavations began in May 2001 in the open air, but as is often the case on archaeological digs, as soon as the team realised there would be 'important finds' tents were ordered to cover the excavation pit (Figure 9.3).

Firstly digging through the sterile soil, the team soon uncovered raw humanity which gave off an unbearably strong smell. 'The stench came from the bodies of what were believed to be Kosovo Albanians murdered during the conflict there with Serbian forces in 1999, and then shipped north as part of an alleged cover-up to make sure the public never knew of the atrocities' (*IWPR, 2002*). Digging up the very recent, decomposing past was a difficult job during the summer months. Apart from the visual dent that was rather powerful, it was the smell that would hardly ever be forgotten. The bodies had been underground for only two to three years at the time of excavation (*ICMP* 2004), so one could still very much feel the rot of the past – the residue and cue of life, people extinguished by one regime.

Excavations at Batajnica

During my first day of work on site we uncovered a mass of plastic bags containing bodies and body fluids in Batajnica 3 grave.[6] The largely intact human remains associated with plastic sheeting were clothed, none found to be wearing military style clothing and no ligatures or definite blindfolds were detected during the excavation (*ICMP* 2004). The single deposit showed no signs of disturbance and was classed as a 'primary' grave (*ICMP* 2004). A large truck panel was also recovered, as well as evidence of intense fire.

After I had been initiated in the minutiae of the recording process, the words of Jon Sterenberg, head of the archaeological group with experience from Bosnia, Iraq and Kosovo (and later Thailand) were the first thing I heard out in the field: 'You have to take it as any other archaeology'. The standard procedure meant that we would take photographs and a point via an EDM Total Station for every joint and the head of each body where possible, for the purposes of post-excavation geo-plotting. Tracks of heavy-duty machines and traces of back-hoe blades could be recorded near the surface and mapped so that a computer simulation of a grave could be made.

Excavating on the first four graves[7] the team found bodies that were buried in layers, some of them had been driven into the grave by the weight of the mass, while others had been shoved in by diggers, or tipped in by camion. It was difficult to be aware of the stratigraphy at every instance and leave the bodies in situ at the same time. There were also attempts to burn the bodies before they were covered up that we recorded – as seen through firing events in the sections and across body remains.

At Batajnica 5 we found evidence of severe fire activity inside the grave, car and lorry tires together with human bones were placed at the bottom and throughout the grave to enable the cremation of the remains (*ICMP* 2004). The damage observed on the bodies was very bad.

War journalists reported on the nature of deposition in the first excavated grave: the method of burning the bodies used in Batajnica 1 was different from that used in the other graves. Car tires had been placed at the bottom of seven metre wide, two and a half metre deep pit, and covered by planks with plastic sheeting on top. The bodies had then been thrown on top of the cover and drenched in petrol (*IWPR* 2002). These contexts suggested attempts to conceal the evidence, but had not been successful. The corpses had previously lain in the water and become so waterlogged that the fire did not destroy them. It was later suspected that some of the bodies from the freezer truck that emerged in the Danube in April 1999 ended up in Batajnica 1 (Ćirić 2001; *IWPR* 2002).

So 'any other archaeology' from the very first day came to represent a curious reference system. I would dare to say that archaeology as a denotation was forever changed for me. Everything else outside the excavation ground bore no resemblance to the life within the compound, either.

Each individual corpse would, after recording, eventually be pulled out and put into a body bag along with the clothing and the remains of soft tissue. We wore surgical gloves at all times and paper suits,

Figure 9.4. Unexcavated body mass, and a body in a body bag at the bottom of pit 5, archaeologists outside of the pit in the background. (Image property of Belgrade District Court)

but the equally obligatory protective masks were impossible to breath through in the summer heat, so we worked without them. The body bags would go to the medical examination and autopsy tables, as well as the on-site team performing anthropological analysis of the skeletons that involved taking samples for DNA (Figure 9.4).

For the Serbian population, myself included, the Albanian population in the nineties was the immediate Other, and there is only so much we can know about the other – but definitely not the most intimate, illicit, personal parts of a life. The risk of sounding overly prosaic and plain stupid here notwithstanding, I have to emphasise that the work on the site had a profoundly revelatory quality for me.

We had to preserve the 'live-ness' of decomposing bodies before they would end up on autopsy tables, but the image was constantly being reconstructed. Furthermore, a corpse would be reconfigured – in visual (iconic) terms – as more and more analyses were performed. Gradually it would be less and less alienated and against all reason, I found myself hoping that it would somehow become alive again once its identity was reconstructed. This in-between situation and the images of a decomposing body[8] – let alone direct contact with the flesh, the fluids and the smell – constituted a strong framework for that kind of thought. Personally, it was extremely defeating to take for granted the fact that a year or two before, the same people could have walked down the streets of Belgrade. On the other end of the thought process, and ultimately on the tail-end of the grim Batajnica reality, was the destruction of those bodies and attempts at destroying the images and thus total eradication. The victims at Batajnica 7 only appear buried en masse, but were killed at different seasons as the clothes and

soil samples suggest, possibly even reburied from the original graves (*ICMP* 2004).

As our aim was always to determine the cause of death, we paid special attention to recognising bullet holes. Wounds caused by firearms were indeed found on a number of male bodies exhumed from Batajnica. We put together a photo-documentation and a video diary of relevant findings that would go to courts. One of the reasons for archaeologists' presence on atrocity sites alike is that the Hague Tribunal accepts evidence recovered by professional excavators/forensic archaeologists – experienced in finding clues and establishing the correct order of events (*ICMP* 2004).

Before long, though, the recording process became too time-consuming as more and more bodies were excavated, and we had to do without extensive interpretations that one would normally offer on a context sheet. The project was hoping to get more data from the independent media, government and non-governmental organisations, and possibly from the inside of the SAJ complex. In order to start writing the history, however minute, reconstitution of events through narrators and (multiple) narratives was necessary. It was, and to the best of my knowledge still is, impossible to figure out the syntactical relationship of the events, the contexts and what connected those events. One would like to argue that from a heuristic point of view it is important to take a relativist stance, but even among us fourteen on site involved in the exhumations, there were many relativisms to choose from.

I clearly remember our early amazement when a projectile hole was spotted in one of the bodies – much like seeing a great find on your 'regular archaeological site'. We soon learned that bullet holes and blanks were littered everywhere inside the SAJ complex due to the close proximity of firing practice ground. Excavation would sometimes be halted for brief periods of time, too – when it overlapped with firing drills. In the same vein, the cause of death became an elusive category because of the nature of data – tertiary archaeological context, multiple deposits, partially or completely burnt individuals, shot to death, hit with a blunt instrument; different soil types with bodies from the same deposit, etc. Among the recovered evidence of Batajnica 5 there were also remains of one coffin complete with a dislodged body (*ICMP* 2004).

The impression of a completely different, skewed reality was further aided by the fact that we would begin and end days at our homes in Belgrade. At seven to eight in the morning we would be transported in a nondescript SUV with shaded windows to the site, only to be back in Belgrade by 5 in the afternoon

Mass graves in three locations in Serbia were found in 2001. At first there seemed to be a single grave with thirty-six bodies, then fifty, and then the next figure was 305. Several witnesses, including security force members, drivers and pit-diggers, testified that close to 800 bodies were taken to Batajnica in five or six trucks in April 1999, probably one vehicle for each grave (*IWPR* 2002). The biggest grave – Batajnica 5 – contained at least 287 bodies (*ICMP* 2004). International committee on Missing Persons in the 2004 reports the figure of at least 705 corpses coming from Batajnica in total.

In general, each discovery and excavation of a mass grave follows a similar pattern. Abnormalities such as depressions in the ground, indicating a filled-in hole, often hint at the presence of a mass grave (Skinner *et al.* 2003). The site is then quickly secured with a tent when machinery comes in to carefully remove the earth, peeling off layer by layer. When the first human remains are uncovered archaeologists take over. The delicate task, according to a textbook, is to excavate subtly, so that no harm is done to the evidence. The contents of the grave, needless to say, are the most important element of the excavation. But while a few bodies or body parts may 'lend themselves' to easy removal from the side of the body mass, eventually one would have to climb on top of the mass to get to bodies – those key top bodies for establishing stratigraphy and contextualising the whole event. Unfortunately, unless a suspension system is employed over the grave, the body mass often has to be stepped on (Tuller and Djurić 2005). One can certainly develop an understanding of when and where to step without damaging the bodies, but the feeling is ghastly all the same. Haglund *et al.* (2001) suggested that maintaining a thirty cm thick layer of soil above a body would be sufficient to protect a buried body from being damaged when treading above it. On the Batajnica excavation team part, we would sometimes reuse the tires found in the compound to construct make-shift bridges to minimise the risk of stepping onto body mass (Figure 9.5).

As the excavation of Batajnica 5 progressed in autumn 2002 we would inevitably go deeper to recover all the bodies, but also effectively spend more time in the grave as going out became increasingly difficult. We conversed more among ourselves enclosed in the trench hole, as if that space became somehow more personal – two coffee breaks for the whole field team, in the morning and early afternoon, were taking place near the autopsy tables. One of the conversations engaged all four archaeologists present in the grave 5 – all four of us had had dreams with haunting images of corpses in them. In the same vein, the stench accompanied sleep overnight. And to me it seemed that that particular smell of decomposing bodies stayed somehow in the pockets of my nostrils and it would regularly cause

Figure 9.5. Body mass and a motor vehicle tire in the foreground, archaeologists working in the background, at the bottom of pit 5. (Image property of Belgrade District Court)

panic when I would accidentally wake up in the middle of the night. On those occasions I would find myself trying to locate a cadaver in my bedroom before realising that it was just a dream. The porosity between reality and dream was disturbingly fascinating.

The finds

Looking back, what was equally horrific, even for senses accustomed to decayed and half-decayed bodies, were the personal belongings – artefacts found in Batajnica graves with or without relation to the bodies.

Some of the artifacts retrieved were (the list can be found at Skrozza 2003):

> two baby pacifiers,
> nail-clippers,
> several bottle-openers,
> marbles,
> pencils and pens,
> combs,
> cigarette holders.
> With many pieces of out-of-circulation former
>   Yugoslav coins we found:
> metal key rings,
> cotton and paper handkerchiefs,
> make-up mirrors,
> 'Bic' shavers,
> several Hoxa's (Muslim priests') writings,
> various pocket knives,
> 'Swiss Army' knife
> battery-powered radio transmitters,
> an address book with phone numbers,
> photographs of two young men and a girl,

buttons,
shoe-spoons,
a screwdriver,
a calculator,
torches,
business cards and amulets,
nails,
safety locks,
loose tobacco,
a bottle of whiskey
tire-valve caps,
power circuit testers,
bus tickets,
keys and key chains,
and dental prostheses (cf. Kaliterna 2006 and
  Skrozza 2003).

It is important to realise that among recovered arte-facts, personal documents were scarce given the number of victims, but were present nevertheless: IDs of the Berisha extended family – forty-eight members including children and a hundred year old woman were killed in Suva Reka – and of another man, a number of drivers' licenses and car and tractor traffic permits (Ćirić 2002; *IWPR* 2002; Kaliterna 2006; Skrozza 2003). There were also health insurance books, two birth certificates and one physically handicapped person's health certificate. What is more important, and what in a particular way sheds light on the very crime, is the fact that not counting the local Serbian money, a considerable number of foreign currency notes was found untouched with the bodies – in the amount of several thousand today's Euros (a fortune in those inflation-plagued days in Serbia). Some of the victims had exactly 1000 Deutche Marks (DM)[9] on them, and the word in the SAJ complex was that 1000 DM was the price of human life in Kosovo in 1999, only the money these people were supposed to buy there lives with was found on them.

This gives an impression of macabre rush killings – random and systematic, like an assembly line (Skrozza 2003). Whether because of hurry or professionalism, a police belt-buckle and part of 'Socialist Party of Serbia' (Milošević's party) delegate's card were also found (Skrozza 2003). This would in turn mean that the killers did not make much difference between 'suitable and unsuitable' victims. Where they came from and through whose command were bodies put in plastic bags prior to deposition is still a mystery. Some of the bodies from Batajnica 5 had small numbered cards incased in plastic and stapled to their clothes (*ICMP* 2004), and the whole highly secretive crime scene conveys a message of panic. According to several reports in *Vreme*, many former and active police officers

were involved and the graves were supposed to give conclusive evidence against the then-president of Serbia Milošević for it was suspected that the ultimate direction for cover-up came from the top.

Where the victims were going or thought they were going is not known, but it is fair to say that they were ordinary people with ordinary problems and ordinary quotidian lives (Skrozza 2003). It is not the intention of this paper to fall into any kind of (inevitable?) pathos, but the very fact that they lay twenty kilometres away from Belgrade, and my parents' home, that people just as ordinary as myself were hideously buried, again, profoundly changed not only my awareness of archaeology as a modern profession (Lucas 2004; Shanks and McGuire 1998), but also my ethical stance in the political climate of the day.

A few days prior to Batajnica excavations and immediately following the early revelatory newspaper articles in 2001, the Serbian public reacted slowly, but still somewhat justified the killings, as if unable to grasp the nature of the crime. In retrospect, I caught myself with an extraordinary capacity to rationalise – as if there was a tiny possibility for just about any approach to justify. When I took part in the exhumation process, however, the kinds of questions that impinged on my Belgrade-Batajnica-Belgrade world were: where to draw the line between where I stand and the rest; how to disagree, how to protest, and what would be the etiquette of disagreement in Serbia of that day? The question of how to be responsible as opposed to be conformist haunted me with all the images and the smell. Ultimately, as I am trying to write this paper, I am asking myself am I really responsive after all to people's actions and concerns? Or, is it the nature of the paper and the conference that pushes me toward the kind of rhetoric that is encompassing empathy,[10] but also exoticism and objectification of victims?

How did the bodies end up in Batajnica?

The bodies recovered from Batajnica are all considered to be victims of atrocities committed in the conflicts in Kosovo during 1999 (Ćirić 2001; *IWPR* 2002; Vasić 2001). The 'clear-out' operation is understood to have been arranged by Milosevic's people to wipe out evidence of killings Serbian forces committed in Kosovo in 1999 (*IWPR* 2002).

The chain of events leading to the revelation began with the article in an obscure local magazine in Zaječar, in eastern Serbia. The *Timočka Krimi Revija* (transl: Timok Criminal Review) monthly reported that a refrigerated truck containing 50 corpses had been pulled out of the Danube at Kladovo, in eastern Serbia,

Figure 9.6. *Archaeologists working in pit 7 (photo by J. Sterenberg)*

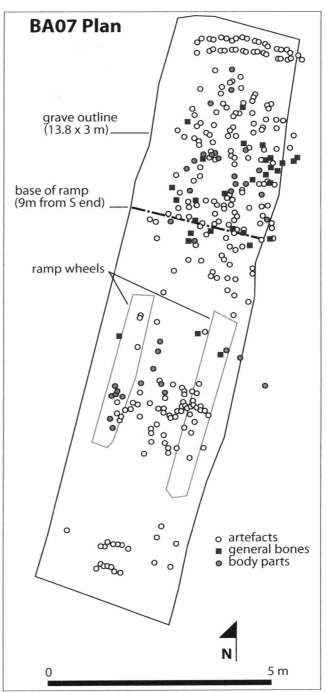

Figure 9.7. *Plotted body parts, artifacts, and tire-marks found in pit 7; retraced after original plan*

in April 1999, and that Milošević's regime had silenced the whole action (Ćirić 2001; *IWPR* 2002; Skrozza 2003; Vasić 2001). The magazine also hinted that the corpses appeared to have come from Kosovo (*IWPR* 2002).The testimonies in the meantime were reporting of two drivers who transported close to two thousand bodies that were buried in Serbia (Ćirić 2001).

Now, the Serbian public had rarely been informed before about true nature of conflicts and Serbian police and paramilitary wrong-doings (*IWPR* 2002). First through a radio station heard in cities only, but at long last the media made the story headline news (*Vreme* 544, 546). Upon serious investigations the name of the diver [sic] who in 1999 had inspected the lorry in the river was found. The type of the lorry and license plates were identified as well. 'After a malfunction a huge stone had been placed on the accelerator pedal to send the truck plunging into the water' (B92 radio interview cited in *IWPR* 2002). Among the corpses pulled out from water were women's and children's bodies, too. Soon, the driver of one of the lorries told his story, how he found out what the transported cargo was, and how he fled the country upon realising what he was shipping, scared of the regime's prosecution. For a long time blocked investigation finally fired up the public, but the chief of police at the time that is now held responsible for the events is hiding in Russia (Ćirić 2002).

The excavations continued in the late autumn and winter[11] of 2002 to uncover Batajnica 7. Although we were excavating under bad conditions and snow at times, the exhumation was completed and marked the end of the process of exhuming bodies from all locations discovered by then in Serbia. The killers

are still unidentified and the list of suspects may well include any or all of the following: the army, the police[12] or paramilitary formations (Tagirov 2005). (Figure 9.6)

(Figure 9.7). The identified objects from grave

sites pointed to places in Kosovo where victims were killed. In May 2002 Belgrade was donated its first DNA laboratory and the first DNA analyses helped identify some of the first bodies recovered from the Batajnica mass graves. Since a parallel DNA analysis of tissue samples of relatives of the victims was needed before any identification could happen, it was necessary to build a database of DNA samples which took a long time. Only in 2004 and 2005 have the bodies been identified in numbers – the remainder of the exhumed bodies being returned to Kosovo in 2006. Corpses are being transported yet again, but this time for proper burial, for, sadly, the paths and shipments of dead bodies have been almost a Balkan privilege (Verdery 1999). In December 2004, Serbia's war crimes prosecutor Vladimir Vučković, in his statement aired on *Radio B92* reported that there were still 3,192 people missing in Kosovo, and out of this number 2,460 Kosovo Albanians, 523 Kosovo Serbs and 203 members of other ethnicities.

Purposefulness and Guilt

The primary goal of the described excavation was to establish identities of the deceased and honor the memory of the dead by bringing closure to living kin and homes. Gil Bailie (1995:228) citing René Girard (1993: 164) proposes that 'murder calls for the tomb, and the tomb is but the prolongation and perpetuation of murder. The tomb of those who died violently is a myth in stone. Both the myths and the tombs relate to the story of past violence and give it meaning. They absolve those who fall under their mythic influence from moral responsibility for collective violence. They edify and unify the mourners.' Tombs are those architectural elements of rituals that make it possible for those who put to death to feel themselves almost united with the suffering. Elias Canetti, when talking about executioners aligning with sufferers, suggests that a tomb 'frees perpetrators from the accumulated guilt of killing and from the fear that death will strike at them too' (Canetti 1981: 145).

We are yet to see the tombs and monuments erected, as well as the ability of people on both sides to mourn the other's victims. In trying to assess the guilt and the crime scene, I propose to consider both individual and collective responsibility. In turn, it is in the context of political tensions that is necessary to consider our events – particularly as it participates in a wider scheme of violations that certain groups perpetrated upon others. Whether there should be such a thing as a collective responsibility for crime against Kosovo Albanians is a major issue among

Serbs. The inability to mourn the victims is interpreted as national egotism, much like in Germany in the aftermath of Second World War (Mitscherlich 1974). On the other hand, it is necessary to understand the graves and events as individual acts, too. We have seen how bodies in this context carry great potential to perpetrate their historicity and extend it well beyond any understanding (cf. Weiss 2005).

Going back to 'the regular archaeological' idiom and without the emotional baggage, working as a forensic archaeologist meant two things to me: the use of forensic science to examine and interpret archaeological finds, and the use of archaeological methods to investigate the crime scene. As archaeologists, we often tie the acts of individual agents to social interests or some other outer causes determined by context. Similarly, classical sociology of which Latour (1996: 199) is critical '… knows more than the *actors*. It sees right through them to the social structure or the destiny of which they are the patients. It can judge their behavior because it has fixed reference frames with respect to which the patients behave in a pathological fashion'. Now, it seems that Latour does not want to reject a social context, but to say that action cannot be explained by context only. Action is not to be found outside or inside individuals as a simple potential, because we cannot know why agents really do what they do. The process that is now (October 2006) taking place in Belgrade for this crime continues to produce evidence from various sources, including the accounts of the surviving members of the Berisha family.

The extended family Berisha were killed on 26 March 1999 – this crime in Suva Reka happened on the third day of NATO bombing of Serbia. During the three days prior to that day there was no evidence that anyone disappeared, was killed or tortured in the area, it was said that there was no reason for revenge against Albanian people, let alone on women and children (Dilparić 2006[13]). The researchers of the case in the meantime reported that someone from the ethnic Albanian paramilitary[14] killed a Serbian man few days before the start of NATO bombing. A day after, the Serbian police and paramilitary forces, armed with heavy weaponry, blocked the town of Suva Reka, killing seven or eight Albanian men. They then started looking for weapons in the part of town where the Berisha were, known as *Berisha mahala*.[15] There policemen and paramilitary first killed Berisha men, then children and women,[16] transported the bodies to Prizren, a bigger town to the south, and from there – in refrigerator-lorries – to Batajnica, where they were buried. The transport was ordered by the aforementioned Serbian police general in hiding.[17]

In his statement, Judge Dilparić called the transporting operation of bodies in refrigerator-lorries 'bestial' and 'completely irrational' (Dilparić 2006), but the whole surreptitious operation that is still coming to light can also be seen as a well-organised maneuver of a group of people, perhaps with the head of state at the helm. Such an (ir)rational behaviour could conceivably be attributed to anything from boredom to panic (Watkins 1986: 103), thus the assumption of purposefulness is constantly made by those who make enormous efforts for the most rigorous analysis of human behavior – practicing psycho-analysts. I am definitely not equipped for such an endeavor, but if we are to 'focus our observations on real people in real life situations' (Barth 1981: 10), at least in the study of mass grave perpetrators and their reasons, we would need that kind of assistance.

Psychiatrist Weine (1999: 77, cited in Weiss 2005), while discussing genocide contexts,[18] offered that '[m]emories can be triggered by a sight, a smell, a sound, or a feeling…[they] can take over the survivor, hurling them out of their involvement in a current situation and dropping them back into the abyss'. I was certainly not the survivor in the described case of mass-grave excavations, but I did feel like a survivor (out of personal egotism, maybe) of the whole project as it was difficult to see through the exhumation process. Recollections take me unwillingly back to the trench sometimes, and I am definitely able to at least empathise with Albanian survivors, and mourn the victims of the Batajnica mass-graves. The whole experience for me highlights the utility of archaeology – while complicating the notion that archaeology, or an archaeologist, can be truly detached from the context of excavation.

Notes

1 My thanks to Jovana Stokić and Christine Folch for making the text appear wholesome, to the reviewer for his/her comments, and to Dušan Borić and John Robb for organising a much-talked about panel at 2006 Society for American Archaeology in San Juan, Puerto Rico, where this paper was first presented.

2 Signed as 'by *IWPR* contributors in Belgrade and London'

3 Much has been written about this, the fragmentation happened for many historico-political, cultural and economic reasons, details of which are impossible to begin to cover in this attempt to give a short historical context, but see Misha Glenny's *The Fall of Yugoslavia* (Penguin Books, 1992) and *The Balkans: Nationalism, War and the Great Powers, 1804–1999* (Penguin Books, 1999) Norman M. Naimark and Holly Case (eds.) *Yugoslavia and its Historians, Understanding the Balkan Wars of the 1990s*, (Standford University Press, 2003); and Dušan Bjelić and Obrad Savić (eds.) *Balkan as Metaphor: Between Globalization and Fragmentation* (MIT Press, 2005) – for more analysis in English.

4 My father is a Montenegrin/Serbian from Ulcinj, a town on the Adriatic coast/the southern most place in Montenegro (and in former Yugoslavia) before the border with Albania. Majority of the population in Ulcinj is Albanian, my father speaks fluent Albanian, and in the past members of his extended family married into Albanian families, thus we have Albanian cousins. This background made the conflicts additionally unsettling.

5 For the position of SAJ complex, map of the firing range and a detailed position of pits, see 'Batajnica Summary Report. Forensic Monitoring Activities', Sarajevo, April 2004 at http://www.ic-mp.org

6 I was not present during excavations of graves 1 and 2, excavated earlier in 2001. The Forensic Monitoring Report 2001 for Batajnica can be found online at http://www.ic-mp.org

7 Batajnica 1, 2, 3, 5, and 7 were graves; pits 4, 6, and 8 did not contain bodies (*ICMP* 2004).

8 If any reference is in place here, I would choose Blanchot's (1982: 257–9) insightful analysis of the image and cadaver

9 German currency before Euro

10 I want to thank professor Vincent Crapanzano for his compelling discussions at the Graduate Center in Spring 2006 course, and for illuminating this complex issue.

11 Excavations were only sealed on 26 December 2002.

12 Trials against former and active police officers that allegedly organised the operation started in October 2006.

13 M. Dilparić, criminal judge of the Belgrade District Court, Department for War Crimes, in a statement given to press agency FoNet, 4 January.

14 *Kosovo Liberation Army* [KLA], in Albanian: *Ushtria Çlirimtare e Kosovës* (UÇK), in Serbian: Oslobodilačka Vojska Kosova (OVK).

15 Incidentally, before the NATO bombing started, in Berisha Mahala was the Organisation for Security and Co-operation in Europe (OSCE) mission.

16 The local population in Suva Reka announced that the place of death of women and children – a pizzeria in Suva Reka should be left untouched and be made into a tomb-museum.

17 June 2007 – After having been on the run for more than three years the police general, Vlastimir Djordjević, was indicted for war crimes to the Hague Tribunal. Arrest came as a result of cooperation between International Criminal Tribunal for the former Yugoslavia (ICTY) and Montenegrin and Serbian police forces.

18 Holocaust and genocide studies recognise psychoanalysis as a major contribution

Bibliography

Arnold, B. 1990. The past as propaganda: Totalitarian archaeology in Nazi Germany. *Antiquity* 64(244): 464–478.

Bailie, G. 1995. *Violence Unveiled: Humanity at the Crossroads*. New York: Crossroads.

Barth, F. 1981. *Process and Form in Social Life*. London: Routledge.

Bjelica, J. 2005. SAJ jeste umešan, ali nije odgovoran? *Danas*, 12 September.

Blanchot, M. 1982. *The Space of Literature*. Lincoln, NB: University of Nebraska Press.

Buchli, V. and Lucas, G. 2001. Bodies of evidence. In *Archaeologies of the Contemporary Past*, edited by V. Buchli and G. Lucas, pp. 121–125. New York: Routledge.

Canetti, E. 1984. *Crowds and Power*. New York: Farrar, Straus and Giroux.

Carmichael, C. 2002. *Ethnic Cleansing in the Balkans: Nationalism and the Destruction of Tradition. Routledge Advances in European Politics*. London: Routledge.

Ćirić, A. 2001. Suočavanje sa zločinima: Arheologija smrti. *Vreme* 548, 5 July.

Ćirić, A. 2002. Druga sezona iskopavanja 'hladnjača': Batajnička arheologija. *Vreme* 618, 11 November.

Cox, M. 1998. Criminal concerns: A plethora of forensic archaeologists. *Archaeologists* 33: 21–22.

Dilparić, M. 2006. Statement given to press agency FoNet, 3 January, 2006. Last seen on-line at the B92 News Agency website http://www.b92.net/info/vesti/index.php?yyyy=2006&mm=01&dd=04&nav_category=64&nav_id=184211&fs=1

Girard, R. 1993. *Things Hidden since the Foundation of the World*. Stanford, CA: Stanford University Press.

Haglund, W.D., Connor, M. and Scott, D.D. 2001. The archaeology of contemporary mass graves. *Historical Archaeology* 35: 7–69.

Haglund, W.D. 2002. Recent mass graves: An introduction. In *Advances in Forensic Taphonomy: Method, Theory and Archaeological Perspectives*, edited by W.D. Haglund and M.H. Sorg, pp. 243–261. New York: CRC Press.

Hunter, J., Roberts, C. and Martin, A. 1999. *Studies in Crime: An Introduction to Forensic Archaeology*. London: Batsford.

International Committee on Missing Persons (ICMP). 2004. Batajnica Summary Report: Forensic Monitoring Activities. Sarajevo. Available at http://www.ic-mp.org

Kaliterna, T. 2006. Batajnica, masovna grobnica. *Monitor*, January 2006.

Latour, B. 1998. *The Pasteurization of France*. Cambridge, MA: Harvard University Press.

Latour, B. 1996. *ARAMIS or the Love of Technology*. Cambridge, MA: Harvard University Press.

Lucas, G. 2004. Modern disturbances: On the ambiguities of archaeology. *Modernism-Modernity* 11(1): 109–120.

Matić, V., Ilić, D. and Stanić, J. 2003. *Po Naredenju: Ratni Zlocini na Kosovu*. Beograd: Samizdat B92; Human Rights Watch/Americas.

Mitscherlich, A.M. 1974. The inability to mourn. In *Explorations in Psychohistory*, edited by R.J. Lifton, pp. 257–271. New York: Simon & Schuster.

Nora, P. 1989. Les Lieux de Memoire. *Representations* 26: 7–24.

Olivier, L. 2001. The Archaeology of the contemporary past. In *The Archaeologies of the Contemporary Past*, edited by V. Buchli and G. Lucas, pp. 175–188. New York: Routledge.

Shanks, M. and McGuire, R.H. 1998. The Craft of archaeology. *American Antiquity* 6(1): 75–88.

Skinner, M. 1987. Planning the archaeological recovery of evidence from recent mass graves. *Forensic Science International* 34: 267–287.

Skinner, M., Alempijević, Dj. And Djurić-Srejić, M. 2003. Guidelines for international forensic bio-archaeology monitors of mass grave exhumations. *Forensic Science International* 134: 81–92.

Skinner, M. and Sterenberg, J. 2005. Turf wars. *Forensic Science International* 151: 221–232.

Skrozza, T. 2003. Dokumenti – masovne grobnice u Batajnici: Tragovi prikrivene smrti. *Vreme* 653, 10 July.

Tagirov, T. 2005. Slučaj Batajnica: Ustajanje Beriša. *Vreme* 774, 3 November.

The Institute for War and Peace Reporting (IWPR). 2002. By IWPR contributors in Belgrade and London, 23 December.

Tuller, H. and Djurić, M. 2005. Keeping the pieces together: Comparison of mass grave excavation methodology. *Forensic Science International* 156(2–3): 192–200.

Vasić, M. 2001. Ekskluzivno – ispovest vozača hladnjače: Mrtvi putuju.., *Vreme* 546, 21 June.

Verdery, K. 1999. *The Political Lives of Dead Bodies: Reburial and Postsocialist Change*. New York: Columbia University Press.

Watkins, J. 1986. Ideal types and historical explanation. In *The Philosophy of Social Explanation*, edited by A. Ryan, pp. 82–105. Oxford: Oxford University Press.

Weine, S.M. 1999. *When History is a Nightmare: Lives and Memories of Ethnic Cleansing in Bosnia-Herzegovina*. New Brunswick: Rutgers University Press.

Weiss, L. (Forthcoming) Terra Incognita: The Role of Landscape in International Tribunal Proceedings. In *Archaeology and Memory*, edited by D. Borić. Oxford: Oxbow Press. (In press, with author's remarks).

Wright, R., Sterenberg, J. and Hanson, I. (Forthcoming) The excavation of mass graves. In *Advances in Forensic Archaeology*, edited by J.R. Hunter, M. Cox and P. Cheetham. London: Routledge.

Meaningless violence and the lived body: the Huron – Jesuit collision of world orders

John Robb

The problem of 'meaningless violence'

Violence is universal in human societies (Ember and Ember 1997; Kelly 2000; Knauft 1987, 1991). It demands explanation, both as a social phenomenon and as a real source of actual harm in modern society. In some ways, the study of violence has been a success. The relationship of violence to political structures is well understood. As Blok (2000) has observed, in state societies, violence is normally understood as instrumental, as a political prerogative used by the state for specific tactical ends such as maintaining order or protecting its foreign interests. Ethnohistorically, a wave of rising warfare accompanied early colonial situations (Ferguson and Whitehead 1992; Wolf 1982), while nineteenth and twentieth century colonialism often entailed the pacification of traditional fighting. Post-modernists have explored the meaning of violence particularly in the context of state terror and genocide (Hinton 2002; Taussig 1984). Moreover, as Rosaldo (1980) has shown so convincingly for the Ilongot, practices of violence such as headhunting are located in specific historical moments and can change their meaning many times during their historical trajectory.

Within the logic of relating violence to the state, non-political forms of violence are understood as irrational social pathologies, as deviations to be abhorred, contained, punished or cured. Yet in many situations, violence is not a pathological deviation from order but part of the constitution of normal social order. There has also been substantial exploration of violence as symbolic action, both worldwide (Aijmer and Abbink 2000; Riches 1986) and in specific areas of the tribal world of which New Guinea is the best explored (e.g.,

Knauft 1985, 1993). Even these studies, however, take little account of the role of the body in violence, not as a neutral executor of instrumental needs or desires but as a locus of lived world order.

Archaeological studies of violence in non-state societies have played an important role in demonstrating that violence is ubiquitous in the human past (Guilaine and Zammit 2005; Keeley 1996; Martin and Frayer 1997; Walker 2001). Yet, theoretically, we have been less successful (cf. Walker 2001). Most studies remain simply at the level of descriptive empiricism, 'rediscovering' violence but leaving it socially untheorised (e.g., Guilaine and Zammit 2005; Martin and Frayer 1997). Studies which theorise violence tend to relate it to simple, generally functional themes such as ecological competition for territory (Keeley 1997). For example, the protracted debate over Anasazi cannibalism has concentrated on either simply establishing whether or not it occurred or relating it to simplistic monocausal determinants such as ecological crisis (White 1992) (though see Darling 1998). Many theoretically minded sectors of archaeology (for example, British Neolithic studies) have generally remained with a pacific vision of the past.

In this paper, my argument is simple and direct. While instrumental, political and symbolic interpretations of violence are often applicable, violence is also and always a symbolically constructed behaviour involving a semantic of the body. One way to demonstrate this is to examine cases when violence cannot be understood as a function of these other factors and must be interpreted upon its own terms.

Throughout Eastern Native North America, from Canada to Georgia, one traditional form of violence was the torture of captives. The best-described single case of it must be the elaborate ritual torture which the Huron Indians inflicted upon war captives in early-mid seventeenth-century Canada. This was not isolated; prisoner torture was also practiced by their neighbours the Iroquois, the Neutral and Wenro (Driver 1969: 324; Fenton 1978; Garrad and Heidenreich 1978; White 1978); several Jesuit missionaries among the Huron in fact underwent painful martyrdom at Iroquois hands during the definitive defeat of the Huron in 1648–1649. However, because of the presence of Jesuit missionaries among the Huron, the ethnohistoric legacy left by the French between 1610 and 1650 is extraordinarily rich (Champlain 1929; Heidenreich 1971, 1978; Kenton 1926; Sagard 1939; Thwaites 1898; Tooker 1964; Trigger 1969, 1976), and the colonial collision in understandings of violence illustrates the problem of meaningful violence particularly well.

By European standards, Huron torture of prisoners was 'irrational' violence *par excellence*. It served no end other than the experiential reproduction of the cultural system which gave rise to it, and to understand it we need to understand deeply buried and different elements of this cultural system, including not only the nature of gender but the nature of human bodies as well.

The Huron torture of prisoners

The Huron Indians were a confederation numbering about 30,000 people who lived near Georgian Bay in Ontario. They were the northernmost Native American group practising maize agriculture, and they lived in palisaded villages of up to 1000 people. In the early seventeenth century the Huron controlled a flourishing trade along the Great Lakes which linked Indians to their west with French fur traders from Upper Canada (Heidenreich 1971; Trigger 1976, 1978). In this period, they were the sworn enemies of the Iroquois, a similar-sized confederation who lived to the south in upstate New York and who traded principally with the Dutch and the English. The Huron and Iroquois fought each other continually throughout the early colonial period, a war which culminated in the total defeat and destruction of Huron in 1649. Many died; the survivors were assimilated as refugees into other groups and lost their cultural identity.

On the 2 September, 1637, twelve years before the Huron's own destruction, two Jesuit priests living as missionaries in a Huron village in Canada witnessed the beginning of what was, to their eyes, a horrifying Calvary. One of them, Father Paul LeJeune, described the events in detail in their annual report to headquarters,

the *Jesuit Relations* (Thwaites 1898: 37–83); similar events are described in many other Jesuit missionary accounts. A Huron party had captured seven Iroquois men out fishing on Lake Ontario. The prisoners were shared out among Huron villages, and one was brought, bound and beaten, to the village where the Jesuit missionaries lived. Here he was given to one of the leading men of the village in compensation for his nephew, who had been captured and killed by the Iroquois. For several days the captive, though tied up, was well-treated, dressed in finery, and given gifts of food. Though everybody knew he was to be tortured to death, the fiction was made that he had been adopted into the tribe and people wept over his torment to come. When all was ready, a feast was held, attended by the entire village and guests from elsewhere. Formally, the victim was sacrificed to the sun, one of the many animistic spirits of the Huron physical world. About nightfall, the man was led among assembled crowds. He was forced to run circuits among them; as he passed, everybody present burned his legs with flaming wood, or broke the bones of his hands, or pierced his ears with sticks. As the night passed, the crowds mocked his cries and became ever more ingenious in finding ways to torment him with fire, until the senior chiefs present told them to desist for fear the man would die before morning. When morning came, the prisoner was tied to post upon a scaffold and fire applied all over his body, in ways calculated to cause the most pain possible. Finally, when he was at the point of death, he was beheaded, and his body torn into pieces and distributed to the crowd to be taken away and eaten.

I have described this encounter in stark detail to convey the immediacy and reality of the violence I will discuss. Violence, whatever the cause, is immediate and compelling. Accounts such as this put faces upon the fragmented human bones scattered in a midden or the isolated skull cached in a pit, and, hopefully, they help dispel both facile explanations and our tendency to mask the human side of violence in the past. However, in the post-colonial era, we must scrutinise not only the natives but ourselves (Gosden 1999). In summarising this episode, both of the standard descriptive ethnographies of the Hurons (Tooker 1964; Trigger 1969), written in the 1960s, screen the Jesuits' own reactions, commentary and interventions out. As a strategy for focusing upon Native American lifeways, this is justified and effective. However, for understanding the logic of violence here, the interplay of Huron and Jesuit points of view is equally illuminating.

Huron warfare is well understood, but, surprisingly, Huron prisoner torture *per se* has never been seriously interpreted. There are normally many reasons why any society goes to war (Maschner 1997). The Huron warred for trade and territory, for prestige and for prisoners. Huron-Iroquois warfare provides a famous example of how colonial contact restructures native societies. There is no doubt that, from the 1630s onwards, the European fur trade unleashed ever-expanding cycles of Indian warfare. The Iroquois, well-organised, adroit at manipulating trade politics, well-supplied with guns, and rapidly exhausting the beaver stock of their own lands, warred aggressively and came to dominate a great swathe of the Great Lakes and Ohio Valley; and this was accompanied by dramatic changes within Iroquoian society (Abler 1992; Trigger 1976, 1978; Wolf 1982). The Huron too were attentive to defend their territory and trade networks. However, we cannot ascribe warfare solely to the effects of colonialism and the pragmatic needs for hunting territory and control of trade. Warfare itself had deep cultural roots (Tooker 1964; Trigger 1969). Warfare was central to gender and status. Visitors before the 1630s, such as Champlain and Sagard, observed that Huron warfare was the traditional test and demonstration of masculine bravery. Men were normally expected to be brave and warlike, and raiding provided an opportunity to accumulate a reputation for boldness and leadership. A fighting career was an important part of a typical male biography. A second motivation was revenge for kin killed by Iroquois raids. A third was to procure captives for torture. Prisoners were prized spoils of war; upon occasion, members of a raiding party even fought over who was responsible for taking a particular prisoner. Although prisoners were turned over to tribal chiefs who disposed of them, capturing them was very prestigious for adult males.

Thus, for the Huron, warfare was often an end in itself, tied into gender and prestige systems. The pattern of warfare these motivations generated defied the European rationality of warfare as the instrumental, controlled use of force. As the Jesuits observed it among the Huron (Trigger 1969: 45), each year's campaign of warfare was often organised not by the senior males who oversaw political relations and controlled trade routes and who often opposed raids, but by rising young men who sought prestige by performing feats of war and from taking captives. Similarly, forces were not concentrated strategically but dispersed into small groups of men intent upon raiding, using tactics such as small-group ambush, for captives or scalps. Indeed, in 1615–1616, Champlain complained because, after he had travelled long distances with the Huron to help them attack the Iroquois, he found that they were satisfied to harass a few villages and return home, without accomplishing what he considered any targeted strategic objective (Trigger 1969: 42).[1]

However we explain Huron warfare, neither warfare, colonialism or gender explain the practice of prisoner torture. Regardless of the extent to which Huron warfare was restructured by European contact, there is no reason to assume that prisoner torture was either encouraged directly or caused indirectly by colonial contact. Unlike the Huron, Europeans clearly found such practices abhorrent, and there was no policy of encouraging them such as giving bounties for enemy scalps or trophies. Moreover, the earliest European observers among the Huron, such as Champlain in 1619 (1929), report prisoner torture as a normal practice among both Huron and Iroquois, which suggests that it had pre-existing roots. Gender was certainly important in how the drama of prisoner torture unfolded. Captured Iroquois women and children were either killed on the spot or adopted in Huron society to replace people killed by the Iroquois; there was no honour or value to be gained in torturing weak victims. Adult men were the prized victims. Captured men were tortured and killed immediately if they could not be taken back safely to Huronia; in this case trophies such as heads or scalps were brought home (Trigger 1969: 47–52). If they underwent the whole course of torment, death and cannibalism, they were observed carefully. If an enemy died particularly bravely, singing his war song and refusing to cry out in pain, it was taken as an ill omen potentially disrupting the meaning of the sacrifice, though men could also drink the victim's blood (as the Iroquois did to Father de Brébeuf (Kenton 1926) or mix the victim's blood with their own to absorb some of his bravery. Violence is a performative arena for masculinity in many societies, including the early modern European world of the Jesuits; but competitive bravery alone does not explain why an entire assembled community, in the security of their homes, should have organised ritualised practices of inflicting pain upon captives unable to defend themselves.

In summary, Huron warfare was certainly motivated by gender ideologies of masculine value and shaped by a history of colonialism and competition over the fur trade. However, these factors are necessary but in no way sufficient to account for why the Huron tortured prisoners.

Contextualising Huron and European bodies

At this point, it is useful to step back and consider how anthropologists and other social scientists have theorised the human body. As many authors have noted, since the Enlightenment, the Western tradition both in theory and in popular culture has been to see humans as divided by a mind-body duality, usually ascribed to Descartes. In this paradigm, the body has tended to be seen as a neutral material instrument for performing the will of the intellect; when the body seems to be acting upon its own, this is understood as threatening to the order of reason. Moreover, historically, social theorists explicitly dealing with the body have tended to adopt either a naturalist or a constructivist approach (Shilling 2003). In a naturalist approach, the body is a self-evident object whose biological properties define the identities and capabilities of persons. For example, females and males are women and men not because of gender socialisation but because they have female or male bodies with certain innate biological properties such as fecundity or strength. Constructivist views, in contrast, view the social body as a symbolic construction whose biological properties are minimally important. For example, Foucault's studies of punishment (1977) and sexuality (1990) in recent European history treat the body as an object of socially constructed discourse (Shilling 2003: 66). As another example, some recent feminist approaches to gender (such as Butler 1993) argue that not only gender but 'biological sex' is culturally defined and constructed, for example by medical practitioners categorising phenotypical variation among newborn children. Constructivist views have helped interpret many bodily practices, for instance bodily education of soldiers, workers and students, sport, dieting and self-image, dress and adornment, and so on, by demonstrating how they are not isolated practices but must be explained with reference to pervasive systems of meaning.

Relatively few theorists of the body have discussed violence *per se*, perhaps from an assumption that violence is pathological or abnormal and the first work of theory should be to explain the normal. Conversely, few theorists of violence have located it as a discourse of the body; as Riches (1986: 21–23) notes, genetic and ethological approaches have treated violence as biological, while and symbolic and political approaches which view violence primarily as the expression or reflection of a symbolic regime or discourse, with little reference to its physical concomitants such as pain or harm. However, as the Huron example shows, violence is normal in many societies other than our own. It is no surprise that the theorists who have dealt with violence as a bodily regime most explicitly, Foucault (1977) and Elias (1994), have both studied the transition from medieval to modern societies.

With this as a starting point, it is important to contextualise Huron torture of prisoners with reference to Huron understandings of the body. These in turn are most apparent when they differ from how the French understood the human body, through reviewing how Europeans and Hurons differed in a wide range of bodily practices.

Bodily civility, dress, sexuality, food

Cleanliness is a matter of enacting boundaries and categories (Douglas 1966). The French found Huron houses crowded, filthy, smoky, and full of fleas and lice. Dogs were everywhere and the floors were muddy with children's urine. In early modern Europe, cleanliness, distance between bodies and regulation of bodily effluvia were important markers of status and social acceptability (Elias 1994). Another distinction involved marking limits between human and non-human bodies, for example in the treatment of dogs. The French were taken aback by the fact that Huron dogs wandered everywhere, eating at will from cooking pots, and by Huron women's feeding favourite dogs with food from their mouths as they did with children. Similarly, the Huron caressed and loved some dogs extravagantly while other dogs (like human war captives) were destined for the cooking pot. Unlike French beliefs, Huron practices did not presume a similarly rigid categorisation between human and non-human bodies, nor between edible and non-edible ones.

Sexuality is another relevant field of action. While the Jesuit's strict concern to regulate sexuality was no doubt not typical of all the French (and they seem to have feared licentious fur traders corrupting the Huron), the French in general seem to have understand sexuality within an opposition between physical pleasure and spiritual morality. In contrast, while the Huron were relatively modest about sexual relations, extra-marital relations were common and apparently did not cause much concern. Similarly, a young couple normally slept together before marrying. Moreover, some healing ceremonies could require the village's assembled youth to perform sexual acts publicly in front of the afflicted person. For the Huron, sexuality seems to have been principally a matter of physical satisfaction, not particularly coupled with either jural relations or a concept of sin. Nudity affords a parallel contrast; the French clearly associated the Huron's exposure particularly of the female body as a provoking temptation to sin, while to the Huron, sexual desire seems not particularly linked to the sight of the body in itself.

If there is a field of action symmetrically opposed to warfare and violence, it seems to concern foodways. To the French, food was an economic commodity, given away outside the family sphere only as an act of ostentation or charity. To people who normally paid for food in inns and lodgings, the Huron's normative hospitality must have seemed an innocent generosity. Conversely, to the Huron, sharing food was normal: visitors to a house or to a village were offered hospitality as an obligatory courtesy whether or not they were hungry. Although not naïve in trade, the Huron were repelled by the haggling of French merchants, and they were amazed to learn that the poor in France begged for food (Trigger 1976). The contrast of rationalities is even more marked at feasts. At Huron feasts, it was important for guests to consume all the food served to them, even at the cost of illness or discomfort. To the French, this marked a bestial and gluttonous dominance of the body over the restraint of reason. However, to the Huron, eating was a form of incorporating elements of the spirit world, for instance to absorb the spirit of corn (Pomedli 1991: 49). Foodways were thus a moral system. To Europeans, the material feeding of the body was regulated within an economic or moral regime involving regualtion of appetite and limited reciprocity. To the Huron, it constituted a common act of basic moral recognition of the other as a human, and a means of interacting with the spirit world.

Spirits, bodies, illnesses and dreams

These practices already intimate that the French and the Huron experienced their bodily worlds differently. Here it is useful to turn to their explicit beliefs about spirituality. Both societies believed in the existence of a spiritual world systematically related to the body, but they did so quite differently.

The French dogma about body and soul forms part of the familiar Western tradition of Christianity (Pomedli 1991). The material world is a transient mask for the eternal, transcendental world of the sacred, which derives from a unitary deity. Humans stand at the juncture between material and spiritual, and can achieve the latter by regulating, transcending or rejecting the former. For example, practices such as fasting, moderation in eating, chastity, restriction of sexuality to married heterosexual couples, cleanliness, and so on were attempts to bring unruly bodies with fleshly appetites in line with spiritual needs – a point otherwise underwritten by beliefs about saintly incorruptibility, the mortification of the flesh in extreme penitence, and other irreplaceable exotica of Christian spirituality.

Huron eschatology was radically different. It is not entirely clear how many souls the Huron thought people possessed, or how differentiated they were (Pomedli 1991; Tooker 1964; Trigger 1969: 103), and there may have been argument among Huron theologians as among Christian ones. What __is__ clear, however, is

that the Jesuits found the Huron difficult to convert in part because the Huron possessed completely different ways of understanding the spiritual world. One basic barrier was that, for the Huron, the spirit world was not opposed to the material world. The Huron's soul is described as 'corporeal' and was assumed to have a physical existence, resembling the body it inhabited. For example, except for some categories of deceased people such as infants, drowned people and victims of violent death, the souls of the dead migrated westwards to the Land of the Dead after the bones were redeposited at the Feast of the Dead. This was not a bodiless, transcendental afterlife, but rather a material world where the dead led a life similar in most respects to their life in the land of the living. The other obstacle was that, unlike Christian souls, the Huron soul was neither unitary nor restricted to humans. People possessed at least two souls, one bound to the body and the other free to move independently of it. This second soul, the *oki*, could also be possessed by a wide range of things Christians would consider inanimate, such as animals, rocks, trees, and winds. The overall effect was to constitute a crowded and busy spirit world which was realer than the world of daily existence but fundamentally parallel to it, not a rejection or inversion of it.

The two Huron planes of existence were not separate. The spirits could interfere in the ordinary world, and often did so for needs not remarkably different than human needs. When people acted, they needed to consider, placate or appease non-human spirits. Moreover, their own souls had autonomous desires which, if not satisfied, could make them ill. One important channel for contacting the spirit world was dreams, which provided guidance to humans on events in the spirit world, problems of daily life, forecasts of wars, hunting, fishing and rituals, and the needs of souls. In dreams, it was believed, the soul ventured forth from the body to the place where the objects of the dream actually existed (Trigger 1969: 114). Hurons set so much store by dreams that the Jesuits, tellingly, commented that the dreams were 'the principal god of the Huron and the 'real masters of the country' (Trigger 1969: 119).

Bodily intervention in the spiritual world

Given the parallel worlds of daily life and of the spirits, the Huron had several well-defined routes for accessing the latter. Several used the body as a medium. For example, illness could be both induced and cured by bodily intervention in the spirit world. Some illnesses were believed to have been inflicted by malicious people. These were cured by extracting spells which had been injected into the patient's body, which were conceptualised as small foreign objects. Shamans were a general category of practitioner who could access the spirit world for particular purposes such as controlling weather, predicting future events, finding lost things and healing (Trigger 1969: 112–6). It is worth noting that shamans accessed the spirit world through a range of physical practices, such as staring into a fire, sweating in sweat lodges, seclusion and fasting. Bodily intervention was also important for other forms of curing; for example, in curing societies, dancing was considered an efficacious way of preventing illness in the community, and dancers sometimes handled hot coals or rocks (Trigger 1969: 97–8).

Burial provided another means of intervening in the spiritual world. After death, a normal deceased person was interred in a bark coffin raised off the ground (Trigger 1969: 106). Here they lay until the next Feast of the Dead, held every ten or twelve years when a village changed location. At this point, the bones and bodies of the normal dead were collected, displayed and mourned over again, and re-interred in large collective ossuaries. Their souls departed westwards for the Land of the Dead, except for souls of the dead too old or young to complete the trip, which lingered in Huronia. Although the Feast of the Dead known ethnohistorically is a florescence of the fur trade period (Trigger 1976), its general principles were shared with neighbouring groups and pre-date this period. The general theme underlying the Feast of the Dead appears to have been promoting unity and solidarity of the group (Trigger 1969: 112).[2] Interestingly, a wide range of deaths did not result in this 'normal' burial. People dying by drowning or freezing were apparently stripped of flesh and their bones deposited in a ditch in an attempt to placate the relevant spirits. Young babies were buried by roads so their soul could re-enter living people. Suicides and people dying a violent death were considered unable to live in peace in the World of the Dead, and hence were burned or buried immediately and excluded from the Feast of the Dead. Effectively, these practices were aimed at reconstituting Huron society harmoniously in the spirit world.

Among other bodily practices designed to have a spiritual effect, fasting and sweating were also part of the general spiritual armoury, carried out to ensure luck at hunting, warfare and other matters. Moreover, men cut themselves to let blood for several reasons: to train themselves to be brave and endure pain, and to ensure hunting or war luck. Cannibalism similarly seems to have been an important part of the destruction of an captive, and if an enemy died especially bravely, his heart could be eaten or his blood drunk or mingled in a Huron warrior's vein in an attempt to acquire some of his fortitude. As Strathern (1988) and Kelly (1993) have shown, bodily substances are central to the constitution and interpretation of relations between people. In practices such as these, blood, flesh and other tissues were used to enact relations such as hostility, dominance, solidarity, bravery, or integration.

Performance and permanence of identity

A final set of contrasts concerns how identity related to the body. The Jesuits believed that the continuity of the individual was based upon the spiritual soul which was housed temporarily in the body. Bodily actions were understood to reflect or demonstrate this constant or permanent inner self. In contrast, the Huron appear to have had a much more performative idea of the self, where the state of the soul mirrored the actions of the body. For example, identities such as masculinity had a performative aspect, requiring participation in hunting and warfare both for esteem and for marriagibility. Similarly, one could change one's identity with a facility difficult for Europeans to believe and possibly to do. For example, the fate of prisoners was not decided by a uniform policy, nor by consideration of each prisoner as a morally regulated individual as in European systems of justice. Rather, the prisoner was either killed or adopted immediately as a complete member of Huron society. Jesuits remarked with amazement that captives who were adopted into Huron families were treated as Huron and considered themselves Huron from that point forward, even to the point of going to war against their former groups.

The same performativity was the case on the scale of individual events. At the Feast of the Dead, for example, participants attempted to induce tears through reciting painful memories; the bodily induced expression of grief did not represent but recreated a genuine spiritual state. Another example of this is the sympathy expressed for captives about to be tortured, something the Jesuits clearly did not understand. In the episode described above, before the prisoner's final torture commenced, the Huron showed him many kindnesses, giving him gifts of food, dressing him splendidly, expressing compassion for him, and assuring him that he was among kin and friends. To this LeJeune comments:

> Good God! What a compliment! All those who surrounded him, with their affected kindness and their fine words, were so many butchers who showed him a smiling face only to treat him afterwards with more cruelty (Jesuit Relations 1637, Thwaites 1898: 43).

LeJeune contrasts the Hurons as 'barbarians whom cruelty alone rendered affable' with the French as 'humane persons who had some real feeling for his misery'. But while the ostensibly kind remarks made later on to the prisoner during his actual torture are clearly cruelly-intended jeers, it is not clear that the sympathetic feelings the Huron demonstrated beforehand were in fact simply dissembling. This perplexed LeJeune, who described how, the morning before the torture was to begin,

> a woman, the sister of the deceased [Huron whom the victim was supposedly adopted to replace], brought him some food, showing remarkable solicitude for him. You would have almost said that he was her own son, and I do not know that this creature did not represent to her him whom she had lost. Her countenance was very sad, and her eyes seemed all bathed in tears (Jesuit Relations 1637, Thwaites 1898: 55).

To the Jesuits, bodily actions were physical evidence of persistent inner states or spiritual constitutions. Hence demonstrating sympathy for someone one is about to torture can only be calculated dissembling; if genuine, it is inexplicable. To the Huron, in contrast, bodily actions such as sorrowing seem to have been understood as the experiential performance of meanings which could vary from context to context.

Back to the infliction of pain: Huron and French (mis)understandings

To summarise this discussion, there are numerous points of contrast between European and Huron understandings of the body. In essence, to Europeans, the human body was a battleground between the spirit and the material, constantly in need of moral monitoring or curbing. To the Huron, body and spirit were not opposed but were parallel or isomorphic. Hence, for both Europeans and Huron, bodily practices had effects in the world of the spirit, but they did so in quite different ways. European bodily doctrines principally involved regulation or restriction of the body, with carefully rational weighing of cost and benefit to the individual in economic or spiritual terms. Huron practices generally involved the performance or exaggeration of bodily values to be affirmed.

Huron torture of prisoners both fascinated and horrified the French, to judge from the numerous accounts of it in the missionaries' annual reports, the *Jesuit Relations*. Huron torture of prisoners is even portrayed as a small inset picture on the ornate neo-Classical frontispiece of Champlain's published description of them, reinforcing the interest this

Figure 10.1. Frontispiece of Champlain's published description of the Huron; note inset scene of prisoner torture. Source: (Champlain 1620), downloaded from on-line version at Early Canadiana Online http://www.canadiana.org/ECO/PageView/90020/0003?id=dc2202f9c9e680cb, accessed 12 May 2005.

practice held for the French and making it an emblem of the Huron's basic nature (Figure 10.1.)(Champlain 1620, frontispiece). As a specimen, let us return to the episode of 2–6 September 1637, witnessed by Father Charles Garnier and his assistant Father Paul LeJeune and reported by the latter. Both Trigger (1969) and Tooker (1964) use LeJeune's report as a quasi-ethnographic account, and it is clear that the two Jesuits witnessed and related circumstantially actual events which they were powerless to derail. Nevertheless, the two Jesuits actively formulated their own interpretation of events.

The theological frame of reference pervades the Jesuit's account. At a basic level, the Jesuits had a universalising view about humanity. To the Huron, the distinction between Huron and Iroquois qualified social relationships. One reacted completely differently to the pain of a fellow Huron and to that of an Iroquois. Similarly, Huron torture of Iroquois was explained, motivated and justified by Iroquois torture of Huron, and vice versa; when Champlain reproved a Huron chief, the answer was 'To which, for sole answer, he replied that their enemies treated them in the like fashion' (Champlain 1929: 65). To the Christian missionaries, on the contrary, all humans were potentially spiritual brothers. Hence they could not witness the pain of the Iroquois victim without feeling compassion (literally, experiencing the passion of the other in the Christian sense of Christ's passion, an image clearly in their mind during this sacrifice of a new convert[3]). The French also equated the excessive and unregulated practice of cruelty with diabolical unreason, and they liken the multitude of Hurons tormenting the victim with fire to 'a living picture of Hell' (Jesuit Relations 1637, Thwaites 1898: 63) with howling demons tormenting a damned soul.

Body and soul: the distinction between the physical torment of the transitory flesh and the spiritual happiness of an eternal soul also helped the Jesuits to give meaning to a scene in which they were active participants, not merely witnessed. They seized this occasion to preach heavenly salvation both to the Iroquois victim and to the assembled Hurons, and they even convinced the victim to accept baptism before his final torture commenced. They used the distinction between passing worldly pain and the eternal happiness of the soul to comfort him repeatedly. When a sympathetic onlooker suggested that he should commit suicide to avoid the pain of torture, they discouraged this, saying that if he did so, he would lose salvation. Finally, their theological beliefs enabled them to see a transcendental spiritual Providence even in the senseless physical barbarism of the Huron. In this period, the Jesuits were unable to preach to the Iroquois, who were unremittingly hostile to them. Hence, LeJeune comments, 'See how the wise providence of God has led this poor Savage into the ways of Salvation. Perhaps if he had remained at Sonongouan [his home village], he might have continued until death in ignorance of his Creator' (Jesuit Relations 1637, Thwaites 1898: 45).

It is hardly surprising to find missionary priests putting a theological spin upon events. But their reactions incorporate more general European attitudes; indeed, many modern European-Americans would no doubt share some of their reactions were we there. This seems most explicit in places where the Jesuits clearly did not understand what they were witnessing. One such inexplicable fact is obviously the motive for the torture itself. Without an explanation for the

Huron's behaviour acceptable in European terms, the Jesuits can only ascribe it to innate barbarism. LeJeune reports a conversation between Father Garnier and a Huron during an intermission in the procedure (Jesuit Relations 1637, Thwaites 1898: 75):

> 'Why art thou sorry,' added some one, 'that we tormented him?'
> 'I do not disapprove of your killing him, but of your treating him in that way.'
> 'What then! How do you French people do? Do you not kill men?'
> 'Yes indeed: we kill them, but not with this cruelty.'
> 'What! Do you never burn any?'
> 'Not often,' said the Father, 'and even then fire is only for enormous crimes, and there is only one person to whom this kind of execution belongs by right; and besides, they are not made to linger so long, – often they are first strangled, and generally they are thrown at once into the fire, where they are immediately smothered and consumed.'

In other words, the French did not object to torturing people to death *per se*, but it had to be on their own terms. For the Hurons, inflicting pain, like warfare, was an end in itself, a moral action or drama. In this context, the individual identity of the victim was irrelevant; it was practiced generically upon an Iroquois adult male, and the more the better. For the French, the infliction of pain was a means towards re-establishing a moral order. Foucault (1977) discusses illuminatingly the nature of French judicial torture in the early modern period, an interpretation which our Jesuit missionaries corroborate faithfully. French victims, like Huron ones, were tortured in a highly ritualised public spectacle. However, individual bodies were not equivalent as victims (as for the Huron, for whom any adult male Iroquois would do); rather, the victims had to be differentiated and judged finely by their particular moral state of guilt or innocence which determined the nature and extent of pain inflicted. Moreover, pain was inflicted as punishment rather than simply as pain *per se*, and the exact proportion between offence and punishment was important. Given this, unmoderated pain inflicted upon those not individually guilty was excessive and an offence against reason. Underlying this view of the social order was a concept of the body as opposed to, and subordinated to, spiritual concerns; reason was the assertion of the latter over the former.

In contrast, the Huron enacted their own theology of the body in torturing the prisoner. At its heart was a ritualised expression of hostility by the entire community; in place of the encumbering Christian idea of the spiritual unity of humans, with the accompanying obligation to feel compassion, was the frequently verbalised certainty that the Iroquois inflicted an identical fate upon Huron captives whenever possible. The ceremony incorporated the idiom of inflicting pain as a test of fortitude, a performative challenge for the victim to bear bravely which men also performed upon themselves and which echoed encouragement given to dying people. The principal participants were adult males, for whom the emotions of bravery and anger were cultivated and closely related (Pomedli 1991: 65). The discursive context may have partially been to induce fortune in war; as a Frenchman commented upon the Iroquois, 'It is a belief among these Barbarians that those who go to war are the more fortunate in proportion as they are cruel toward their enemies' (Kenton 1926: 193). The actual dynamic followed the pattern of fasting, dancing, curing and eating: that positive spiritual values could be accessed performatively by repeated and exaggerated collective bodily action. As Pomedli (1991) notes, such actions did not represent spiritual states and deeds; rather, they created or performed them, in a way impossible to translate fully into a theology which divorced spirit from body.

If this interpretation is correct, it is no accident that the Huron mode of spiritual intervention required bodily action, while the French mode of spiritual intervention required the restriction, denial or redefinition of action through invocation of an immaterial sign, the word. This contrast is epitomised poignantly in the cacophony of competing meanings as Fathers Garnier and LeJeune lurked on the margins of the scene of torture, baptising and comforting the victim, uselessly reproaching the torturers and onlookers, constantly attentive to subvert the spiritual efficacy of the Huron's physical act through the Christians' spiritually efficacious word.

Discussion: violence, the body, and world orders

'Violence is not an unchanging, "natural" fact but a historically developed cultural category that we have to understand primarily as symbolic activity, as meaningful social action. To define violence as senseless or irrational is to abandon research where it should start: exploring meaning, interpreting symbolic action, and mapping out the historical and social context of activities defined as violent' (Blok 2000: 33) Violence is never meaningless, because the body is never meaningless. However, the rationality governing it need not be the same as our own. My rhetorical strategy here has been to proceed from apparently disparate practices to general principles of thought underlying them, but this strategy itself is rooted in a tradition of a faith in a unifying, rationalising word. It is immensely difficult to discuss a radically different ontology without reducing it.

Huron prisoner torture cannot be understood simply with reference to warfare, with or without the effects of European colonialism, nor simply through the idiom of warfare and violence as a gendered practice. Rather, it originated in a systematic distinction between how Europeans and Huron understood the human body. Cosmological logic and orientations toward the world are embodied in physical gestures, actions and movements; the body serves as one of the primary means for understanding humans' place in the world and their possibilities of action within it. Consequently, the habitus, or generative logic of a culture (Bourdieu 1977) is never simply reducible to abstract principles. Instead it must be understood as modality of action continually taught and reproduced through apparently disparate actions contextualised in all the fields of action members of a society engage in.

While we must be careful of sweeping characterisations about how medieval and early modern Europeans understood the body (Bynum 1995), as Knauft (1993) shows convincingly, generalisations in comparative analysis are scale-dependent (cf. Strathern and Lambek 1998). Although there were certainly serious theological controversies within Christianity over matters of body and soul, in contrast with completely distinct cultural systems, there was a common set of terms of argument to European ways of understanding the body. For example, although there were controversies opposing an Aristotelian view of the unity of body and soul to a neo-Platonic view of their separation and problems reconciling a neo-Platonic view of death as liberating the soul from the body with the New Testament doctrine of the resurrection of the body, Christians all worked within a hierarchical dualism opposing body and soul and linking the latter to divinity (Pomedli 1991). This dualism provided the tools for delimiting human and non-human bodies, and for understanding how the body was to be inhabited. The body was a battleground between flesh and spirit, a theatre of regulation, and actions such as eating, sexuality, and violence had to be carefully controlled in accordance with a spiritual order.

The Huron's ontological principles – enacted rather than codified – ran counter to European ones. As in many Native American traditions, the border between human and non-human entities was more complex; both could possess souls and enter into social relations. Unencumbered by a matter-spirit opposition, to the Huron, bodily action was a performative way of accessing a spiritual or moral order fundamentally similar to that of the physical world but more real or enduring. In this context, prisoner torture was part of a broad modality of efficacious body practices including giving food, eating and fasting, dancing, sweating and healing, dreaming, burying the dead, inflicting pain, and circulating bodily substances such as blood and flesh. Through such actions moral values were created and a spiritual economy based not on regulation but upon reciprocity within an animistic world was curated.

Notes

1 Champlain helped the Huron fight the Iroquois because he was trying to lay the basis for a French-Huron fur trade centred upon the St. Lawrence Valley, to compete with the nascent Iroquois-Dutch/English trade centred on the Mohawk and Hudson valleys.

2 Parenthetically, the Feast of the Dead demonstrates that collective burial need not be associated with ancestor veneration, as in recent archaeological treatments of funerary ritual; the point of the Feast of the Dead appears not to have been to venerate ancestors as transcendental beings permanently present in the affairs of the living, but rather to have given the dead a large-scale, sentimental and permanent farewell.

3 'Yet a soul closely united to God would have here a suitable occasion to meditate upon the adorable mysteries of the Passion of our Lord, some image of which we had before our eyes. One thing that consoled us was to see the patience with which he bore all this pain. In the midst of their taunts and jeers, not one abusive or impatient word escaped his lips' (Jesuit Relations 1637, Thwaites 1898: 71). Interestingly, what the French interpreted here as the patience of a Christian martyr seems actually to have been a traditional Huron and Iroquois comportment, a stubborn impassivity, enacting a defiant bravery by steadfastly refusing to acknowledge pain.

Bibliography

Abler, T.S. 1992. Beavers and muskets: Iroquois military fortunes in the face of European Colonization. In *War in the Tribal Zone: Expanding States and Indigenous Warfare*, edited by R.B. Ferguson and N.L. Whitehead, pp. 151–174. Santa Fe: School of American Research.

Aijmer, G. and Abbink, J. (eds) 2000. *Meanings of Violence*. Oxford: Berg.

Blok, A. 2000. The enigma of senseless violence. In *Meanings of Violence: a Cross-cultural Perspective*, edited by G. Aijmer and J. Abbink, pp. 23–37. Oxford: Berg.

Bourdieu, P. 1977. *Outline of a Theory of Practice*. Cambridge: Cambridge University Press.

Butler, J. 1993. *Bodies that Matter: On the Discursive Limits of 'Sex'*. London: Routledge.

Bynum, C. 1995. Why all the fuss about the body? *Critical Inquiry* 22: 1–33.

Champlain, S.d. 1620. *Voyages et descouvertes faites en la Nouvelle France, depuis l'année 1615, jusques à la fin de l'année 1618: oáu sont descrits les moeurs, coustumes, habits, façons de guerroyer, chasses, dances, festins & enterremens de divers peuples sauvages, & de plusieurs choses remarquables qui luy sont arrivées audit paèis, avec une description de la beauté, fertilité & temperature d'iceluy*. Paris: Chez Claude Collet, au Palais, en la gallerie des Prisonniers.

Champlain, S.d. 1929. *The Works of Samuel de Champlain. III: 1615–1618*, edited by H.P. Biggars. Toronto: The Champlain Society.

Darling, J.A. 1998. Mass inhumation and the execution of witches in the American Southwest. *American Anthropologist* 100: 732–752.

Douglas, M. 1966. *Purity and Danger*. London: Routledge Kegan Paul.

Driver, H.E. 1969. *Indians of North America*. 2nd ed. Chicago: University of Chicago Press.

Elias, N. 1994. *The Civilizing Process: the History of Manners, and State Formation*. Oxford: Blackwell.

Ember, C.R. and Ember, M. 1997. Violence in the ethnographic record: results of cross-cultural research on war and aggression. In *Troubled Times: Osteological and Archaeological Evidence of Violence*, edited by D.L. Martin and D. Frayer, pp. 1–20. New York: Gordon and Breach.

Fenton, W.N. 1978. Northern Iroquoian culture patterns. In *Handbook of North American Indians, Volume 15: Northeast*, edited by B.G. Trigger, pp. 296–321. Washington, DC: Smithsonian Institution.

Ferguson, R. and Whitehead, N. 1992. *War in the Tribal Zone: Expanding States and Indigenous Warfare*. Santa Fe: School of American Research Press.

Foucault, M. 1977. *Discipline and Punish: The Birth of the Prison*. London: Allen Lane.

Foucault, M. 1990. *History of Sexuality* 1. New York: Vintage.

Garrad, C. and Heidenreich, C.E. 1978. Khionontateronon (Petun). In *Handbook of North American Indians, Volume 15: Northeast*, edited by B.G. Trigger, pp. 394–397. Washington, DC: Smithsonian Institution.

Gosden, C. 1999. *Anthropology and Archaeology: a Changing Relationship*. London: Routledge.

Guilaine, J. and Zammit, J. 2005. *The Origins of War: Violence in Prehistory*. Oxford: Blackwell.

Heidenreich, C.E. 1971. *Huronia: A History and Geography of the Huron Indians*. Toronto: McClelland and Stewart.

Heidenreich, C.E. 1978. Huron. In *Handbook of North American Indians, Volume 15: Northeast*, edited by B.G. Trigger, pp. 368–388. Washington, DC: Smithsonian Institution.

Hinton, A.L. (ed) 2002. *The Annihilation of Difference: the Anthropology of Genocide*. Berkeley: University of California Press.

Keeley, L. 1996. *War before Civilization: The Myth of the Peaceful Savage*. New York: Oxford University Press.

Keeley, L.H. 1997. Frontier warfare in the Early Neolithic. In *Troubled Times: Osteological and Archaeological Evidence of Violence*, edited by D.L. Martin and D. Frayer, pp. 303–319. New York: Gordon and Breach.

Kelly, R. 1993. *Constructing Inequality: The Fabrication of a Hierarchy of Virtue among the Etoro*. Ann Arbor, MI: University of Michigan Press.

Kelly, R.C. 2000. *Warless Societies and the Origins of War*. Ann Arbor, MI: University of Michigan Press.

Kenton, E. (ed.) 1926. *The Jesuit Relations and Allied Documents: Travels and Explorations of the Jesuit Missionaries in North America 1610–1791*. London: Brentano's.

Knauft, B. 1985. *Good Company and Violence: Sorcery and Social Action in a Lowland New Guinea society*. Berkeley: University of California Press.

Knauft, B. 1987. Reconsidering violence in simple human societies: homicide among the Gebusi of New Guinea. *Current Anthropology* 28: 457–499.

Knauft, B. 1991. Violence and sociality in human evolution. *Current Anthropology* 32: 391–428.

Knauft, B. 1993. *South Coast New Guinea Cultures: History, Comparison, Dialectic*. New York: Cambridge University Press.

Martin, D.L. and Frayer, D. 1997. *Troubled Times: Archaeological and Osteological Evidence of Violence and Warfare*. New York: Gordon and Breach.

Maschner, H. 1997. The evolution of Northwest Coast warfare. In *Troubled Times: Archaeological and Osteological Evidence of Violence and Warfare*, edited by D.L. Martin and D. Frayer, pp. 267–302. London: Gordon and Breach.

Pomedli, M.M. 1991. *Ethnophilosophical and Ethnolinguistic Perspectives on the Huron Indian Soul*. Lewiston/ Queenston/ Lampeter: Edwin Mellen.

Riches, D. 1986. *The Anthropology of Violence*. Oxford: Blackwell.

Riches, D. 1986. The phenomenon of violence. In *The Anthropology of Violence*, edited by D. Riches, pp. 1–27. Oxford: Blackwell.

Rosaldo, R. 1980. *Ilongot Headhunting: a Study in Society and History, 1885–1974*. Stanford, CA: Stanford University Press.

Sagard, G. 1939. *The Long Voyage to the Country of the Huron*. Toronto: The Champlain Society.

Shilling, C. 2003. *The Body and Social Theory*. 2 edn. London: Sage Publications.

Strathern, A. and Lambek, M. 1998. Embodying sociality: Africanist-Melanesianist comparison. In *Bodies and Persons: Comparative Perspectives from Africa and Melanesia*, edited by A. Strathern and M. Lambek, pp. 1–25. Cambridge: Cambridge University Press.

Strathern, M. 1988. *The Gender of the Gift: Problems with Women and Problems with Society in Melanesia*. Berkeley: University of California Press.

Taussig, M. 1984. Culture of terror, space of death. *Comparative Studies in Society and History* 26: 467–497.

Thwaites, R.G. 1898. *The Jesuit Relations and Allied Documents: Travels and Explorations of the Jesuit Missionaries in New France 1610–1791. Volume XIII: Hurons: 1637* 13. Cleveland: Burrows.

Tooker, E. 1964. *An Ethnography of the Huron Indians, 1615–1649*. Bureau of American Ethnology Bulletins 190. Washington, DC: Smithsonian Institution.

Trigger, B.G. 1969. *The Huron: Farmers of the North*. New York: Holt, Rinehart and Winston.

Trigger, B.G. 1976. *The Children of Aataentsic: a History of the Huron People to 1660*. Montreal: McGill-Queen's University Press.

Trigger, B.G. 1978. Early Iroquoian contacts with Europeans. In *Handbook of North American Indians, Volume 15: Northeast*, edited by B.G. Trigger, pp. 344–356. Washington, DC: Smithsonian Institution.

Walker, P.L. 2001. A bioarchaeological perspective on the history of violence. *Annual Review of Anthropology* 30: 573–596.

White, M.E. 1978. Neutral and Wenro. In *Handbook of North American Indians, Volume 15: Northeast*, edited by B.G. Trigger, pp. 407–411. Washington, DC: Smithsonian Institution.

White, T. 1992. *Prehistoric cannibalism at Mancos 5MTUTR-2346*. Princeton, NJ: Princeton University Press.

Wolf, E. 1982. *Europe and the People Without History*. Berkeley: University of California Press.

Bodily beliefs and agricultural beginnings in Western Asia: animal-human hybridity re-examined

Preston Miracle and Dušan Borić

Introduction

One of the chronic problems in the field of body studies has been the persistence of nature-culture dichotomies, even in the works that consciously address or try sidestepping this conceptual determinism. A common critique of such dichotomies between 'Nature' and 'Culture' emphasises the historical and cultural embeddedness of this Cartesian way of thinking in the Western philosophical episteme. Related to this critique is the defamiliarisation of taken-for-granted and common-sense conceptual categories in our thinking that has been mentioned by both social anthropologists working in non-Western cultural contexts (e.g., Ingold 2000; Strathern 1988) and historically minded philosophers (e.g., Foucault 1970; Latour 1989). Anthropologists and philosophers respectively have either provided examples of indigenous ontologies different from those dominating Western thought or exposed the genealogy of the specifically Western trajectory in the constitution of the subject and the individual. Ethnographic examples show that in numerous non-Western cultural contexts, mind-body and culture-nature polarisations are less sharply drawn, or point to a complete inversion of these categories (see below). Mind, consciousness and the sense of being, it has been emphasised, are situated in the material world, while the body can hardly be separated from objects such as prosthetic devices that constitute it. Latour (1989) and other authors have even gone so far as to argue that our own thought is far from the post-Enlightenment, modernist dream of an absolute separation of mind and matter, and that the constitution of Western subjects largely depends on their situatedness in the world of material

things. Lambek (1998), on the other hand challenges the argument about the purely constructed nature of our own and other ontologies when it comes to the persistence of nature-culture, body-mind polarities by arguing that the persistence of mind-body dichotomies is more universal and cross-cultural than the current anthropological and sociological critique allows.

In this paper we focus on the problem of the culture-nature divide by tackling what on the surface appears to be the most critical material for examining this problem: relationships between animal and human bodies. This area, with some exceptions (e.g., Borić 2005; Conneller 2004; Ingold 1988, 1996; Meskell and Joyce 2003: 79-94), has been inadequately researched and the first goal of our contribution is to contextualise the difference drawn between animal and human bodies and indicate the relevance of this material for the constitution of the categories 'cultural' and 'natural' in Western, non-Western and past contexts. The second goal of this paper is to examine how categories of human and animal bodies are played out in a regionally and chronologically situated sequence of archaeological case studies, focusing on the process commonly described as the transition to agriculture in Western Asia. This area provides the classic Old World example for constructing the meta-narrative of a human separation from the natural order and the development of 'Culture' as part of a larger social evolutionary trajectory and, hence, is of particular importance in following the genealogy of human–animal relationships. We begin by discussing analytic tools and methodologies that are context specific, attempting to sidestep partly the familiar discussions of domestication, as a separation from nature, that have dominated archaeological narratives from the region. We then use these tools to examine changing past beliefs with regard to animal and human bodies throughout the development that covers the span from the Natufian to the end of Pre-Pottery Neolithic periods, i.e., 12,000–6300 cal BC.

Animal and human bodies: nature-culture divide reconsidered

Body studies in archaeology have been traditionally focused on the human body, animal bodies are thought of primarily in utilitarian terms, whether as sources of food, as draft animals, means of transport, and so forth. When the other dimensions of animals are considered, it is primarily in terms of animals as symbols or metaphors, through the abstraction of an animal's essence or reference to bodily characteristics and behaviours of an animal. Like human bodies, however, animal bodies in the past might have also been partitioned, modified, combined, and reconstituted through a variety of practices and representations (examples – butchery, taxidermy/trophies, ornaments made from body parts, use of skins/hides, imaginary beasts, representations of above through rock art, figurines made on body parts or other media). One way of approaching the topic of changing beliefs about bodies would thus be to widen the scope to include animal and human bodies, comparing the treatment of one to the other. However, this falls into the trap of assuming the existence of the various categories that we wish to examine: to what extent and in what ways were bodily boundaries defined and defended? Can we conceive of bodies in ways that move beyond our own familiar and comfortable assumptions as to what a body is, and what limits it has?

In fact, even in those mythological universes that are related to our own there are images and concepts of bodies that challenge a simple division between 'human' and 'animal' – human-animal hybrids abound, whether through composite bodies such as those presented by a satyr, minotaur, Anubis, etc., the sort of transforming bodies we bring out to scare ourselves – e.g., werewolves, Dracula, or explain the world around us – e.g., the raven 'trickster' common to many Native American cosmologies. These animal-human hybrids are often conceived of as 'dangerous' precisely because they break down boundaries and question categories (e.g., Aldhouse Green 2001; Bynum 2001; Douglas 1966). Here again, the discussion is predicated on assumed and accepted 'natural' categories of 'human' and 'animal'. As several different ethnographic examples, show, however,

these categories are not 'natural', but rather culturally constructed. Human-animal hybrids apart from being considered 'dangerous' might also have been accepted and expected part of the flow of the life cycle.

Human attitudes toward animals represent one of the important topics of early ethnographic works that allowed the introduction of the analytical concept of *animism* in anthropological literature with regard to the origins of religious thought (Tylor 1871; cf. Stringer 1999). Lévi-Strauss's famous explanation for the importance of both animals and plants in religious, 'speculative thought' is 'that natural species are chosen not because they are "good to eat" but because they are "good to think"' (1964: 89). Such importance of animals and plants for the development of religious and sacred is based on the human meta-narrative of its place in nature and the nature of existence.

One particular strand of thought in western thinking about the relationship between animals and humans is provided by the philosopher George Bataille. Bataille, fascinated by the Upper Palaeolithic parietal art, suggested that the notion of animality can usefully be considered in following the trajectory of human separation from nature, in what he calls the 'passage from animal to man' (1955, 2005). Bataille sees Upper Palaeolithic art with its 'naturalistic' depictions of a large variety of animals and often schematic and sometimes hybrid depictions of humans as both underlying the difference between the animal and man, and, at the same time, as media of transgression – through cave paintings the realm of animality is revealed, while paintings on cave walls become entry points into the *animality*, seen as religiously sacred. Although Bataille's discussion on animality can usefully be considered to relativise our common sense understanding of whether humanity or animality can be related to the idea of sacred, his discussion very much remains confined to the meta-narrative that sees a universal and cross-cultural, in his words 'tragic', separation between humans and animals, with human acquiring of consciousness and 'Culture'.

That such an understanding of animal-human separation is not universally shared and widely accepted can most aptly be shown on the basis of indigenous understandings known as Amerindian perspectivism. It has been emphasised that across South America and particularly among various Amazonian peoples the main site of differentiation between different classes of beings is not the culture or spirit but the body. Here, animals and radically differentiated categories of humans, such as once kin, foreigners, enemies etc., share the same culture. Their true differences lie in different perspectives they occupy which depend on the type of body they have (e.g., Vilaça 2005; Viveiros de Castro 1998). To have a different body means to see different things: '…where we see a muddy salt-lick on a river bank, tapirs see their big ceremonial house' (Viveiros de Castro 2004: 6). In this ethnography, a 'properly human' body must constantly be constructed and negotiated. This is done through the practices of sharing food, or by inhabiting the same living space, by sleeping side by side. Our common-sense biological understanding of relatedness is of no relevance in Amazonia, as kinship is rather seen as a process of relating to and communicating with the 'exterior', inhabited by other classes of beings (Vilaça 2002). Furthermore, human and animal bodies in Amazonia are characterised by the 'chronic' instability of form: '…the possibility of metamorphosis expresses the … fear of no longer being able to differentiate between the human and the animal, and, in particular, the fear of seeing the human who lurks within the body of the animal one eats …' (Viveiros de Castro 1998: 481). This metamorphic capacity of all beings derives from an essentially hunting ideology that is based on the predator-prey balance of powers in the world. In such an ontological universe, every event is intentionally caused in the interplay of agencies that abound (Gell 1998: 16–17; cf. Ingold 2000a, 2000b).

By evoking this example of one specific ethnography with its set of ontological principles (some of which are not only confined to Amazonia, cf. Ingold 2000b on the Ojibwa), one relativises the separation along the animal-human axis. If one imagines an ontology in the past that, similarly to the Amazonian example, considered animals and humans to share the same culture and transform into each other through the metamorphosis of the body form, the relevance of aligning the category 'animal' with 'nature' and the category 'human' with 'culture' means that this particular alignment is relative to context. Such an understanding suggests that some of the meta-narratives that persist in the archaeological writings about the processes of domestication as involving a gradual human departure from nature need to be reconsidered.

In the field of research that focuses on the process of agricultural transition in western Asia such meta-narratives abound in emphasising the process of settling down, domestication of animal and plant species and the 'explosion' of symbolism. Authors such as Cauvin (2000) and Hodder (1990), with somewhat different perspectives, have most forcefully argued for an important shift with the start of the Holocene toward increasingly individuated human agency that tames 'Nature' and allows a human-like god image. In the core of their arguments, these authors suggest that there is the symmetry between our meta-narrative of social evolutionary, progressive move away from

'Nature' and the self-representation among societies of western Asia at the 'dawn of agriculture', i.e., in the period from around 12,800 to 6500 cal BC. Two main media for expressing such indigenous understandings are frequently considered: a) the treatment of human and animal bodies in the mortuary record, and b) depictions of images of human and animal bodies by painting, carving and moulding a range of materials.

In the next section of this paper, we examine whether one could sustain this implicit idea of the symmetry between our own meta-narratives that glorify the separation and individuation of human agency from the natural order, on the one hand, and what particular bodily beliefs might have been like at the beginning of the Neolithic, on the other hand. We discuss a range of analytical categories with which to approach animal-human mixtures in search of an adequate research methodology for the set of theoretical issues previously developed.

Western Asian sequences: From the Natufian through Pre-Pottery Neolithic B

The region of western Asia as we consider it here encompasses a huge territory that includes parts of the present-day countries of Turkey, Syria, Jordan, Israel and Iraq (Figure 11.1). In our Natufian case study we examine mortuary evidence from the Early (12,800–11,000 cal BC) and Late Natufian (11,000–10,000 cal BC) periods from Israel. Here, with the Natufian we see the emergence of what are considered to be more sedentary base camps with the evidence of domestic architecture and associated human burials, along with a proliferation of ground stone and bone artefacts, ornaments and 'art' objects (e.g. Bar-Yosef 1998; Bar-Yosef and Valla 1990). For the Pre-Pottery Neolithic (10,000–6750 cal BC) we discuss evidence from the larger region of western Asia, which exhibits shared elements in various aspects of mortuary practices and symbolic and ritual expression (Goring-Morris and Belfer-Cohen 2002, 2003; Kuijt 2000; Kuijt and Goring-Morris 2002). There are three phases that can roughly be applied to this larger territory that we consider: PPNA (c. 10,000–8,550 cal BC), PPNB (c. 8550–6750 cal BC) and PPNC/early Pottery Neolithic (c. 6750–6300 cal BC). Although the cultural unity of the subdivisions of the PPN is debated, there are some widely shared traits in the region. Features commonly shared during the PPNA include oval to circular huts and primary human burials with secondary skull removal. During the PPNB period we often find a shift to rectangular buildings with plastered, red-coloured, limestone

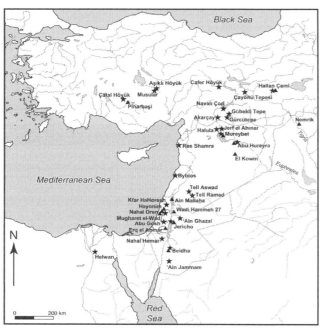

Figure 11.1. Map of south-west Asia with principal sites mentioned in the text. Natufian sites and other epi-palaeolithic sites marked by triangles and PPNA-B sites marked by stars (drawn by Dora Kemp)

floors; there is also an increase in various aspects of symbolic expression (e.g., large plastered statues, clay figurines, the secondary removal and circulation of skulls that are sometimes plastered, etc.).

Animal-human hybridity: Developing methodologies and case studies

There is clearly a strong case for examining both human and animal bodies and examining how these bodies were created and defined. Our core thesis is that beliefs about human and animal bodies have varied in time and space, and that our own assumptions about bodies provide only one lens for examining these past beliefs. A critique of 'western' body categories and concepts is relatively easily made; see the work of innumerable anthropologists and social theorists over the last several decades. While archaeologists have increasingly accepted this critique, with a few exceptions aside, they have made only modest contributions to the question of 'what were bodily beliefs in the past' beyond the banal observation that 'the past was different'. Our goal in the rest of this paper is to outline an approach for examining human-animal hybridity, which we will illustrate with a few case studies taken from the 'dawn of agriculture'

in Western Asia. We focus on the burial record and representations (pictorial and sculptural) of humans and animals.

A first step is to consider human and animal bodies as two ends on a continuum, and the ways in which we might define the space in between them. Next we can examine the process by which humans and animals might be combined. Questioning 'human' and 'animal' as categories is not to deny their existence. By examining the conditions and contexts in which these categories are undermined, reconstituted, and in which new categories are introduced should tell us something about bodily beliefs and how/when they changed. If we accept that 'human' and 'animal' are two ends on a continuum, what do we have in between them? It is a spectrum of human-animal hybridity. In trying to develop an adequate methodology for the examination of this spectrum of animal-human hybridity in the archaeological record, we shall compare the 'human' and 'animal' elements through their combinations. We have chosen to examine following analytical categories: association, substitution, and transformation.

Association

Association refers to a deliberate juxtaposition or association of humans and animals. Examples are many and include the following: the use of animal parts (e.g., teeth) as ornaments/clothing on human bodies, the use of animal representations as grave goods, the inclusion of human and animal bodies (or parts) in a single grave, the inclusion of human and animal burials in the same cemetery, the association of humans and animals in rock art, on stelae, and so forth. A whole series of choices are reflected in such associations, including the choice of species, whole bodies versus body parts, unmodified versus modified parts, fleshed versus defleshed, the association with particular parts of human body (e.g., head, neck, arm, torso, pelvis, feet, etc.), and the association through mediating elements (e.g., clothing) or through direct contact with the skin.

For example, a number of Early Natufian burials from el-Wad, Hayonim Cave, Mallaha, Erq el Ahmar, and Wadi Hammeh 27 have associated beads made out of animal parts, commonly dentalium shells (Figure 11.2), but also made out of gazelle phalanges, partridge tibia-tarsus bones, and rarely fox teeth (only at Hayonim Cave) (Belfer-Cohen 1995; Sellars 2001). The dentalium beads were interpreted by Wright (1978) and Henry (1989) as status markers, and the decorated burials are central to their interpretation of social ranking during the Early Natufian. Belfer-Cohen (1995: 15), as part of a wider critique of Wright's model of Natufian social ranking, notes that dentalium shell beads are unlikely to have served as prestige goods because dentalium shells are readily available and can be made into beads with little effort. Perhaps the dentalium shell garments had magical/ritual significance, for instance protective or apotropaic properties. These beads, particularly the dentalium shell caps, necklaces, bracelets, and leggings, were in very close contact with human bodies. Were they an extension of the body or were body boundaries extended to incorporate them? What is interesting is that during the Late Natufian beads are no longer used to decorate dead bodies, even though the raw materials for bead production are still widely available (e.g., dentalium shells, gazelle toes, partridge bones). Since beads were not manufactured out of other materials, it would seem that this change has more to do with bead use rather than changing beliefs about human-animal bodies.

More rare human-animal associations come from the inclusion of animal parts, apparently as grave goods, in human graves. The species and parts used are tortoise carapaces (el-Wad, Hayonim Terrace), gazelle horn cores (el-Wad, Hayonim Terrace, Mallaha), horse teeth (only at Erq el Ahmar). This practice is not very common, but does show continuity from Early to Late Natufian.

With current data, it is not possible to study in detail if particular species are associated with particular body parts, skeletal sexes or ages – the general impression is that dentalia are associated particularly with the head and long bones, and probably were sewed onto caps and garments. Gazelle phalange beads are associated with head (young child, adult male), neck (adult male and female), pelvis (belt – adult female), arm (bracelet – adult female). Gazelle phalange beads may occur on their own or mixed with dentalia or partridge bone beads. Partridge bone beads are less common than either of the other bead types. They are found in association with dentalium shells in headdresses, or on their own forming bracelets. Partridge bone beads have not been found at Ain Mallaha; they appear to be associated with adult males.

Also, it is important to ask the question whether shells were important as animals or as a raw material – would these be thought of as animal remains in regions distant from the coast – where animals were not encountered 'alive' but disassociated with the living animals – in this case a chunk of shiny or colourful mineral? To what extent could one make similar arguments about the use of animal teeth as pendants. Is the material transformed when disassociated from animals? – so that people in donning the pendants would not see them as some association with animals,

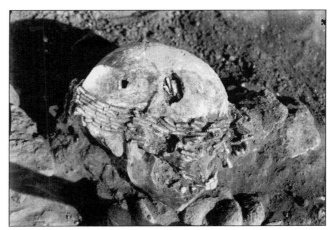

Figure 11.2. Natufian dentalium shell headdress on Homo 25 from Garrod's excavation at Mugharet el-Wad (photograph by D. Garrod, 1929, Pitt Rivers Museum 1998-294-301, University of Oxford)

but rather with 'hard' or 'white' or 'thing with hole' or some other category. Put slightly differently, when do things like pierced shells, teeth, worked bone, etc. stand for bodies (of animals), are recognised and thought of as parts of a body, or were thought of in completely different ways? How would one distinguish between these different possibilities?

One famous example of this dilemma from the study region is the puppy buried with an old woman at Ain Mallaha during the Early Natufian period (*c.* 9300 BC) (Figure 11.3). Domestic dogs buried with people may also be present at el-Wad and are definitely present in Late Natufian contexts at Hayonim Terrace (Belfer-Cohen 1995). The intimacy implied by this association has received considerable comment, and this burial is pivotal to discussions of the domestication of the dog and human-animal relations in general. To the best of our knowledge, the puppy burial at Mallaha is the first case of a complete animal body buried with a human body – where people have consciously respected the integrity of a non-human body. Likewise, the positioning of the puppy near the woman's head, their analogous burial position – crouched and facing left, and the position of her left hand on the animal were deliberate and probably significant, a point we return to below.

Within the southern Levant region of Western Asia, while there is widespread evidence of the manipulation of human bodies after death, including deliberate skull removal starting at least in the Late Natufian and continuing through the PPN, these practices were mostly about the partibility and boundaries of human bodies; animals play only a minor role in these practices. Exceptions include 'votive offerings' of animals in human graves during the MPPNB at

Figure 11.3. Puppy burial with Burial H104 from Ain Mallaha, c.9300 BC (photograph by Simon Davis)

Kfar HaHoresh (Kuijt and Goring-Morris 2002: 422), and during the PPNC the inclusion of pig tusks and bones with two secondary human burials in Building C2 at 'Ain Ghazal (Kuijt and Goring-Morris 2002: 416). Other examples of human-animal associations are grave goods such as shell necklaces that apparently were placed on bodies starting in the MPPNB after 9250 BP (Kuijt and Goring-Morris 2002: 411).

In Anatolia, at the Pre-Pottery Neolithic site of Çayönü Tepesi, directly associated with a special purpose building called the Skull Building, due to a continuing interment of around 450 individuals in several successive levels for at least a thousand years if not longer (9200/8400 to 7500 cal BC), there were pits containing secondary human burials and aurochs skulls with horns (Özdoğan 1995, 1999; Özdoğan and Özdoğan 1998; Schirmer 1999). These pits were found in the first building phase (BM1), below the floor where detached human skulls were placed. In the following phase of this building (BM2a), similarly to the earlier levels, there was a depression in the floor of the building containing aurochs horns along with ninety skulls and postcranial bones in piles found on the floor level within specially constructed cellars. In the southern area of the Skull Building, on a large stone slab blood residues of both humans and aurochs have been identified (Loy and Wood 1989; Wood 1998). In addition, in Grill-Building Sub-phase (PPNA-EPPNB

period) at Çayönü a male burial was accompanied by a dog burial and boar skull (Özdoğan 1999: 47).

Another example of spatial-temporal contrasts within the study area involves the use and deposition of clay and stone figurines. In the southern Levant, during the PPNA the few figurines are mostly anthropomorphic, although a few birds are also represented at sites like Gilgal I and Salibiya IX (Kuijt and Goring-Morris 2002: 377). Clay animal figurines, primarily of cattle (but perhaps also sheep/goat and equids) are much more frequent during MPPNB, and are commonly associated with residential architecture. Such examples are also found at the site of Çatalhöyük in south-central Anatolia (Hodder 2006; Mellart 1967). Interestingly, some of these cattle figurines appear to have been ritually 'killed' with flint blades. Moving on into the LPPNB and PPNC, the few figurines are mostly anthropomorphic (Kuijt and Goring-Morris 2002: 411, 417). From our standpoint, however, what is significant is that although the representation of animals is clearly important, it is temporally restricted within the PPNB and these figurines are not directly associated with human bodies – whether in graves or through the association with human representations. This pattern is in stark contrast to that found in southeast Anatolia where at sites like Göbekli Tepe and Nevalı Çori animals are frequently carved on stelae and T-shaped monoliths that have been interpreted as representing humans (Peters and Schmidt 2004: 182). Do these associations constitute animal-human hybrids? This question only makes sense by taking a narrow view of what hybridity is all about – and misses our very point about opening up the interpretive spaces among human-animal-hybrid.

Substitution

Substitution refers to cases where animal bodies are being substituted for human bodies. One example would be the burial of animals with grave goods, for example some of the dog burials at Mesolithic sites like Skateholm in Sweden (Larsson 1990), or other cases where the personhood of animals is particularly underlined in a manner analogous to humans.

In this light, the Natufian burial of a puppy with a young woman at Ain Mallaha also hints at substitution. The analogous treatment of the bodies in terms of burial position, and the emphasis on the intact body of the puppy implies that the boundaries of the social 'body' also included the puppy, and the puppy may in fact be a substitute for a young human, as there are occasional Natufian burials of adults with children (e.g., el-Wad H. 23, H. 28; Hayonim Cave Grave VII [Belfer-Cohen 1995: 11–13]).

Other examples of substitution would include the

substitution of animal parts for human parts in a grave, or the substitution of animal bones for human bones in the manufacture of bone artefacts. We are not aware of any evidence of substitutions of these sorts during the Natufian period. Slightly later during the MPPNB at Kfar HaHoresh there is a plastered human skull 'directly associated with an otherwise complete but headless gazelle carcass' (Goring-Morris 2000: 110). Gazelles continued to receive special treatment during the LPPNB, at 'Ain Jammam a gazelle skull was placed in a small niche at eye level, while a group of charred gazelle horns on a building floor at 'Ain Ghazal led Rollefson to suggest the presence of a gazelle cult at the site during the LPPNB (Rollefson 1998: 113). In both cases, the treatment of gazelle heads is reminiscent of the special treatment given to human skulls during the MPPNB at a number of sites in the wider region (Rollefson 1998: 112). These examples suggest a certain interchangeability between humans and gazelles, and that in some contexts one was a substitute for the other. We are not aware of any human bone artefacts; in many cases, however, it may be impossible to determine the species used to make bone artefacts in the absence of genetic/chemical tests.

Transformation

Transformation is seen to involve a more thorough or complete combination of human and animal bodies than either association or substitution. Of course, it is quite possible that many of the 'pure' animal or human bodies and images that we have might have been conceived of as 'transformed' humans or animals. For this reason, we think it is most profitably to examine cases where the process of transformation is emphasised. From this perspective, the referent of an animal-human 'hybrid' may be the *process* of transforming from animal to human rather than the outcome. Animal-human 'hybrids' can be documented through the iconography; there is also evidence of their creation through the combination of animal and human remains. In the former case, there is considerable ambiguity as to whether significance was attached to the 'finished' hybrid or to the transformational process within which a hybrid is simply in an intermediate state.

We are not aware of any human-animal hybrids from Early or Late Natufian contexts. The same is also true for the PPNA. The situation changes provocatively during the MPPNB. Now there is clear evidence of human-animal hybrids in both the burial and figurative records. One possible case, that of Kfar HaHoresh, was briefly discussed earlier. This is a headless gazelle skeleton associated with a plastered human skull (Goring-Morris 2000: 110). Together

they constitute a hybrid body. Human and animal bodies, partially articulated but lacking skulls, were also commingled at Kfar HaHoresh (Goring-Morris 2000: 115). Examples include gazelle-human and aurochs-human. Goring-Morris (2000: 115) suggests this selection and symbolic treatment of wild animals may have significance in the context of incipient animal domestication (of the goat). Another possible example, again from Kfar HaHoresh that points to the arrangement of disarticulated gazelle and human bones into a pattern that when viewed from above resembles the profile of an animal (aurochs?, wild boar?, lion?) (Verhoeven 2002: 238, also Kfar HaHoresh web site) is not adequately published and, at face value, needs to be taken with some caution. However, if the excavator's interpretation is correct, these gazelle remains are thus commingled to create a new body of yet another species – a human-animal hybrid with different levels of metaphorical associations.

Imagery of human-animal hybrids

Some of the most potent examples of human-animal hybrids come from images executed on stone, particularly from the sites of Göbekli Tepe and Nevalı Çori in southeastern Anatolia. Göbekli Tepe has important ritual structures from the Late PPNA/Early PPNB (9100–8500 BC), along with later components from the Middle and Late PPNB. The site is on a large limestone ridge and consists of several large mounds; the location is somewhat unexpected as it is not close to either water or arable land. To date, at least six semi-subterranean 'ritual' structures have been exposed, although the site contains neither clear 'domestic' structures nor human burials (Peters and Schmidt 2004; Schmidt 2001; 2003; Schmidt and Hauptmann 2003). These ritual structures contained numerous, large, T-shaped pillars; the T-shape has been interpreted as anthropomorphic, and this interpretation is supported by engravings of human arms and fingers on the narrow sides of some pillars (Figure 11.4). Many of these pillars are decorated, and to these we can also add a number of large limestone sculptures. Some of the themes include: an animal with human head, an animal on human head, wolves, reptiles, boar, dog, a headless lion, turtle, sceptre, giant phallus, incised snake, snake relief, and discussed previously, a human body, human arms, and human fingers. Excepting a clear representation of a woman on a stone slab from the 'lion pillar' enclosure, the remainder of unambiguous gender depictions on animals and objects are male. If such an anthropomorphic understanding of these stelae is accepted, carvings of animals are thus inscribed on/in human bodies. Such

Figure 11.4. T-shaped pillar with the carvings of human arms, Enclosure D, central pillar 18, Göbekli Tepe (photograph by Irmgard Wagner, Deutsches Archäologisches Institut)

interpreted as anthropomorphic (Hauptmann 1999; Verhoeven 2002). There are eleven other limestone sculptures, many of which depict human-animal hybrids. Examples include a snake on the back of a human head, two humans with raised arms on either side of a tortoise (?) similarly depicted (the tortoise is a human transformed?), and a large carnivore (lion?) with bared, human-like teeth. There is particular emphasis at the site on human-bird combinations; the most provocative image (compared to a totem pole by Hauptmann) is of a bird (raptor?) missing its head (decapitated?) perching on top of a human-bird hybrid (human head with flowing hair on a bird body and tail) (Hauptmann 1999; Voigt 2000: 271). The same human head/bird body hybrid is represented in a second sculpture (Hauptmann 1999; Voigt 2000: 272). All of these representations were incorporated into the walls and foundations (in the case of the limestone bowl with three figures) of ritual structures at the site. Hauptmann (1999) and Voigt (2000) focus on rounded stomachs and interpret the imagery in terms of fertility and abundance. We are struck, instead by the implied instability and transformation of bodies suggested by these hybrids. Furthermore, the images may have been used in various rites until they either lost their efficacy, or were needed to found/construct ritual buildings, at which time they were incorporated into the very fabric of these structures. Although unclear from published descriptions, these hybrid images may have remained visible once incorporated into walls, niches, and benches, or accessible through other bodily senses (e.g., touch) during the use of these structures. Although immobile, these incorporated images may have still served as props in rituals.

Similar images to those hybrid beings with raised arms and legs found at Nevalı Çori and other sites in southeast Anatolia (Figure 11.5) and the Levant were also found at the site of Çatalhöyük in south-central Anatolia (Hodder 2006; Mellaart 1967). Here, many buildings have moulded headless figures with raised legs and arms that since the time of Mellaart's first discoveries have been interpreted as pregnant women, thus promoting the widely accepted meta-narrative about the Mother Goddess that, along with the bull, was one of the main figures in the Çatalhöyük's religious pantheon. However, in 2005 season, a discovery of a stamp seal in the infill of one of the buildings at the site shows a similar iconography to those images moulded on building walls, this time with an animal's head that is interpreted by team members as a bear (Hodder 2006: 201). This example possibly indicates that all of the headless moulded figures with raised arms and legs on building walls at Çatalhöyük represent similar hybrid beings.

associations can perhaps be interpreted as a way of releasing these animals or hybrid beings onto the surface that represented the interface between different realities. At Göbekli, these human-animal hybrids and transformations are also gendered male. There is a temporal shift in depictions on pillars and sculptures; animals predominate in earlier layers, while humans predominate in later layers. However, there remains the question whether right from the inception of these T-stelae the idea was to represent a stylised human body or if this shape became anthropomorphised through the interpretive acts of carving human arms, fingers, etc. (Figure 11.4)

Many of these themes are repeated at the PPNB site of Nevalı Çori, also in southeastern Anatolia, where there is rich imagery of human-animal hybrids executed on stone stelae and sculptures. Again we have T-shaped stelae, sometimes carved with arms and hands (Lewis-Williams and Pearce 2005: 30),

Figure 11.5. T-shaped pillar with the carving of a splayed hybrid human-animal or reptile figure, Göbekli Tepe (photograph by Michael Morsch, Deutsches Archäologisches Institut)

Discussion

In our survey of evidence for animal-human hybridity in the Natufian and Pre-Pottery Neolithic A and B periods in southwest Asia, we have, on the one hand, pointed out a permeable character of categories animal and human for the type of societies we have discussed, and, on the other hand, we have suggested analytical categories that can be used to examine this archaeological data set. Animal-human mixtures in the pre-Neolithic eastern Mediterranean speak of a distinct ontology that might have been characterised by a 'multi-naturalist' position, i.e., where the true difference between different categories of beings was grounded in the body as the main site of ontological differentiation. The change of the body in death or through various stages of life cycle might have been emphasised by comparing such changes with the most radical examples of shape-shifting, such as a transformation into an animal. This position seems to have characterised many non-Western societies (e.g., Aldhouse Green 2001; Borić 2005, 2007; Ingold 2000; Vilaça 2005; Viveiros de Castro 1998). Such transformations might have had both positive and negative connotations. Many ethnographies, including the European medieval beliefs in shape-shifting (Bynum 2001), express a fear of metamorphosis that is frequently equated with the death as a radical change of topological orders. At the same time, individuals and groups were often equated with certain animals that could have been considered to have apotropaic character, due to their strength, potency or other positive attributes. Examples of such associations can

perhaps be seen in a metonymic placement of specific animal parts in burials or bucrania on the walls of houses, seen as bodies of a collective agency, in the (pre-)Neolithic eastern Mediterranean.

Some representatives of the embodiment paradigm suggest an anti-Cartesian or pre-Cartesian model of the self for non-Western societies. Meskell and Joyce suggest 'that the intellectual legacy of Cartesianism pervades the dualism of human/animal...' (2003: 89). It is certainly true that our own Western view of animal-human or plant-human relatedness depends on 'the rigid taxonomies that we have constructed and naturalized' (Meskell and Joyce 2003: 88). However, it could hardly be claimed that various boundaries between humans and animals in non-Western and past social contexts were not constructed in various ways. While many such ontologies allow for permeable boundaries between animal and human worlds, it does not mean that the change is a comfortable place and that the maintenance of boundaries between humans and various categories of beings such as animals, enemies, the dead as well as other forms of alterity is not necessary or needed. Hence, we can imagine that in the Neolithic eastern Mediterranean specific ontologies of relatedness as well as processes of constructing and naturalising differences between diverse kinds of beings, including animals and plants, must have characterised the social reality.

There are three important questions that should be posed on the basis of the existing evidence of animal-human mixtures for the given period and region. First, can the material of human-animal mixtures and the context of their placement or deposition tell us something about specific aspects of long-term structures of beliefs that might have persisted for a very long period of time across this vast region? Second, can one identify decisive moments that prompted alterations of such beliefs and practices in the diachronic perspective? And, third, can certain aspects of animal-human, or even supposed plant-human, hybridity be related to changes that the period from 12800 to 6750 cal BC saw with regard to the process of the domestication of plant and animal species?

The obvious difference in the diachronic perspective relates to a change from the Natufian to the Pre-Pottery Neolithic A period. In the Natufian period animal human mixtures appear primarily by metonymical kinds of association with a spectrum of species by attaching animals' body parts to the garment or by incorporating a skeleton of a puppy into a human burial. It seems that the primary focus here is the body itself where ornaments seem to be conceived as extensions of the body. Only with the beginning of the PPNA one encounters a clear change toward the depiction of animal-human hybridity and a specific elaboration of the context of the placement or deposition of such an explicit narrative form. It should be noted that the depiction of such hybrid beings is widespread during the Palaeolithic period in Europe through various media (cf. Bataille 1955; Borić 2007; Lewis-Williams 2002). Even though such hybrids are not known from the Upper Palaeolithic and Natufian of western Asia, one could still argue that human-animal transformation has been part of the human cognitive repertoire for tens of thousands of years. Clearly what makes the PPNA-B cases interesting and significant is not simply the novelty of the practices, but the cultural contexts within which they occur.

Most of the hybrids achieved through manipulation of bodies/skeletons come from the Levant, although the prominence given to cattle heads is more widespread. Images of human-animal hybrids, on the other hand, appear to be more common to the north, i.e., southeastern Anatolia at the sites of Göbekli Tepe and Nevalı Çori (and other unexcavated sites from the Urfa region – Karahan Tepe [Verhoeven 2002: 253]), or moving farther to the west, at Çatalhöyük.

Verhoeven (2002) dicusses human-animal linkages as part of a wider study of the function and meaning of rituals during the PPNB in the Levant and southeastern Anatolia. He (Verhoeven 2002: 252) notes that evidence of human-animal linkages comes from clear ritual contexts. For instance, Kfar HaHoresh and Göbekli Tepe have been interpreted as specialised ritual sites without any domestic structures. Variability in the association of particular animal representations and structures at Göbekli Tepe (Figure 11.6) has been interpreted through the idea of totemism to imply different clan or ritual groups aggregating at the site from a wider region (Peters and Schmidt 2004: 210–212). The Nevalı Çori evidence for the most part comes from special ritual structures (Buildings II and III), although House 3 (with stone bowl with three figures in foundation) was domestic. At Çayönü the treatment of aurochs skulls and horns is from ritual structure – 'Skull' building. While all of this may suggest restricted access to these human-animal hybrids and depictions, perhaps by a newly emerging elite of priests-shamans during the Pre-Pottery Neolithic period (Lewis-Williams and Pearce 2005: 81–82; Peters and Schmidt 2004: 213), Verhoeven (2002: 247) argues that at Nevalı Çori the repetition of images from the large sculptures/stelae on small carvings deposited in houses undermines interpretations of these special ritual structures as restricted to 'secret societies'.

The species chosen for human-animal links are almost always wild and male (Verhoeven 2002; Peters and

Figure 11.6 T-shaped pillar 33, with the carving of a fox, Enclosure D, Göbekli Tepe (photograph by Irmgard Wagner, Deutsches Archäologisches Institut)

Schmidt 2004). Verhoeven (2002: 251) offers a functional interpretation for the explosion and evocativeness of ritual symbolism in the PPNB, compared to both the preceding PPNA and the succeeding Pottery Neolithic; it is a response to the massive changes and uncertainties introduced with the new, Neolithic way of life. The specific symbolism is thought to derive from beliefs of domestication/control, whether of land, settlement space, people, or food. Another influential perspective comes from Hodder (2006) who interprets humans represented at Çatalhöyük teasing wild and dangers animals as a celebration of human agency in the Holocene that mastered the Nature and the wild.

Yet, these interpretations do not move very far from the domestication meta-narrative that has dominated archaeological accounts of this evidence to-date. An alternative explanation for the predominance of wild and dangerous animals in the described contexts would be to argue that increasing mixing of human groups of different origins across this wide region from

Figure 11.7. T-shaped pillar 12 with the carvings of birds in a landscape (?), wild boar and fox, Enclosure C, Göbekli Tepe (photograph by Dieter Johannes, Deutsches Archäologisches Institut)

the beginning of the PPN prompted the necessity of defining individual and group identities in relation to the plenitude of emerging social 'Others'. In the course of this period, we see an increase in interactions between cultures 'with a consequent need for transferability and intercultural validity' (Sherratt 1995:16–17; see 2004). Yet, one should be warned that the very category of 'the human body' may be problematic to sustain since the bodily resemblance, as we understand it did not have to be understood necessarily in terms of 'humanity'. To put it differently, non-human beings (e.g., animal and plant species) sometimes could have been more understood as 'us' within a given group of humans than other humans themselves. Thus, interactions of quite diverse groups of people and new ways of relatedness in the course of the PPN period might have triggered the emphasis on the depiction of wild, dangerous and transformations (Figure 11.7), in other words, the exterior, beyond the confines of here and now.

The exterior could have been a stretchable category; something beyond this landscape, this settlement, this house or this wall. The fear of shape-shifting and the emphasis on the mutability of the body might have been entangled with an increasing mutability of individual and group identities that had started being reshaped through new forms of sociality.

Conclusion

Concepts of what constituted human and animal bodies and how they could be combined were clearly not stable in time and space over the period from the Natufian to PPNB in western Asia. During the Early Natufian, boundaries of human bodies were marked through shell and animal bead decorations; emphasis was on the integrity of human bodies or members of the wider social body (e.g., dogs), although the very focus on body boundaries may suggest that these boundaries were contested or perceived to be under threat.

Beliefs about the human body and its boundaries, as expressed in the mortuary record, clearly changed in the Late Natufian and PPNA; some human bodies were now clearly divisible and distributable and animal bodies/parts were not involved in these transactions. In the PPNB, there is a return to animal imagery and animal-human combinations. Humans, aurochs, and gazelle were in specific, ritually framed contexts interchangeable. Aurochs and gazelle may at times have served as ancestors or stood in for other members of the human social group. We also have true hybrids that emphasise the instability of human and animal bodies; these beings do not fit simple animal/human categories. When we turn to representations of humans and animals, however, a different pattern emerges. Animals inscribed on anthropomorphic, T-shaped pillars during the PPNA at Göbekli Tepe and Nevalı Çori represent a new development compared to the animal figurines of the Natufian. These human-animal associations suggest transformations of bodies, if not actual hybrids.

These data undermine narratives of the transition to agriculture that treat domestication as a progressive separation of humans from nature or a 'taming' of the wild. Instead of thinking of the process of agricultural beginnings in terms of such a simplistic cause-effect relationship, we rather see overlapping trajectories of changes in mortuary rites as opposed to visual depictions that do not necessarily correlate with changing human-animal-plant relations involved in the process of domestication. Throughout the period there is an almost paradoxical emphasis on wild and dangerous animals in representational media, despite an increasing reliance on domestic plant and animal species. This pattern may alternatively be interpreted as an increasing concern with defining one's identity in relation to other beings that was a corollary of living in aggregated agricultural villages. These villages engendered new human socialities grounded in more intense interactions among people from distant regions, which resulted in a mixing of human groups with diverse origin myths and social values. Categories of human-animal and culture-nature in such a social context might have become more blurred in the course of our temporal sequence. Human-animal combinations were yet another way of creating identities and differences, that, along with the bodies themselves, were perpetually constructed and transformed throughout western Asia.

Acknowledgements

This paper represents the first results of our ongoing research into early prehistory as part of the Leverhulme Research Programme *Changing Beliefs of the Human Body*. We thank Karina Croucher for her comments on earlier drafts of this paper. We are also grateful to Klaus Schmidt and Simon Davis for their help in obtaining images from Göbekli Tepe and Ain Mallaha.

Bibliography

Aldhouse Green, M. 2001. Gender-bending images: permeating boundaries in ancient European iconography. In *A Permeability of Boundaries? New Approaches to the Archaeology of Art, Religion and Folklore*, edited by R.J. Wallis and K. Lymer, pp. 19–30. BAR International Serices 936. Oxford: BAR.

Bataille, G. 1955. *Lascaux or the Birth of Art*. Geneva: Skira.

Bataille, G. 2005. *The Cradle of Humanity. Prehistoric Art and Culture* (edited by Stuart Kendall). New York: Zone Books.

Bar-Yosef, O. 1998. The Natufian Culture in the Levant, threshold to the origins of agriculture. *Evolutionary Anthropology*: 159–174.

Bar-Yosef, O. and Valla, F.R. 1991. *The Natufian Culture in the Levant*. International Monographs in Prehistory, Archaeological Series 1. Ann Arbor, Michigan.

Belfer-Cohen, A. 1995. Rethinking social stratification in the Natufian culture: The evidence from burials. In *The Archaeology of Death in the Ancient Near East*, edited by S. Campbell and A. Green, pp. 9–16. Edinburgh: Oxbow Monographs.

Borić, D. 2005. Body metamorphosis and animality: volatile bodies and boulder artworks from Lepenski Vir. *Cambridge Archaeological Journal* 15(1): 35–69.

Borić, D. 2007. Images of animality: hybrid bodies and mimesis in early prehistoric art. In *Material Beginnings: A Global Prehistory of Figurative Representation*, edited by C. Renfrew and I. Morley, pp. 89–105. Cambridge: The McDonald Institute for Archaeological Research.

Bynum, C.W. 2001. *Metamorphosis and Identity*. New York: Zone Books.

Cauvin, J. 2000. *The Birth of the Gods and the Origins of Agriculture*. Cambridge: Cambridge University Press.

Conneller, C. 2004. Becoming deer: corporeal transformations at Star Carr. *Archaeological Dialogues* 11(1): 37–56.

Douglass, M. 1966. *Purity and Danger: An Analysis of the Concepts of Pollution and Taboo*. London: Ark Paperbacks.

Foucault, M. 1970. *The Order of Things. An Archaeology of the Human Sciences*. London: Routledge.

Foucault, M. 1986. *The Archaeology of Knowledge*. London: Routledge.

Foucault, M. 1985. *The Use of Pleasure: The History of Sexuality*, vol. 2. London: Penguin Books.

Foucault, M. 1986. *The Care of the Self: The History of Sexuality*, vol. 3. London: Penguin Books.

Gamble, C. 1991. The social context for European Palaeolithic art. *Proceedings of the Prehistoric Society* 57(1): 3–15.

Gell, A. 1998. *Art and Agency. An Anthropological Theory*. Oxford: Clarendon Press.

Goring-Morris, A.N. 2000. The quick and the dead: The social context of aceramic Neolithic mortuary practices as seen from Kfar HaHoresh. In *Life in Neolithic Farming Communities: Social Organization, Identity, and Differentiation*, edited by I. Kuijt, pp. 103–136. New York: Kluwer Academic/Plenum.

Goring-Morris, N. and Belfer-Cohen, A. 2002. Symbolic behaviour from the Epipalaeolithic and Early Neolithic of the Near East: Preliminary obsrervations on continuity and change. In *Magic Practices and ritual in the Near Eastern Neolithic*, edited by H.G.K. Gebel, B.D. Hermansen and C.H. Jensen, pp. 67–79. Studies in early Near Eastern production, subsistence and environment 8.

Goring-Morris, N. and Belfer-Cohen, A. 2003. Structures and dwellings in the Upper and Epi-Palaeolithic (ca 42–10k BP) Levant: profane and symbolic uses. In *Perceived Landscapes and Built Environments*, edited by S.A. Vasil'ev, O. Soffer and J. Kozlowski, pp. 65–81. British Archaeological reports series 1122. Oxford: BAR.

Hauptmann, H. 1999. The Urfa region. In *Neolithic in Turkey: The Cradle of Civilization: New Discoveries*, edited by M. Özdoğan and N. Başgelen, pp. 65–86. Istanbul: Arkeoloji ve Sanat Yayinlari.

Henry, D.O. 1989. *From Foraging to Agriculture*. Philadelphia: University of Pennsylvania Press.

Hodder, I. 1990. *The Domestication of Europe. Structure and Contingency in Neolithic Societies*. Basil Blackwell, Oxford.

Hodder, I. 2006. *Çatalhöyük. The Leopard's Tale: Revealing the Mysteries of Turkey's Ancient 'Town'*. London: Thames & Hudson.

Kuijt, I. 2000. Keeping the peace. Ritual, skull caching, and community integration in the Levantine Neolithic. In *Life in Neolithic Farming Communities: Social Organization, Identity, and Differentiation*, edited by I. Kuijt, pp. 137–164. New York: Kluwer Academic/Plenum.

Kuijt, I. and Goring-Morris, N. 2002. Foraging, farming, and social complexity in the Pre-Pottery Neolithic of the southern Levant: a review and synthesis. *Journal of World Prehistory* 16: 361– 440.

Ingold, T. 1988. Introduction. In *What Is an Animal?*, edited by T. Ingold, pp. 1–16. London: Unwin Hyman.

Ingold, T. 1996. Growing plants and raising animals: an

anthropological perspective on domestication. In *The Origin and Spread of Agriculture and Pastoralism in Euroasia* edited by D.R. Harris, pp. 12–24. London: UCL Press.

Ingold, T. 2000a. A circumpolar night's dream. In *The Perception of the Environment. Essays on Livelihood, Dwelling and Skill*, edited by T. Ingold, pp. 89–110. London: Routledge.

Ingold, T. 2000b. Totemism, animism and the depiction of animals. In *The Perception of the Environment. Essays on Livelihood, Dwelling and Skill*, edited by T. Ingold, pp. 111–131. London: Routledge.

Lambek, M. 1998. Body and mind in mind, body and mind in body: some anthropological interventions in a long conversation. In *Bodies and persons. Comparative Perspectives from Africa and Melanesia*, edited by M. Lambek and A. Strathern, pp. 103–123. Cambridge: Cambridge University Press.

Larsson, L. 1990. Dogs in fraction – symbols in action. In *Contributions to the Mesolithic in Europe*, edited by P.M. Vermeersch and P. van Peer, pp. 153–160. Leuven: Leuven University Press.

Latour, B. 1989. *We Have Never Been Modern*. Cambridge, MA: Harvard University Press.

Lévi-Strauss, C. 1964. *Totemism*. London: Merlin Press.

Lewis-Williams, D. 2002. *The Mind in the Cave: Consciousness and the Origins of Art*. London: Thames & Hudson.

Lewis-Williams, D. 2004. Constructing a cosmos: architecture, power and domestication at Çatalhöyük. *Journal of Social Archaeology* 4(1): 28–59.

Lewis-Williams, D. and Pearce, D. 2005. *Inside the Neolithic Mind*. London: Thames & Hudson.

Loy, T. and Wood, A.R. 1998. Blood residue analysis at Çayönü Tepesi, Turkey. *Journal of Field Archaeology* 16(4): 451–460.

Mellaart, J. 1967. *Çatal Hüyük: A Neolithic Town in Anatolia*. London: Thames & Hudson.

Meskell, L.M. and Joyce, R.A. 2003. *Embodied Lives: Figuring Ancient Maya and Egyptian experience*. London: Routledge.

Mitthen, S.J. 1991. Ecological interpretations of Palaeolithic art. *Proceedings of the Prehistoric Society* 57(1): 103–14.

Özdoğan, A. 1999. Çayönü. In *Neolithic in Turkey*, edited by M. Özdoğan, pp. 35–63. Istanbul: Arkeoloji ve Sanat Yayınları.

Özdoğan, M. 1995. Neolithic in Turkey: the status of research. In *Reading in Prehistory, Studies Presented at Halet Çambel*, edited by J. Roodenberg, pp. 41–59. Istanbul: Graphis.

Özdoğan, M. and Özdoğan, A. 1998. Buildings of cult and the cult of buildings. In *Light on Top of the Black Hill: Studies Presented to Halet Çambel*, edited by G. Arsebük, J. Machteld Mellink and W. Schirmer, pp. 581–601. Istanbul: Ege Yayınları.

Peters, J. and Schmidt, K. 2004. Animals in the symbolic world of Pre-Pottery Neolithic Göbekli Tepe, south-eastern Turkey: a preliminary assessment. *Anthropozoologica* 39(1): 179–218.

Rollefson, G.O. 1998. The Aceramic Neolithic. In *The Prehistoric Archaeology of Jordan*, edited by D.O. Henry, pp. 102–126. Oxford: Archaeopress.

Rollefson, G.O. 2001. The Neolithic period. In *The Archaeology of Jordan*, edited by B. MacDonal, R. Adams and P. Bienkowski, pp. 67–105. Sheffield: Sheffield Academic Press.

Schirmer, W. 1990. Some aspects of building at the 'Aceramic-Neolithic' settlement of Çayönü Tepesi. *World Archaeology* 21(3): 363–387.

Schmidt, K. 2001. Göbekli Tepe, southestern Turkey. A preliminary report on the 1995–1999 excavations. *Paléorient* 26(1): 45–54.

Schmidt, K. 2003. 'Kraniche am See'. Bilder und Zeichen vom früneolithischen Göbekli Tepe (Südosttürkei). In *Der Turmbau zu Babel. Ursprung und Vielfalt von Sprache und Schrift*, edited by W. Seipel, pp. 23–29. Eine Ausstellung des Kunsthistorischen Museums Wien für die Europäische Kulturhauptstadt. Graz: Band IIIA.

Schmidt, K. and Hauptmann, H. 2003. Göbekli Tepe et Nevalı Çori. *Dossiers d'Archéologie* 281: 60–67.

Sellars, J.R. 2001. The Natufian of Jordan. In *The Prehistoric Archaeology of Jordan*, edited by D.O. Henry, pp. 83–101. Oxford: Archaeopress.

Sherratt, A. 1995. Reviving of the grand narrative: archaeology and long-term change. *Journal of European Archaeology* 3(1): 1–32.

Sherratt, A. 2004. Fractal Farmers: Patterns of Neolithic Origin and Dispersal. In *Explaining Social change: Studies in Honour of Colin Renfrew*, edited by J. Cherry, C. Scarre, and S. Shennan, pp. 53–63. The McDonald Institute for Archaeological Research: Cambridge.

Strathern, M. 1998. *The Gender of the Gift. Problems with Women and Problems with Society in Melanesia*. Berkeley: The University of California Press.

Stringer, M.D. 1999. Rethinking animism: thoughts from the infancy of our discipline. *Journal of the Royal Anthropological Institute* (N.S.) 5: 541–556.

Tylor, E.B. 1871. *Primitive Culture: Researches into the Development of Mythology, Philosophy, Religion, Art and Custom*. London: John Murray.

Verhoeven, M. 2002. Ritual and ideology in the Pre-Pottery Neolithic B of the Levant and southeast Anatolia. *Cambridge Archaeological Journal* 12: 233–58.

Vilaça, A. 2002. Making kin out of others in Amazonia. *Journal of the Anthropological Royal Institute* (N.S.) 8: 347–65.

Vilaça, A. 2005. Chronically unstable bodies: reflections on Amazonian corporalities. *Journal of the Anthropological Royal Institute* (N.S.) 11: 445–64.

Viveiros de Castro, E. 1998. Cosmological deixis and Amerindian perspectivism. *Journal of the Anthropological Royal Institute* (N.S.) 4: 469–88.

Viveiros de Castro, E. 2004. Perspectival anthropology and the method of controlled equivocation. *Tipití* 2(1): 3–22.

Voigt, M.M. 2000. Çatal Höyük in context: ritual at Early Neolithic sites in central and eastern Turkey. In *Life in Neolithic Farming Communities. Social Organisation, Identity, and Differentiation*, edited by I. Kujit, pp. 253–293. London: Kluwer Academic/Plenum Publishers.

Wood, A.R. 1998. Revisited: blood residue investigations at Çayönü, Turkey. In *Light on top of the Black Hill: Studies Presented to Halet Çambel*, edited by Güven Arsebük, Machteld J. Mellink and Wulf Schirmer, pp. 763–764. Istanbul: Ege Yayınları.

Wright, F.A. 1978. Social differentiation in the Early Natufian. In *Social Archaeology: Beyond Subsistence and Dating*, edited by C.L. Redman, M.J. Berman, E.V. Courtin, W.T. Langhorne, Jr., N.H. Versaggi and J.C. Wasner, pp. 201-223. New York: Academic Press.

12

Is it 'me' or is it 'mine'?
The Mycenaean sword as a body-part

Lambros Malafouris

Or was the sword thought to have a life all of its own, to be extinguished when its owner died?
(Desborough 1972: 312)

Before you know it, your body makes you human
(Gallagher 2005: 248)

Introduction

The main idea of this paper derives from the recent phenomenologically grounded archaeological conceptualisations of the body as a site of lived experience and embodied agency (Fowler 2002, 2003; Hamilakis *et al.* 2002; Knappet 2005, 2006; Thomas 2000). Adopting the perspective of the Material Engagement approach (Malafouris 2004, 2008a; Renfrew 2004; Malafouris and Renfrew in press) I shall attempt to clarify the possible cognitive and neuronal mechanisms that underpin our experience of *being* and *having* a body as an ongoing phenomenological intertwining between brains, bodies and things. To this end I shall be focusing on the idea of the extended and embodied mind and discuss some important recent findings in the cognitive neurosciences of self and the body that may help archaeology re-conceptualise some of the ways that the human physical body is usually understood.

The argument I intend to make is that material culture (tools for the body) has the ability to change and shape our bodies by transforming and extending the boundaries of our *body schema*. I should clarify at the outset that the notion of 'body schema' does not relate to our beliefs about the body – i.e. 'body image' (Cambell 1995) – but to the complicated neuronal action map associated with the dynamic configurations

and position of our body in space (Cambell 1995; Gallagher 1995; 2005). As I shall be discussing below the body schema is not a simple percept of the body, but it is closely associated with cortical regions that are important to self recognition and recognition of external objects and entities (Berlucchi and Aglioti 1997: 562). Thus the body schema cuts across the reflexive and pre-reflexive levels of our bodily experience and having a concrete biological basis offer a powerful means for linking neural and cultural plasticity within the general frame of embodied cognition and the Material Engagement approach (Malafouris 2004, 2008a).

To explore these ideas from an archaeological perspective I shall be concentrating on the relationship between the Mycenaean body and the Mycenaean sword. Focusing on the early Mycenaean period I shall be arguing that the sword becomes a constitutive part of a new extended cognitive system objectifying a new frame of reference and giving to this frame of reference a privileged access to Mycenaean reality and to the ontology of the Mycenaean self.

The embodied mind

The general idea behind embodied cognition is quite simple: the body is not as conventionally held, a passive external container of the human mind that has little to do with cognition *per se* but a constitutive and integral component of the way we think. In other words, the mind does not inhabit the body, it is rather the body that inhabits the mind. The task is not to understand how the body contains the mind, but how the body *shapes* the mind (Gallagher 2005; Goldin-Meadow 2003; Goldin-Meadow and Wagner 2005). To give a simple example, for the embodied cognition paradigm the development of the five-fingered precision grip and the opposable hand implies much more than a simple evolutionary curiosity. The hand is not simply an instrument for manipulating an externally given objective world by carrying out the orders issued to it by the brain; it is instead one of the main perturbatory channels through which the world touches us, and which has a great deal to do with how this world is perceived and classified. The interdependence of hand and brain function appears to be so strong that according to Frank Wilson any theory of human intelligence which ignores 'the historic origins of that relationship, or the impact of that history on developmental dynamics in modern humans, is grossly misleading and sterile' (Wilson 1998: 7). For embodied cognition, the very structures on which thinking is based emerge from our bodily sensorimotor experiences. Our brains are structured so as to project activation patterns from sensorimotor areas to higher cortical areas. Instead of abstract mental processes, cognitive processes are directly tied to the body (Lakoff 1987: 386; Johnson 1987: Lakoff and Johnson 1999: 77).

Viewed from the perspective of Material Engagement approach the case of embodied mind, although promising as a model for the study of human cognition, is not without problems. No doubt, by grounding cognition in bodily experience a successful step has been made towards resolving the traditional mind-body dichotomy. Nevertheless, what this step essentially implies for the proponents of embodied cognition approach, is simply an expansion of the ontological boundaries of the *res cogitans* rather than the dissolution of those boundaries altogether (Malafouris 2004; 2008a).

The point I am trying to develop here is that if some bodily pre-conceptual structure is to be accepted as the experiential foundation of the human mind, then it has to be recognised also that such a structure cannot emerge but only within some context of material engagement. In such a context of embodied and situated activity however, the boundaries of the mind are not determined solely by the physiology of the body, but also from the available constrains and affordances of the material reality with which it is constitutively intertwined. In other words, if the body shapes the mind then it is inevitable that the material culture that surrounds that body will shape the mind also. As Warnier phrases the question: '[I]s not material the indispensable and unavoidable mediation or correlate of all our motions and motor habits? Are not all our actions, without any exception whatsoever,

propped up by or inscribed in a given materiality?' (2001: 6) (Malafouris 2008a).

The sword

Every artefact, as Gell characteristically points out, 'is a "performance" in that it motivates the abduction of its coming-into-being in the world. Any object that one encounters in the world invites the question "how did this thing get to be here?"' (Gell 1998: 67). The Mycenaean Shaft Graves (Karo 1930–3; Mylonas 1973; Schliemann 1880) preserved for us a unique funerary constellation of such artefacts that for more than a century now invites this sort of abductive reasoning maybe more than any other assemblage in Mycenaean prehistory. The unique quantity and quality of artefacts deposited in the two Mycenaean Grave Circles A and B marks the transition between the Middle and the Late Helladic period and the emergence of a new cultural trajectory which for more than a century now, remains one of the most debated issues in Aegean prehistory (e.g., Dickinson 1977; Rutter 1993; Voutsaki 1997).

The change from single contracted to collective extended inhumations that took place between the Middle and the Late Helladic period in the mainland, provides a new interactive area for depositional display and motivates the construction of new cognitive schemas and categories of valuation. The depositional choices of material arrayed around the dead body constructed a durable network of somatic extension and predication. This network brings forth a whole new 'range of biographical possibilities' (Kopytoff 1986: 66) which speak about a new phenomenal awareness of the lived body. This new embodied awareness is also testified in the important changes in the depiction of the human figure where the icon of the Mycenaean person starts to become visually narrated and emblematised. The limited and schematic representations of the human figure from the Middle Helladic period indicate that the Middle Helladic social *habitus* lacked the motivation necessary for the warrior's image to become visually narrated and commemorated. Consequently the emergence of the human figure in the Shaft Grave period signifies important changes in the perception and experience of the Mycenaean body and the Mycenaean person. Being narrated and commemorated is thus objectified. This new embodied as well as gendered awareness of the Mycenaean self is constituted in a dialectical relationship with the construction and social appropriation of a new sensory environment emphasising certain properties, media and themes of representation with a crucial bearing for the cognitive operations active in that period.

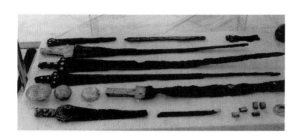

Figure 12.1. Mycenaean swords and a gold signet ring depicting a battle scene (The Mycenaean Shaft Graves) (National Museum)

More relevant to my purposes in this paper, prevalent in the material culture of this transitional phase is the emergence of a new Mycenaean *ethos* the focus of which is the warrior's body. The material instatiations of this *ethos* are many but the most important is undoubtedly the Mycenaean sword (see Figure 12.1), '[o]ne of the most far-reaching inventions of the ancient world, and more particularly of the Aegean' (Sandars 1961: 17; 1963). The unique assemblage of swords deposited in the two Mycenaean Grave Circles A and B testifies to the special significance of the former in the cognitive and social landscape of this transitional period. It should be remarked that a variety of other recently introduced military technologies (chariot, shield, helmet, spear) must have played also an important role in the construction of this new personal and cultural Mycenaean identity. Nevertheless, their striking under-representation in the funerary context, in comparison to the salient distribution of the Mycenaean sword, indicates the special significance of the latter in the cognitive and social landscape of this transitional period. This observation is also reflected in the iconography of this early phase of the Mycenaean becoming where the victory of the swordsman is a central theme in all battle or *agonistic* scenes (see Figure 12.1). Indeed, there is no example of a spearman defeating a swordsman. More important than that however, is the following association that Kilian Dilmeier among others has pointed out in relation to the Shaft Grave material: Although not all male burials contain swords, only burials with swords are accompanied with other valuable material, and the more the swords the richest the funerary assemblage (1987: 162–3). This evident correlation between swords and funeral gifts indicates that wealth and prestige

in the early Mycenaean period might have been intimately connected with a certain military quality or lifestyle (1987: 163). 'We might therefore already see in the heaps of swords deposited in the Shaft Graves', as Voutsaki characteristically observes in her extensive examination of the funerary record of that period, 'the establishment, or at least the outward expression, of an agonistic ethos, a moral scheme which is to glorified in the Homeric epics' (1993: 161). Indeed, this is an important statement about the moral entailments of the Mycenaean sword, which will be unfortunately subsumed by Voutsaki under a generalised mechanism of conspicuous consumption and gift exchange. What, I believe, Voutsaki fails to realise here is that the *ethos* of the sword precedes the *ethos* of accumulation that she identifies as the principal characteristic of early Mycenaean funerary behaviour and the defining parameter in the dialectics of power of the early Mycenaean society. More specifically, the point she misses is that '[t]he claim of social and political leadership, as well as the chance of accumulating wealth by monopolising the access to the economic recourses seems to have rested upon the performance of military excellence' (Deger-Jalkotzy 1999: 122). This is a statement that clearly, and to my mind also appropriately, indicates that it is the sword that constitutes the principal shaping factor of this new lifestyle, or what Voutsaki calls 'mode of prestige' characteristic of the early Mycenaean period. Let me clarify: I do not disagree with Voutsaki's argument that the processes of gift exchange and conspicuous consumption that we see in the funerary context of the early Mycenaean period should be understood as active strategies of value acquisition – i.e., a 'central mechanism for the creation *rather than expression or legitimation* of status' (Voutsaki 1997: 44, authors italics). I simply believe that this line of argument, though correct in emphasising the active role of the funerary context in the process of social stratification, contains a deductive oversimplification that cannot help us understand the cognitive life of the sword and its relation with the 'military excellence' or 'quality' already noted. This relationship I argue is the key feature of Mycenaean personhood and of the Mycenaean becoming.

The introduction and development of the Mycenaean sword (type A and B) may be considered as one of the primary distinguishing features of the early Mycenaean warrior and of the Mycenaean person in particular. But how precisely do Mycenaean brains, bodies and swords relate? This question has never been raised or systematically pursued despite its crucial bearing on our understanding of the Mycenaean self and the body (see however Molley 2008; Gosden 2008). The critical issue here is where do you draw the boundary between persons and things. And if we press the question of the boundary between the sword and the Mycenaean person two major possibilities can be seen to arise: The first is to retain the boundary of the skin, and the second, is to traverse the ordinary Mind/Body/World divide and view the sword as a dynamic integral component of the emerging Mycenaean embodied cognitive system. As an advocate of the second option, in what follows I want to develop my position more thoroughly.

Swords with a life of their own?

No doubt the recent proliferation of anthropological studies on the nature and boundaries of self and the body has made it all the more difficult to succumb to the gravitational pull of our own Westernised images and prototypes of personhood and individuality (e.g., Strathern 1988). Nonetheless, from an archaeological perspective many problems remain. It may well be, for example, that within Melanesian networks of social relation 'people and things have mutual biographies' (Gosden and Marshall 1999: 173), but on what basis can those mutual biographies be projected in the past, and if they are so projected how can we penetrate their culturally specific unfolding? As Strathern comments in a similar instance '[t]his was not a logic that the anthropologist had to excavate. People acted openly by it' (Strathern 1998: 139). Relations of this sort cannot be easily extrapolated from the material remains of the past.

I suggest that the following remark by E. Vermeule might offer an interesting alternative starting point: '*There is a sense that weapons are partly alive*' (Vermeule 1975: 13, my emphasis). What are we to make of this statement? In what possible sense can the Mycenaean sword be conceived as being 'partly alive'?

People with a strong inherent tendency for 'natural dualism' based on their strong conviction for the undisputable presence of a natural boundary between persons and things or else living and non-living things, would most certainly dismiss the heuristic value of such a statement as being an anthropomorphism of the 'empty words and poetic metaphors' type. Although some, might be willing to recognize the '*emic*' possibility that the Mycenaeans might have treated the sword as a living thing. From the '*etic*' viewpoint this possibility is perceived as a sign of some 'primitive mentality' or symbolic behaviour rather than as a sign of material agency (Malafouris 2008b). For the 'natural born dualist' to ascribe agency to the Mycenaean sword is simply a metaphoric way of looking at or speaking about things that carries with it no epistemic credit or real explanatory force. The animate character of the sword is a figment of the Mycenaean imagination and not a property of the sword itself.

The above line of criticism, legitimate as it might seem, carries with it, a number of problematic assumptions. To exemplify what I mean by that very briefly, it is that anthropomorphism – or what we may call *hylozoism* in this case – arises as a problem only for an external observer who presupposes the universal presence of a definite boundary that clearly articulates the ontological contours of the human *form – form* here is used in the Aristotelian sense of *morphe* meaning actuality – and which places agency at the center of this form in a soul-type manner. What such an observer fails to recognise is the possibility that it is this very boundary between humans and nonhumans that has been canceled or at least contested by the presence of the phenomenon that he or she construes or translates as anthropomorphism. In other words, my suggestion is that if from the perspective of a modern observer the previously quoted statement of Vermeule may seem a form of naïve anthropomorphising, this is simply because such an observer adheres to those boundaries that, as I intend to show in the following, the Mycenaean sword transgresses.

Indeed, we might think we know what a sword is and what it looks like but we need to go beyond the obvious if we are to grasp what it is like to be a Mycenaean sword. By that of course, I do not mean to imply either that we should construe the Mycenaean sword as being 'alive' in the conventional biological sense or in some other mystical or symbolic sense. The life of the sword neither breach the laws of physics nor require the intervention of some supernatural agency. The sword I want to suggest is 'alive' in a more basic albeit far more significant sense. It is 'alive' as a *material agent* that leads a cognitive life (Malafouris 2008b; Malafouris and Renfrew in press) by directly participating in the distributed cognitive system that defines the boundaries and contours of the Mycenaean lived body. The sword is 'alive' by having the role of a dynamic attractor that draws out of the Mycenaean body a novel predisposition for action not previously available. To deny the agency of the sword is to misconstrue the essence of the cognitive efficacy of material culture. Although things do not contain their principle of motion within them they may well operate as a 'final cause'. That is they operate as end-points, eliciting and drawing cognitive phenomena into being. The isolated object may not be in position to move in itself, but neither does the human hand in the absence of some 'intention in action' that arises only in the presence of such an object. The Mycenaean sword is full of intentions, urging the hand that grasp it or the eye that is staring at it to act in some way or another.

Alfred Gell has well illustrated the diverse ways in which agency 'can be invested in things, or can emanate from things' (Gell 1998: 18) and despite my disagreement with his distinction between 'primary' and 'secondary' agency an analogy between the Mycenaean sword and the Trobriand canoe 'prow-boards' might be useful. Focusing for example upon the highly elaborate and complex motifs that we often see inscribed on the gold pommels of the Mycenaean swords, one may identify techniques of visual 'captivation' effecting a 'cognitive blockage' similar to the one Gell 1998 illustrated in relation to the Trobriand canoe prowboards: 'the spectator becoming trapped within the index because the index embodies agency which is essentially undecipherable'.

Of course, it would be wrong to assume here that the animistic element that the Mycenaean sword incorporates is simply a by-product of human perceptual gestalts and of surface decoration. Visual captivation is only one instance of how the Mycenaean sword 'touches' the mindful body of the Mycenaean person. Indeed, beyond its function as a potent aesthetic object and fighting weapon, the sword is also a psychological weapon, that is, a cognitive artefact. It is important however, that this should not be understood in the usual symbolic/representational terms. The Mycenaean sword is not the passive symbolic conduit for some social statement of status or power which flows through the sword's midrib like electricity flows through a copper wire; it is not the vehicle for the transmission of a message but participates in it. The sword does not convey a message; the sword, *is the message* (see also McLuhan 1964). The Mycenaean sword is not simply a passive denomination 'in terms of which status came to be measured towards the end of the Middle Helladic period within mainland Greek societies' (Rutter 1993: 790), but redefines what Mycenaean status and value means as well as how they should be ascribed and measured. It is not the potential information content, not even the actual military or other use, of the sword that matters most from an embodied perspective. What matters, is primarily the change in inter-personal dynamics that the sword as a new technology of meaning brings with it.

For instance, I want to argue that the most important cognitive function of the Mycenaean sword relates to the ability of this cognitive artefact to promote the perception of powerful identifications between disparate phenomenal domains of experience. By this I mean that the Mycenaean sword can be seen as a 'boundary artefact' that operates in-between spaces, practices and realms. For example, the sword is a boundary artefact that establishes links between the Minoan and the Mycenaean worlds, but also between the sacred and the mundane, between the male and the female, between memory and oblivion, between life and death. But most importantly for my present concerns, the sword is a boundary artefact linking the realms of persons and things, the human and the nonhuman. It is this unique capacity of the sword to construct new affective ties that renders it the enactive sign *par excellence* of the Early Mycenaean world (see also Malafouris 2007). The early Mycenaean warrior is not simply using a new weapon but is extending and transforming his very self. He is not the same warrior in possession of a better weapon but a substantively different human/non-human hybrid. The sword does not merely represent a new aspect of the emerging Mycenaean world, but constitutes a novel concrete situational perspective of being-in-the-Mycenaean world. The intentional stance of the Mycenaean person is partially determined by the skilled embodied engagements made possible by the use of the sword. Representational content and 'aboutness' are not to be found inside the cabinet of the Mycenaean head they are instead negotiated between the hand and the sword (see also Malafouris 2008b).

The extended body: A sword for the body schema

But in what sense can we conceptualise the sword as a part of the Mycenaean body? In what other way if not that of pure metaphor can we conceive the Mycenaean sword as a body-part? In what other sense can this organic relation be understood in any proper sense without reducing it to some sort of symbolic representation inside the Mycenaean 'savage mind'? One part of the answer, I suggest, has been around for many decades. It can be found in Levy-Bruhl's *Notebooks* (1975) under the name 'law of participation' the crux of which can be summarised as follows: Human and non-human entities can be at the same time themselves and something else joined by connections that operate at a pre-conceptual level in a non-representational manner. As well summarised by Cazeneuve:

> By virtue of this law, things can be at the same time themselves and something else, and they can be joined by connections having nothing in common with those of our logic. What Tylor and Frazer explained by animism is in reality an effect of participation….[T]he body is not distinguished from the mind, and the self is not confined within the boundaries of the body but extends to what Levy-Bruhl calls the *appurtenances* (for example, hair, footprints, and clothing) (Cazeneuve 1972: 5–8).

The 'law of participation' has two major implications: On the one hand, it directly violates the logical principle of non-contradiction already established from the time of Aristotle, and on the other it collapses the distance between signifier and signified in an essentially non-representational manner. As long as participation exists there can be no representation, 'it is only when participation ceases to be felt directly that there is a symbol' (1975: 18). But how are we to account for this identity of substance? Levy-Bruhl has no systematic answer to offer. Instead he considers the phenomenon of participation as the characteristic of some 'pre-logical' mode of thinking. We need not succumb to this fault. There is nothing 'primitive' about the cognitive operations that the 'law of participation' describes, it is the 'law of participation' that is rather a 'primitive' – yet insightful and ethnographically grounded – exposition of what we call the *extended mind hypothesis* (Clark and Chalmers 1998). Indeed, stripped of its unfortunate 'evolutionary' and 'prelogical' connotations, the notion of participation furnishes us with an excellent means to conceptualise the complex affective linkages that underlie the co-substantial unity between brains, bodies and things. This ontological unity is very often elusive and difficult to pin down, but, I want to suggest, it can be brought into sharp focus by introducing another interesting notion that this time goes by the name of 'body schema' (Holmes and Spence 2004; Poeck and Orgass 1971). The notion of the 'body schema' was first introduced by Head and Holmes (1911–1912) (Oldfield and Zangwill, 1942) and currently denotes in cognitive neuroscience the complicated neuronal network responsible for continually tracking the position of our body in space, the dynamic configurations of our limb segments and the shape of our body surface. In other words it can be understood as an unconscious body map responsible for the constant monitoring of the execution of actions with the different body parts. According to Melzack (1990) the body schema although largely prewired by genetics it is open to continuous shaping influences of experience, and what is important to note in this context is the effect that external objects and prostheses appear to have in the cognitive topography of this space. More specifically, not only behavioural and imaging studies of visuotactile interactions have shown that tool-use extends the 'peripersonal space' – i.e. the behavioural space that immediately surrounds the body – but more important, recent neuroscientfic findings suggest that the systematic association between the body and inanimate objects (like clothes, jewelerly, tools, etc.) can result into a temporary or permanent incorporation of the latter into the body schema (Berti and Frassinetti 2000; Farnè and Làdavas, 2000; Farnè *et al.* 2005;

Flugel 1930; Graziano *et al.* 2002; Holmes and Spence 2006; Holmes *et al.* 2005: 62, 2004; Iriki *et al.* 1996; Maravita and Iriki 2004; Maravita *et al.* 2002, 2003). An observation which essentially means *that objects and tools attached to the body can become a part of the body as the physical body itself*. Head and Holmes referred to this phenomenon with their famous comment that 'a woman's power of localization may extend to the feather in her hat' (1911–12: 188).

However, to understand the drastic implications of the above in our conventional understanding of the active and embodied character of material culture and its relation to the lived body I want to use the following quote from Berlucchi and Aglioti summarising one of their recent breakthrough findings published originally at *Neuroreport* in 1996:

> After a large right hemisphere stroke, a 73-year-old woman, while showing no sign of being demented, exhibited a total unawareness of her severe left-arm paralysis and in fact repeatedly affirmed that the paralysed hand belonged to someone else. The peculiarity about this patient was that while she was able to see and describe the rings she had worn for years and was currently wearing on her left, now disowned hand, she resolutely denied their ownership. By contrast, she immediately recognized these rings as her own (and produced much veridical autobiographical information about them) when they were shifted to her right hand, or displayed in front of her. Similarly, she promptly acknowledged ownership of other personal belongings that, in her previous experience, had not been ordinarily associated with the left hand (for example, a keyholder or a comb), even when she saw such objects in contact with that hand. Denial of ownership of the left-hand rings was thus conditional not only on their being seen on the disowned hand, but also on the existence of a previous systematic association between them and that hand. It was as if a conjoint visual representation of the left hand and its rings had been retained in her memory but expunged from her self awareness, implying that before the stroke the rings thus represented had become part of an extended, primarily visual body schema (Berlucchi and Aglioti 1997: 561).

I recognise, of course, that findings from neuropathology, like those described above, cannot be easily extrapolated to fit the archaeological constructions and conceptualisations of the human body. Nonetheless, I suggest they deserve explicit archaeological and anthropological attention for two main reasons: The first reason is that neuropathology has the power to expose the hidden interior of many hermetically sealed 'blackboxes' of what Knappett calls, drawing on Mauss, human *bio-psycho-social* reality (2005: 11). We all, under normal circumstances, share a common intuition that we own and control our bodies. Luckily, under normal conditions, we do not question whether it is actually our hands that move or our fingers that press the keyboard of our PC. We might very often experience a certain 'neglect', as for example, when getting 'immersed' in a certain act to such a degree that we loose any conscious awareness about what certain parts of our bodies are doing or about how they do what they are doing, but nonetheless, the moment we think about the act we immediately regained our 'partially' lost sense of body ownership. Whether we have been modern or not (Latour 1993), we certainly have a body the ownership and control of which we may sometime question at the social or symbolic/conceptual level, but never at the physical level. This is precisely what the neuropathology of bodily disorders does.

Brain lesions can induce profound changes in the body schema and our bodily awareness. Simply imagine that intending to move your index finger you see instead your thumb move and one can easily understand the implications of such phenomena in our sense of agency and self-recognition. *Anosognosic* stroke patients would deny that they are impaired at all and right brain damage may result in the denial of ownership of a body part (Aglioti *et al.* 1996). In this context one would certainly add the so-called *phantom limb* phenomena very often reported among amputees (Melzack 1992; Ramachandran *et al.* 1995). The opposite phenomenon, that is, of multiple *supernumeracy* of body parts (mostly hands or feet) is also reported not the case of amputees but brain-damaged patients (Halligan *et al.* 1993, 1995; Sellal *et al.* 1996). Indeed, disturbances of body schema that are caused by brain lesions can radically alter the way the body is perceived and represented and challenge our concepts of agency, self and the body by exposing the underlying complexity and fluidity of things that we often conceive as fixed, given and natural. That those insights will usually be subsumed under some Western medical categories of normality/abnormality to serve the purposes of our modern laboratories of life need not deter anthropology and archaeology from exploring the possibilities that those data offer in the context of our own hypotheses. This brings me to the second, and probably more important reason for looking at these phenomena, which is that although current neuroscientific and neuropathological studies may possess this unique experimental capacity of demystifying the anthropologically and archaeologically inaccessible parts of human bodily experience, more often than not, they lack the theoretical framework and conceptual background to understand the wider consequences of their findings. We should bear in mind that notions like 'partibility' and 'dividuality' (Strathern 1988) do not figure either in the vocabulary or the general mind

frame of a neuroscientist although in some cases, I suggest, they offer a possible explanatory avenue for a great deal of neuroscientific data that are usually subsumed in one or another 'homuncular' hypothesis of body representation.

Final discussion

Let us go back to the Mycenaean swords and bodies: Does our previous discussion implies that the Mycenaean sword has left a permanent and distinguishable mark on the soft tissue of the Mycenaean cerebral architecture? The neuroscience of self and the body has left little room for doubting that this was probably indeed the case. We should bear in mind that according to the perspective of *neural constructivism* 'the representational features of the cortex are built from the dynamic interaction between neural growth mechanisms and environmentally derived neural activity' (Quartz and Sejnowski 1997: 537). But why is this important? How does it help us to answer our question of what is it like to be a Mycenaean self and body?

Let me clarify, that 'what is it like to be' questions are phenomenological questions, and phenomenological questions when raised from an archaeological perspective do not invite or afford definitive answers. Phenomenological questions, at least in archaeology, serve a different role: they have a critical function. In the context of this paper, this function is to remind us that (a) physical bodies, rather than simply our ideas about bodies, are changing; and (b) that bodies do not change in isolation but in relation to the material reality they become attached in different historical contexts. The major implication of that, and this is what constitutes the crux of my argument in this paper, is that the common distinction between a physical and a social body – the first being the domain of life sciences and the second of anthropology/archaeology – can no longer be sustained.

Indeed, the act of grasping the Mycenaean sword involves much more than a purely mechanical process of visuo-proprioceptive realignment of the Mycenaean body; it is also an act of incorporation which provides a new basis for self-recognition and awareness. If the Mycenaean sword looks as if it is 'alive' this is because in this case the boundary between biology and culture as well as between mind and matter has been transgressed. In the words of Alfred Gell, 'Internal (mental processes) and outside (transactions in objectified personhood) have fused together, mind and reality are one' (Gell 1998: 231).

The centre of consciousness and bodily awareness for the Mycenaean person, and for the warrior in particular, is not some 'internal' Cartesian 'I', but the tip of the sword. Through the tip of the sword the Mycenaean person is simultaneously reach out, makes sense of and apprehends the world. The sword as an enactive sign brings about a whole new semiotic field of embodied activity offering a new means of engaging the world and as such a novel understanding of what is to be a Mycenaean person and body. Of course, my suggestion does not mean to imply that the complex phenomenological map of the emerging Mycenaean self can be reduced solely to the cognitive space articulated between the sword and the warrior's body. I simply propose that this association offer us an instance – albeit, a very significant one – of what it is to become a Mycenaean person.

Acknowledgements

I want to thank John Robb and Dušan Borić for the invitation to contribute in this volume. I want to thank also Barry Molloy and an anonymous referee for the valuable comments. Research was funded by the Balzan Foundation and also supported by a 'European Platform for Life Sciences, Mind Sciences and the Humanities' grant by the Volkswagen Stiftung for the 'Body Project: interdisciplinary investigations on bodily experiences'.

Bibliography

Aglioti, S.A., Smania, N., Manfredi, M. and Berlucchi, G. 1996. Disownership of left hand and objects related to it in a patient with right brain damage. *NeuroReport*, 8: 293–296.

Berlucchi, G. and Aglioti, S.A. 1997. The body in the brain: Neural bases of corporeal awareness. *Trends in Neurosciences*, 20: 560–564.

Berti, A. and Frassinetti, F. 2000. When far becomes near: Remapping of space by tool-use. *Journal of Cognitive Neuroscience*, 12: 415–420.

Campbell, J. 1995. The body image and self-consciousness. In *The Body and the Self*, edited by J.L. Burmúdez, A.J. Marcel and N. Eilan, pp. 29–42. Cambridge, MA: MIT Press.

Cazeneuve, J. 1972. *Lucien Levy-Bruhl*. Oxford: Basil Blakwell.

Crowley, J.L. 1989. Subject matter in Aegean art: The crucial changes. Iin *Transition. Le Monde Egéen du Bronze Moyen au Bronze Récent*, (*Aegaeum 3.*), edited by R. Laffineur, pp. 203–214. Liège: Universitè de l'Etat à Liège.

Clark, A. and Chalmers, D. 1998. The Extended Mind. *Analysis* 58 (1): 10–23.

Deger-Jalkotzy, S., 1999. Military prowess and social status in Mycenean Greece. In *Polemos: Le Contexte Guerrier en Egée a l' Age du Bronze*, (*Aegeum 19*), edited by R. Laffineur, pp. 121–131. Austin: University of Texas at Austin Program in Aegean Scripts and Prehistory.

Dickinson, O.T.P.K., 1977. *The Origins of Mycenean Civilisation*. Studies in Mediterranean Archaeology 49. Göteburg: Paul Åströms Förlag.

Douglas, M. 1970. *Natural Symbols: Explorations in Cosmology*. Barrie & Jenkins.

Farnè A, Iriki A and Làdavas E. 2005. Shaping multisensory action-space with tools: Evidence from patients with cross-modal extinction. *Neuropsychologia*, 43: 238–248.

Farnè, A. and Làdavas, E. 2000. Dynamic size-change of hand peripersonal space following tool use. *NeuroReport*, 11: 1645–1649.

Fowler C. 2002. Body parts: personhood in the Manx Neolithic. In *Thinking Through the Body: Archaeologies of Corporeality*, edited by Y. Hamilakis, M. Pluciennik and S. Tarlow, pp. 47–69. New York: Kluwer Academic/Plenum.

Fowler C. 2003. *The Archaeology of Personhood: An Anthropological Approach*. London: Routledge

Flugel, J.C. 1930. *The Psychology of Clothes*. London: Leonard & Virginia Woolf.

Gallagher, S. 2005. *How the Body Shapes the Mind*. Oxford: Oxford University Press.

Gallagher, S. 1995. Body schema and intentionality. In *The Body and the Self*, edited by J. L. Burmúdez, A.J. Marcel and N. Eilan, pp. 225–244. Cambridge, MA: MIT Press.

Gell, A. 1998. *Art and Agency: An Anthropological Theory*. Oxford: Oxford University Press.

Goldin-Meadow, S. and Wagner, S.M. 2005. How our hands help us learn. *Trends in Cognitive Sciences* 9 (5): 234–241.

Goldin-Meadow, S. 2003. *Hearing Gesture: How Our Hands Help Us Think*. Cambridge, MA: Harvard University Press.

Gosden, C. 2001. Making sense: archaeology and aesthetics. *World Archaeology* 33(2): 163–7.

Gosden, C., 2008. Social ontologies. *Philosophical Transactions of the Royal Society of London B* 363: 2003–2010.

Gosden C. and Marshall Y. 1999. The Cultural Biography of Objects. *World Archaeology* 31 (2): 169–178.

Graziano, M.S.A., Alisharan, S.E., Hu, X.T. and Gross, C.G. 2002. The clothing effect: Tactile neurons in the precentral gyrus do not respond to the touch of the familiar primate chair. *Proceedings of the National Academy of Sciences USA*, 99: 11930–11933.

Hamilakis, Y., Pluciennik, M. and Tarlow, S. (ed) 2002. *Thinking Through the Body: Archaeologies of Corporeality*. New York: Kluwer Academic/Plenum

Halligan, P.W., Marshall, J.C. and Wade, D.T. 1993. Three arms: A case study of supernumerary phantom limb after right hemisphere stroke. *Journal of Neurology, Neurosurgery and Psychiatry* 56: 159–166.

Halligan, P.W., Marshall, J.C. and Wade, D.T. 1995. Unilateral somatoparaphrenia after right hemisphere stroke: A case description. *Cortex* 31: 173–182.

Head, H. and Holmes, G. 1911–12 Sensory disturbances from cerebral lesions. *Brain* 34: 102–254

Holmes, N.P. and Spence, C. 2004. The body schema and the multisensory representation(s) of peripersonal space. *Cognitive Processing* 5: 94–105.

Holmes N.P., Calvert G.A. and Spence, C. 2004. Extending or projecting peripersonal space with tools: Multisensory interactions highlight only the distal and proximal ends of tools. *Neuroscience Letters* 372(1–2): 62–67.

Iriki, A., Tanaka, M. and Iwamura, Y. 1996. Coding of modified body schema during tool use by macaque postcentral neurones. *NeuroReport* 7: 2325–2330.

Johnson, M. 1987. *The Body in the Mind: The Bodily Basis of Meaning, Imagination, and Reason*. Chicago: University of Chicago Press.

Karo, G. 1930–3. *Die Schachtgraber von Mykenai*. Munich: Bruckmann.

Knappett C. 2005. *Thinking Through Material Culture: An Interdisciplinary Perspective*. Pennsylvania: University of Pennsylvania Press.

Knappett, C., 2006. Beyond Skin: Layering and Networking in Art and Archaeology. *Cambridge Archaeological Journal* 16: 239-251.

Kopytoff, I. 1986. The cultural biography of things: Commoditization as process. In *The Social Life of Things*, edited by A. Appadurai, pp. 64–91. Cambridge: Cambridge University Press.

Lakoff, G. 1987. *Women, fire, and dangerous things: what categories reveal about the mind*. Chicago, IL; London, UK: University of Chicago Press.

Lakoff, G. and Johnson, M. 1999. *Philosophy in the Flesh: The Embodied Mind and Its Challenge to Western Thought*. New York: Basic Books.

Latour, B. 1993 *We Have Never Been Modern*. Cambridge, MA: Harvard University Press.

Levy-Bruhl, L. 1975. *The Notebooks on Primitive Mentality*. Oxford: Blakwell.

Malafouris, L. 2004. The Cognitive Basis of Material Engagement: Where Brain, Body and Culture Conflate. In *Rethinking Materiality: The Engagement of Mind with the Material World*, edited by. E. DeMarrais, C. Gosden and C. Renfrew, pp. 53–62. Cambridge: The McDonald Institute for Archaeological Research.

Malafouris, L., 2007. Before and Beyond Representation: Towards an enactive conception of the Palaeolithic Image. In *Image and Imagination: A Global History of Figurative Representation*, edited by C. Renfrew and I. Morley, pp. 289–302. Cambridge: McDonald Institute for Archaeological Research.

Malafouris, L., 2008a. Between brains, bodies and things: tectonoetic awareness and the extended self. *Philosophical Transactions of the Royal Society of London B* 363: 1993–2002.

Malafouris, L. 2008b. At the Potter's Wheel: An argument for Material Agency. In *Material Agency: Towards a Non-anthropocentric Approach*, edited by C. Knappett and L. Malafouris, pp. 19–36. New York: Springer.

Malafouris, L. and Renfrew, C. (eds.), forthcoming. *The Cognitive Life of Things: Recasting the Boundaries of the Mind*. Cambridge: The McDonald Institute for Archaeological Research.

Maravita, A. and Iriki, A. 2004. Tools for the body (schema). *Trends in Cognitive Sciences* 8: 79–86.

Maravita, A., Spence, C. and Driver, J. 2003. Multisensory integration and the body schema: Close to hand and within reach. *Current Biology* 13: 531–539.

Maravita, A., Spence, C., Kennett, S. and Driver, J. 2002. Tool-use changes multimodal spatial interactions between vision and touch in normal humans. *Cognition* 83: 25–34.

McLuhan, M. 1964/2001. *Understanding Media: The Extensions of Man*. London: Routledge & Kegan Paul.

Melzack, R. 1992. Phantom limbs. *Scientific American* 266 (April): 120–126.

Molloy, B., 2008. Martial arts and materiality: a combat archaeology perspective on Aegean swords of the fifteenth and fourteenth centuries BC. *World Archaeology* 40(1): 116–134.

Mylonas, G.E. 1973a. *O Taphikos Kyklos B ton Mykenon*. Athens: Archaeological Society.

Oldfield, R.C. and Zangwill, O.L. 1942. Head's concept of the schema and its application in contemporary British psychology. Part I. Head's concept of the schema. *British Journal of Psychology* 32: 267–286.

Poeck, K. and Orgass, B. 1971. The concept of the body schema: A critical review and some experimental results. *Cortex* 7: 254–277.

Quartz, S.R. and Sejnowski, T.J. 1997. The neural basis of cognitive development: a constructivist manifesto. *Behavioral and Brain Sciences* 20(4): 537–96.

Ramachandran, V.S., Rogers-Ramachandran, D. and Cobb, S. 1995. Touching the phantom limb. *Nature* 377: 489–490.

Renfrew C. 2004. Towards a theory of material engagement. In *Rethinking Materiality: The Engagement of Mind with the Material World*, edited by E. DeMarrais, C. Gosden and C. Renfrew, pp. 23–31. Cambridge: The McDonald Institute for Archaeological Research.

Rutter, J.B. 1993. The prepalatial Bronze Age of the southern and central Greek Mainland. *American Journal of Archaeology* 97 (4): 745–97.

Sandars, N.K. 1963. Later Aegean Bronze Swords. *American Journal of Archaeology* 67: 117–53.

Sellal, F., Renaseau-leclerc, C. and Labrecque, R. 1996. The man with 6 arms. An analysis of supernumerary phantom limbs after right hemisphere stroke. *Revue Neurologique* (Paris) 152: 190–195.

Schliemann, H. 1880. *Mycenae. A Narrative of Researches and Discoveries at Mycenae and Tiryns*. New York: Charles Scribner's Sons, Bell & Howell Co.

Strathern, M. 1988. *The Gender of the Gift*. Berkeley, CA: University of California Press.

Strathern, M. 1998. Social relations and the idea of externality. In *Cognition and Material Culture: the Archaeology of Symbolic Storage*, edited by C. Renfrew and C. Scarre, pp. 131–145. Cambridge: The McDonald Institute for Archaeological Research.

Thomas J. 2002. Archaeology's humanism and the materiality of the body. In *Thinking Through the Body: Archaeologies of Corporeality*, edited by Y. Hamilakis, M. Pluciennik and S. Tarlow. pp. 29–45. New York: Kluwer Academic Press.

Vermeule, E. 1975. *The Art of the Shaft Graves of Mycenae*. Cincinnati: University of Cincinnati.

Voutsaki, S. 1993. *Society and Culture in the Mycenean World: An Analysis of Mortuary Practices in the Argolid, Thessaly and the Dodecanese*. PhD Diss., University of Cambridge.

Voutsaki, S. 1997. The Creation of Value and Prestige in the Aegean Late Bronze Age. *Journal of European Archaeology* 5(2): 34–52.

Warnier, J.P. 2001. A Praxeological Approach to Subjectivation in a Material World. *Journal of Material Culture* 6(1): 5–24.

Wilson, F.R. 1998. *The Hand: How its use shapes the brain, language, and human culture*. New York: Pantheon Books.

13

Embodied persons and heroic kings in Late Classic Maya imagery

Susan D. Gillespie

Embodied persons and heroic kings in Late Classic Maya imagery

Current perspectives in social theories of the body come into play in interpreting anthropomorphic images created by the Maya civilisation, spanning southern Mexico, Guatemala and Belize. In the Classic Period (ca. AD 250–900) Maya artists put great emphasis on the human body in monumental and portable media, depicting both idealised and historical persons. Their artworks have long been considered the most 'naturalistic' within the Mesoamerican culture area, whereas styles of neighboring peoples are characterised as abstract or schematic (Pasztory 1990–91). Despite the appearance of verisimilitude, however, Maya artists eschewed portraiture and adhered to certain visual conventions, especially in monumental imagery (Houston 2001: 207; Schele and Miller 1986: 66). For example, basic body and facial types are sexually neutral (Joyce 1996: 169), and rulers known to have lived well into old age are never shown as elderly (Grube 2004: 248).

These anthropomorphic images should therefore not be taken as faithful depictions of reality, even where accompanying inscriptions may name the pictured persons as unique individuals. Nevertheless, we can consider how their production and display 'actively constituted theories of the body' (Joyce 1998:147). Because most of the depictions in stone sculpture are of rulers, we can use them to explore Maya theories about the body of the king. Images of kings and other courtly figures present stereotypes of, and insights into, those 'aspects of ancient Maya personhood [that] were most highly charged, the subjects of greatest interest and, potentially, of most contestation' (Meskell and Joyce 2003: 23).

Among the insights gained in recent studies of the bodies of Maya kings, as discussed below, is the totalising quality referenced by their regalia. Certain symbols worn or held by the king indicated his singular ability to unite social and cosmic differentiation within his person (Houston *et al.* 2006: 6). I suggest that this symbolic use of the body – as a framework for inscribed messages – was paralleled by a growing artistic emphasis on embodiment – practices and experiences that had physical consequences for the body. I further argue that these bodily consequences were incorporated into the artistic repertoire as part of a well-recognised stylistic change in figural representations in the Late Classic period starting in the seventh century.

These two analytical perspectives conform to distinguishable traditions in contemporary theorising about the body. One is the 'semiotic use of the body' to serve 'as representations of the identity of the social person' (Turner 1995: 146). In post-structuralism the body is treated as a system of meaning and conceptual object of discourse – 'a kind of readable text upon which social reality is "inscribed"' (Csordas 1994: 12; Turner 1994: 28). An alternative view emphasises bodiliness, lived experience, and processes of self-productive activity (Csordas 1990, 1994; Meskell 1996; Turner 1994; Turner 2003). This contrast in perspectives has been characterized by Csordas (1994) as the distinction between body and embodiment, representation and being-in-the-world, and more generally, semiotics and phenomenology.

Treating these perspectives as complementary (following Csordas 1994), and recognizing an analytical separation of 'body' and 'person' (e.g., Douglas's [1970] 'two bodies'; see also Kantorowicz 1957) instead of merely substituting the former for the latter (e.g.,

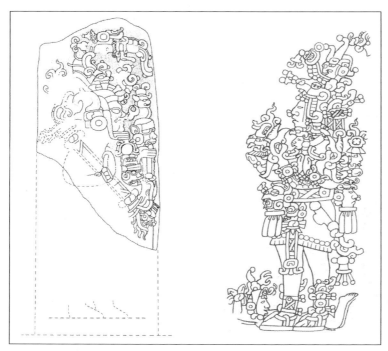

Figure 13.1. Early Classic images of kings. Left: Tikal St. 29 (AD 292), front side, top portion only. Limestone. Fragment length approximately 1.4 m. (Jones and Satterthwaite 1982: Fig. 29a; reprinted with permission of the University of Pennsylvania Museum of Archaeology and Anthropology, Philadelphia) Right: Image of a ruler on the Leiden Plaque (AD 320). Although not a monumental portrayal, the depiction of the ruler matches those on stelae of this time period. Incised jade. Length 21.7 cm. Rijkismuseum voor Volkenkunde, Leiden, Holland. (Drawing by Linda Schele, © David Schele, courtesy Foundation for the Advancement of Mesoamerican Studies, Inc., www.famsi.org, Linda Schele Archive #2007)

Strathern 1994: 43), raises an investigative question: To what extent and in what contexts do semiotic and phenomenological aspects (body and embodiment) coincide or cohere within a society? More specifically, how can we understand the construction of an 'embodied person'? In the case of Classic Maya kings, the quality of totality claimed by royal persons and referenced via the symbols on their bodies should have been realized in appropriate bodily practices that may also have been signaled in imagery. I endeavor to show how the greater degree of 'naturalism' attributed to Late Classic figural representations is a clue to the importance of the embodiment of kings as an index of their totalising agency and their capacity for action.

Symbolic and indexical signs of totality

In a seminal art historical study Proskouriakoff (1950) detailed important changes in Maya sculptural traditions from the Late Preclassic through the Classic periods. The most important sculptural type was the free-standing limestone stela with bas-relief carving on one or both of its broad faces, usually depicting a single standing human figure now recognizable as a paramount lord, the ruler of a polity. Accompanying

inscriptions typically name the ruler and provide a date for the event(s) commemorated on the stela in the Long Count calendar. In the Late Preclassic (early centuries BC–ca. AD 250) through the Early Classic (250–600), the king was most often shown in stiff profile with frontal shoulders, rather comparable to Egyptian dynastic art (Kubler 1984: 248), or alternatively in a pure profile posture.

The rulers are garbed in costume elements and carry regalia iconographically identifiable as 'supernatural insignia and deity representations' (Pasztory 1978: 125). In the Late Preclassic and Early Classic periods these power-charged objects were often visually overwhelming (Figure 13.1). On the fragmentary Tikal St. 29 (AD 292), for example, the ruler 'stands in profile, obscured by a veritable thicket of ornament, including feathers, scrolls, and masks' (Pasztory 1978: 116). The king's body was a framework upon which to hang valued and sacred objects – heirlooms of the royal house and other signs of rank or title. Only facial features and glimpses of appendages serve as minimal reference points to his bodily presence.

Among the items on the king's body were objects and signs that represented the totality of the cosmos, indicating the king's positioning at the cosmic center. They include icons of the 'world tree' as axis mundi

(Baudez 2000; Schele and Miller 1986). Baudez (2000: 135) thus suggested that 'the king's costume presents his body as a metaphor for the universe.' This quality Baudez deemed fitting for the king, 'not only because he stands above all men, but because he is the man *par excellence*, the representative and quintessence of his community and of all the men that compose it' (2000: 135).

In this manner the Maya king's body referenced the 'body politic', incorporating all other members of his state (following Kantorowicz 1957). Tarlow (this volume) makes a similar use of Kantorowciz's study of the king's 'two bodies' in medieval Europe to argue that the effigy of Oliver Cromwell represented the body politic. The effigial body in European royal funerary practice wore the symbols of state while the literal body, subjected to natural processes of decay in contradistinction to the uncorrupted effigy, was kept out of sight.

In Baudez's (2000: 143) interpretation, important women (usually mother or spouse of the king) associated with some of the same regalia as depicted on the stone carvings would have functioned as the ruler's alter ego. However, a reading of royal totality was also indicated via gendered *difference*. Joyce (1996, 2000a) has shown that on Maya sculptures 'male' and 'female' were treated as complementary qualities, divorced from sexual reproduction and signaled principally by costume and titles that together formed a unity. These images 'simultaneously convey gender difference and encompass it' (1996: 182). In the Late Classic it became more common to couple male and female depictions, putting them individually on paired stelae or together in a single scene (1996: 172ff). In the typical depictions on these monumental images, royal women's costume references the earth's surface and sea – the totality of horizontal space. Royal male dress includes the world tree symbol, such that their bodies formed a vertical axis that, paired with the female, formed a spatial cosmic totality: the horizontal and vertical extent of the universe, the periphery and the center (Joyce 1996: 172, 2000a: 76–77).

Significantly, a few Late Classic male rulers were occasionally shown wearing items of female costume (e.g., Palenque's Tablet of the Temple of the Foliated Cross, Copan's Stela H). Joyce interpreted the wearing of an item of female dress by the male ruler as 'a symbolic assertion of totalizing ability' (Joyce 1996: 187) via an innovated 'encompassing gender that ... transcended and unified bodily differences of all kinds' (Joyce 2000a: 79). These depictions evidenced 'the common claim of Classic Maya rulers to unite in themselves all the social differences that divided their people' (2000a: 81).

Concern for social difference was also referenced by the affective aspects of bodily experience. Houston (2001; see also Houston *et al.* 2006: 189–190) noted that another Late Classic innovation in monumental imagery was the depiction of certain emotions by secondary figures, often shown in more active, even contorted poses compared to passive primary figures. In Classic figural art as a whole, rulers and their queens are usually depicted as 'expressionless', no matter what their personal situation might be (Houston *et al.* 2006: 189). However, in Late Classic scenes of rulers with defeated enemies taken in battle (elite personages themselves), the victorious paramount remains impassive but now the captives lose control of themselves and thereby 'accentuate their humiliation and drastically reduced status' (2001: 211). Houston (2001: 215) suggested this contrast in depictions of emotional expression in the Late Classic 'may reflect a growing concern with social differentiation' in the more complex and competitive political arenas of that time period, while adhering to the ideal of 'unexpressed emotion and rigid self-control' of lords and other members of the royal court (Houston *et al.* 2006: 198).

Thus, Late Classic representations especially were concerned with expressing, in stereotypical ways, sociocosmic differences and their encompassment by the ruler in terms of signs on the body and the presence/absence of emotion, a bodily affect. Furthermore, emotions and other physical aspects of the body differed depending on the immediate experience; for example, whether the lord was victor or humiliated captive. Increasing social distance in the Late Classic and the resort to both symbolic and affective aspects of the body to simultaneously indicate difference and its abrogation thus became incorporated into Maya sculptural styles.

The emergence of the body of Late Classic Maya kings

It was also in the Late Classic that images of kings on stelae began to be depicted with full frontal view of the body, although the face was more often still in profile (Proskouriakoff 1950: 112) (Figure 13.2a). This pose persisted until the end of this sculptural tradition at about AD 900 (Kubler 1984: 248). Concomitant with this modification in body posture from profile to frontal were significant changes in composition and greater use of figural imagery on other sculptural media (lintels and wall panels) as well as portable objects. Principal figures were often shown engaged in restrained action, sometimes with secondary persons,

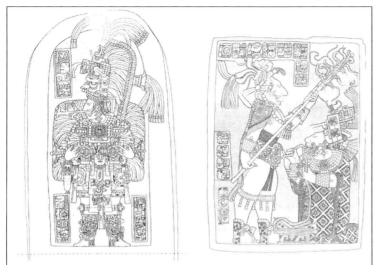

Figure 13.2: Late Classic images of kings. Left: Tikal St. 16 (AD 711), front. Limestone. Height above ground level approximately 2.23 m. (Jones and Satterthwaite 1982: Fig. 22; reprinted with permission of the University of Pennsylvania Museum of Archaeology and Anthropology, Philadelphia) Right: Yaxchilan Lintel 24 (AD 725). Limestone. Height 1.1 m. British Museum. (Graham and von Euw 1977: 53; Drawing, YAZ: Lnt. 24 from Corpus of Maya Hieroglyphic Inscriptions, Vol. 3, Part 1, Yaxchilan, reproduced courtesy of the President and Fellows of Harvard College)

such that these artworks are considered narrative rather than merely hierarchic (Pasztory 1978: 127).

Pasztory (1978) related the change in the depiction of king's bodies described by Proskouriakoff to the influence of historical contacts with Teotihuacan, the great capital in central Mexico. In Teotihuacan painted murals, artists maintained a sharp distinction between figures of humans and deities: humans were shown in profile and deities in frontal view, and humans were noticeably smaller when shown together with deities (Pasztory 1978: 117). In Pasztory's view, this divine/mortal separation effected via body size and position made the shift to the frontal depictions of rulers on Late Classic Maya stelae signally important. It indicated 'a conscious attempt to associate the ruler with the supernatural rather than the human world' (1978: 117), i.e., 'an equation of the ruler with the gods' (1978: 125).

Nevertheless, Maya kings were sacred long before the Late Classic period. From the beginning of the dynastic era (the Late or Terminal Preclassic), images of their bodies, as noted above, were loaded down with power-filled objects, and rulers were shown manipulating small deity images themselves, including the sun deity. References to their persons included the name of the sun (deity) *k'in* (Colas 2003). The ruler also assumed the epithet *k'uhul ajaw*, meaning 'sacred' or 'holy' lord. This titular reference to qualities shared with the divine served to differentiate the paramount lord from the other *ajawob* (lords) in his and rival courts. Although this title has been traced back to the Late Preclassic, it became common only after about AD 500 (Houston and Stuart 1996: 295–296).

Pasztory's (1978) thesis was that the change in posture on stelae was a different means for linking divine and mortal qualities in the bodies of Maya kings than that used previously, when he was covered with sacred objects. However, there is more to the seventh-century change in representational conventions than the adoption of frontality, and its simple explanation as a foreign-derived sign of divinity appears unlikely. Greater attention to the human body was also being accomplished by other stylistic innovations. As Pasztory (1978: 121) noted, beginning in the Late Classic 'the corporeal quality of human figures was indicated by an emphasis on the rendering of unbroken body outlines and on the revival of three-dimensional sculpture.' Natural body curves are quite discernable even where clothing covers the body (Figure 13.2b). On Palenque's bas-relief stone and stucco tablets, male figures wear little clothing, showing increased artistic emphasis on 'elegant body outlines' and musculature (1978: 121). Within Late Classic sculpture more generally flat relief gave way to rounded, and deep relief as well as three-dimensional techniques were developed, in some cases appearing rather suddenly (1978: 122).

In sum, in these artworks 'the ruler has a physical presence, due either to high relief, carving in the round, or the unobstructed outlines of the body, and the supernatural insignia and deity figures surround him without impinging on his person' (Pasztory 1978: 125). This is an inversion of the Early Classic scalar relationship between body and regalia, the inner essence and its outer covering. In the seventh century the body as a unified entity emerged out from behind the trappings of regalia that previously had almost obliterated it or had made it appear to be composed of discrete anatomical parts strung together with costume items. With some exceptions, the monumental representations still tended to give prominence to costume elements, but those objects were arranged on a unified and noticeably corporeal body, giving the impression that they are actually being held or worn. Thus, it is the Late Classic images that achieved what Westerners appreciate as a greater sense of 'naturalism', both in depictions of human figures and in their settings and narrative compositions. Such naturalism of the body may have concealed the exercise of power (Joyce 1998: 157); indeed, these media 'were part of the material apparatus' through which such concepts of embodiment were naturalised (Joyce 2005: 147).

Greater attention to the physical body (including emotions as described above) implies that the embodied individual was important to representational conventions, despite the general impression–stated explicitly by Baudez (2000: 135) – that the focus on costume 'contrasts with the neglect of the royal person's anatomy.' As already noted, depictions of persons were still generic rather than individualised, and even gender was indicated in monumental images by costume and naming conventions rather than by physical differences. Nevertheless, the body became important in the Late Classic as more than just a framework for the right assortment of symbols.

These artworks seemingly take into account what current social theorists have come to realise: the body is not a naturally prior, blank surface for inscription; instead, bodies are produced out of intersubjective performances and practices in interactions with the material world and other social persons (Grosz 1994: x; Turner 1994). Given the semiotic use of the king's body as a carrier of royal regalia referencing unity and encompassment of difference, it is worth investigating whether the production of the king's body would have included life experiences appropriate for a totalising person. Were the Maya king's 'two bodies' treated as contrasts of one another – the immortal symbol of the political collective versus the individual 'mortal coil' subject to decrepitude and death – or did their qualities coincide? Were both aspects revealed in the imagery, or only the 'body politic'?

The evidence indicates that in the Late Classic period the semiotic and phenomenological aspects were entwined in the production and representation of the royal body.[1] The setting for the production of the king's body was the royal court, and protocols of body management were an important aspect of Maya courtly life (Inomata and Houston 2001; Miller and Martin 2004). The palace was notably a place of

consumption – of food and drink, music, dance, ritual and other performances, and cloth along with finely crafted objects (Webster 2001: 147–148). These latter objects – especially painted pottery vessels intended for serving food and beverages – form a significant additional medium for depicting court personnel and courtly life. Made by and for aristocrats, they were exchanged among noble families and deposited in elite tombs. In the Late Classic, hieroglyphic inscriptions in additional to figural images were painted on vessels destined for aristocratic consumption. Many of the texts state the vessels' intended contents – especially maize or chocolate drinks (Houston *et al.* 2006: 108; Reents-Budet 2001: 75) – indicating the important roles played by individual food items in courtly cuisine.

As Tarlow (this volume) observes, the movement of substances into or out of the body constitutes an exchange between the body and the world. Feasting is characteristic of royalty in many premodern societies, indicative of 'the prodigious appetites expected of the royal body, which summons foodstuffs that no mortal could consume at one sitting' (Houston *et al.* 2006: 7). Whatever the pragmatic function of courtly banquets in terms of allocating resources and loyalties between a ruler and his subjects, Classic Maya imagery is notable in appearing 'to have stressed royal needs and royal satiety, not what others received from royalty' (2006: 130). In other words, 'ingestion by the ruler' is the principal event depicted in images of courtly consumption (2006: 130).

The most frequently portrayed individual on this corpus of elite painted pottery is the *k'uhul ajaw*, who 'occupies the greatest amount of pictorial space' (Reents-Budet 2001: 213). His body is often painted in a different color than those of other figures in the same scene (2001: 213). Significantly, within these non-monumental images some rulers' bodies show what look like the effects of over-consumption of food and drink. They are so depicted on the vessels that held their comestibles, especially cylindrical pots for serving chocolate beverage (cocoa beans were a major tribute item owed to the lords [Houston *et al.* 2006: 108]). An extreme example is a Late Classic ruler of Motul de San José, nicknamed the 'Fat Cacique' (chief) by art historians because of his corpulence (Figure 13.3). He is so consistently depicted on various vessels as to suggest a rare attempt at portraiture (Reents-Budet 1994: 173).[2]

Consumptive practices, which would have been essential to the lived experiences of kings, could have been considered a performative indication of the totality of the king's being – his literal bodily encompassment of difference at the cosmic center (the court) – but these practices had specific consequences as a result of bodily

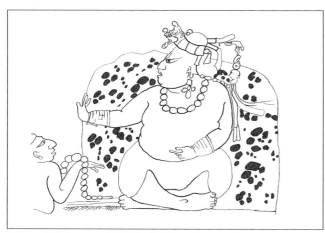

Figure 13.3: Image of the "Fat Cacique" from a polychrome painting on a cylindrical ceramic vessel, Late Classic (AD 600-800). The king is seated on a bench throne with a jaguar pelt-covered cushion behind him. Height of vessel 22.3 cm. Kimbell Art Museum, Ft. Worth, Texas. (Drawn by the author from a photograph by Justin Kerr, K1452)

processes. Increasing girth is a physiological index of such processes over time, and it was an outcome of acts of social agency (following Gell 1998: 15).[3] It was thus subject to the vicissitudes of political life, not an immutable characteristic of the king's body, in contrast with the semiotic qualities invoking the body politic. War captives shown in imagery – most of them lords or nobles – appear emaciated in Late Classic imagery, the presumed outcome of the withholding of food (Houston *et al.* 2006: 131). This is the same difference in bodily representation between victor and loser that was marked by the absence or presence of emotion, noted earlier.[4]

In sum, the lived experience of (over) ingestion and its physical effects on the king's body was shown in Late Classic depictions – primarily on portable objects utilised in aristocratic contexts – together with the inscriptive marking of the king's body through attached insignia – primarily on monumental imagery in courtly settings – despite the otherwise generalized and emotionless portrayals of bodies and faces.

Encompassing persons and heroic kings

Another indication of totality is the extension of the ruler's body in various forms – both as his physical body and his 'distributed' personhood (following Gell 1998). This aspect is complex and cannot be covered here in the detail it deserves, especially in

terms of how the human body served as a node in a production cycle that transformed substances. Suffice it to say that the boundaries of Maya persons were relatively permeable – 'stench, scent, breath, speech, song, and noise' are shown emanating from human bodies in Classic Maya artworks (Meskell and Joyce 2003: 26; see also Houston *et al.* 2006). Various souls or animating spirits also inhabited, if only temporarily, human bodies (Gillespie 2002; Houston and Stuart 1989). Tangible and intangible aspects of personhood painstakingly constructed during life, including elements contributed by the mother's and father's families to an individual, were deconstructed after death concomitant with the physical decomposition of the corpse (Gillespie 2001).

Rulers also were able to extend their personhood through material references to themselves in monumental imagery and texts, which became another kind of index of their actions (Looper 2003: 28). This aspect of their being, recorded as *baah* and interpreted as 'self', was shared with images of the king and also of gods, and included representations of rulers in deity costumes, merging mortal and divine qualities thereby (Houston and Stuart 1998: 81; see also Houston *et al.* 2006: 72–74). Houston and Stuart (1998: 86) suggest there was 'an extendable essence shared between images and that which is portrayed' and that 'portraits contained part of the royal essence, in ways that multiplied his presence' (1998: 95). These images allowed the king to be in multiple places at the same time and to continue to exert influence even after death (1998: 90).

These images and texts also served to integrate 'a physical person with a history,' another important aspect of Classic Maya royal personhood (Meskell and Joyce 2003: 28). Significantly, history written on stone monuments was monopolised by the paramount lords, and frequently it was used in conjunction with depictions of their bodies or statements of their names/titles. An important function of the stelae was to present 'images whose specific historical identity is precisely delimited by texts with dates in the Maya "Long Count" calendar' (Bachand *et al.* 2003: 242); both the stelae and their Long Count dates are hallmarks of the Classic period. Indeed, time (as a phenomenon) and royal bodies 'were processed by similar rituals,' including tying and wrapping with cloth (Houston *et al.* 2006: 81). Even on painted vessels secondary texts recording an event are often rendered in an architectonic way that frames or supports the body of the king: 'This enframing solidifies the royal body within the recorded event, immortalizing both' (Reents-Budet 2001: 214).

The totalising quality and consumptive actions of

the king's body, together with the ability to extend his selfhood outward – all of which enabled him to unify difference through performance – were integral to the king's person and would therefore have implicated his agency and historical effectiveness. As a living exemplar of totality (of society, history, the cosmos), indicated by both the symbolic and experiential connotations of his body, the Classic Maya ruler was comparable to the 'heroic kings' of Polynesia described by Sahlins (1985, 1991) whose 'heroic capacities and actions summarize, unify, encompass and thus expansively *internalize* the relations of society's members as a *whole*' (Mosko 1992: 698). Although Classic Maya society and culture are dissimilar in many ways from historic period Fiji and Hawaii, aspects of chiefly personhood in such societies may have analogues among the Classic Maya.

According to Sahlins, the political power of the Fijian chief or Hawaiian king derived from the 'symbolic magnification of the person. People so endowed with the power to embody a larger social order become *social-historical individuals*. ... persons whose own acts unfold a collective history ... because they personify the clan or the land and because their acts, universalized through the acquiescence of the historic group, then signify its dispositions' (Sahlins 1991: 63). Following from a concept of hierarchy based on 'the encompassing of the contrary' (Dumont 1980: 239), the heroic king's hierarchical position derives from his ontology as a totality that encompasses the rest of society, incorporating into himself all its social divisions (Sahlins 1985: 35). Furthermore, 'to include the existence of others in one's own person' is a concept of hierarchy reminiscent of *mana* in Polynesia, often construed as sacredness, 'implying a life-power of the chief that extends to and activates others, whether people or objects' (Sahlins 1991: 64).

Sahlins's reference to 'the symbolic magnification' of the heroic king recalls Kantorowicz's notion of the king's body as signifying the body politic, although in the Maya case the king's 'two bodies' are not so easily distinguished. Furthermore, the lived indexes and the inscribed symbols of Maya royal encompassment are not merely assertions of political legitimacy – of why the king is the king. They derive from a theory of embodied personhood and thus of agency, of how the king constructs himself – and is constructed by – his relationships with other persons, and therefore, how he is able to act. The ethno-logic of this theory can be characterised by a relational approach to personhood, agency, and the body, one that is different from Strathern's (1988) Melanesian 'dividual', which has become rather popular in archaeological interpretations (e.g., Borić and Robb this volume; Fowler 2004; Jones 2005).

Strathern modeled two modes of plural personhood. In the case of the 'dividual,' plurality is eliminated in social interactions via the detachment of elements, while in the other, plurality or difference is 'encompassed or eclipsed' (Strathern 1988: 15). It is the latter mode that better matches Sahlins's 'heroic king' (and also Wagner's [1994] 'fractal person'). As Mosko (1992: 699–700) explained, with Strathern's 'dividual',

> social practice is portrayed as a fundamentally 'subtractive' process ... and it is with incompleteness rather than completeness that agency is effected, [whereas] in Sahlins's conception, practice is rendered as essentially 'additive' or 'expansive' ... [and] it is in the very presumption that certain persons *do* incorporate other persons and relations *completely*, even to the extent of embodying or encompassing the entire society or cosmos, that the capacity and realization of agency lie. Persons of lesser order, as incomplete or less complete by comparison, are to that degree of lesser historical efficacy.

Relational constructions of plural personhood therefore vary in terms of what is being related and how, and how intersubjectivities thereby come into being (e.g., Busby 1997; Fowler 2004).[5] Modes of relational personhood are also expected to differ between more egalitarian and hierarchical societies, and the Classic Maya clearly exemplified the latter (Jones 2005: 197).

Sahlins was more concerned with history and historicities than with personhood *per se*, but the comparison is still apt for the Classic Maya. In his description of Fijian 'heroic history' that follows from these conceptions of hierarchy and the encompassing nature of the chief, 'the chief lives the life of the group. He is the principle of the group's existence, a kind of living ancestor, and accordingly its history is his own' (Sahlins 1991: 64). While historiography in these societies seems superficially to resemble the 'great man' history characteristic of modern Western societies, there is an important difference: 'This really *is* a history of kings and battles, but only because it is a cultural order that, multiplying the action of the king by the system of society, gives him a disproportionate historical effect' (Sahlins 1985: 41).

As noted above, the Maya employed a calendar and writing system beginning in the Late Preclassic – coincident with the development of depictions of rulers on stelae and dynastic kingship – to extol the events in kings' lives. By the Late Classic, there was an explosion of texts and images relating the paramounts' accessions, battles, and rituals associated with important buildings (e.g., Stuart 1998), along with cosmic events and creation myths seemingly localized to each capital. This monumental attention to the lives and exploits of Maya kings has typically been explained as the result of strategic intentions of an increasing number of rival aggrandizers seeking self-magnification and operating within a 'network' strategy of political-economic ties (e.g., Blanton *et al.* 1996). These ties are presumed to have been based on kinship or alliance relationships linking royal and subroyal noble houses, separated thereby from concepts of incorporation with the mass of commoners.

However, from the viewpoint of embodied kings as heroic figures, the life of the king (and all the other paramounts with whom he is enchained) *is* the history of his capital. He incorporates all of his polity and the multidimensional social differences it entails within himself – his person and his consumptive body.[6] Using images and inscriptions Late Classic Maya aristocracy emphasised how the encompassing capacity and agency of the *k'uhul ajaw* made history. It was at this time, starting in the seventh century, that they developed monumental images with a narrative quality that focused visual attention on the wholeness and integrity of the king's body as a naturalised index of his totalising person.

Conclusion

The encompassing capacity of the Maya paramount lord was a source of his sacredness and key to his hierarchical standing and that of his royal house. Stylistic shifts in the portrayal of the king in Late Classic sculpture–with increasing emphasis on the unity and corporeality of the body – can be correlated with the semiotic overlay on the king's body indicating his status as a totalising figure whose agency and historical effectiveness were predicated on actions of encompassment of sociocosmic divisions. These depictions of the body in both monumental and portable artworks demonstrate its indexical sign status, a reference to natural bodily processes and lived experiences, and not just to the inscription of symbols onto the body as framework. The imagery and the textual references to the actions of kings in history further suggest the notion that Maya kings were comparable in their intersubjective relationships with both nobles and commoners to Sahlins's 'heroic' kings.

These developments, evident in Maya imagery and inscriptions, implicate significant changes between Early and Late Classic political ideologies despite a superficial appearance of cultural continuity. They may also provide clues to the Classic to Postclassic transition (the Maya 'collapse' beginning in the ninth century), when this 'heroic' quality of embodied encompassment was modified, if not lost altogether. The erection of figural stelae with inscriptions and Long Count calendrics ceased, replaced by new architectural and sculptural media of political representations marked by the absence of the king's body.

Notes

1   See Joyce (2000a, 2000b, 2003) on the production of gendered bodies through performance in Classic Maya art.

2   Portraiture is also noted among some of the monumental depictions of paramounts at Palenque (Schele and Miller 1986: 66), one of the Late Classic centers whose artworks greatly emphasised the corporeality of the ruler and which were the focus of attention in Pasztory's (1978) analysis.

3   Noble women's girth was also depicted on some painted pots and Late Classic figurines (Miller and Martin 2004: 25), as consumption characterised all of the court as an extension of the king's person. Obesity can signal other meanings and functions besides over-eating or sloth, but it is a known index of consumption of rich foods, and royal eating was a principal event as shown in the imagery. Ingestion through the rectum and the ritual and social use of enemas (e.g., Houston *et al.* 2006: 117) are related activities that cannot be addressed here.

4   As Tanner (2001) has observed, such 'naturalism' in figural imagery is not merely a stylistic choice but a means to engage the senses. The viewers' bodies as well as the body of the figure depicted come into play. By combining cultural codes with bodily experiences, these artworks may elicit 'affective projections on the part of viewers grounded in their sense of their own bodies' (Tanner 2001: 271). Kus (1992: 172) argued that such 'an appeal to "sensuousness" (or some combination of the physical and emotional as well as the mental character of human existence)' should not be ignored in the dominant semiotic approaches to the body favored by archaeologists.

5   The encompassment of different attributes of personhood was displayed in a variety of ways among the Late Classic Maya rulers, as I (Gillespie, in press) have suggested utilising an analytical dichotomy employed by Strathern (1994). Among the western Maya (Usumacinta River area), including Palenque and Yaxchilan, there was greater emphasis on shared substantive and 'horizontal' linkages of a person to other living embodied individuals, such as kinsmen, and the artworks more often name or depict the king's parents or spouse. At Copan and Tikal, further east in the Maya lowlands, the totality of the king was more often referenced according to Strathern's (1994) 'vertical perspective', emphasising the enchainment (*sensu* Wagner 1994 – a mechanism of fractality) between the living king and his predecessors back to the founding of a specific ruling line.

6   According to Mosko's development of Sahlins's heroic kings, their 'hierarchical supercomposition' is constructed out of additive or expansive practices (Mosko 1992: 697, 699). Such kings or chiefs should thereby have extraordinary qualities of detachability or decomposition compared to ordinary people (1992: 701). Joyce (1998: 152) has argued that acts of mutilation, decapitation, or sacrifice of kings and other noble war captives shown in Late Classic imagery are aspects of such detachability –practices that make the depictions of kings with unified bodies all the

more meaningful. Elaborate secondary funerary rituals were involved in the social decomposition of Maya kings (Gillespie 2001). In addition, Houston and Stuart (1998: 95) discussed the risk of extending 'royal essence' to monumental images or texts given that these objects were subject to mutilation and destruction as well as to reuse in innovated settings. Further development of this converse aspect of the Maya king's totalising being is beyond the scope of this paper.

Bibliography

Bachand, H., Joyce, R.A. and Hendon, J.A. 2003. Bodies moving in space: Ancient Mesoamerican human sculpture and embodiment. *Cambridge Archaeological Journal* 13: 238–247.

Baudez, C.-F. 2000. The Maya king's body, mirror of the universe. *Res: Anthropology and Aesthetics* 38: 134–143.

Blanton, R. E., Feinman, G.M., Kowalewski, S.A. and Peregrine, P.N. 1996. A Dual-processual theory for the evolution of Mesoamerican civilization. *Current Anthropology* 37: 1–14.

Busby, C. 1997. Permeable and partible persons: a Comparative analysis of gender and the body in South India and Melanesia. *Journal of the Royal Anthropological Institute* 3(2):261–278.

Colas, P.R. 2003. K'inich and king: Naming self and person among Classic Maya rulers. *Ancient Mesoamerica* 14:269–283.

Csordas, T.J. 1990. Embodiment as a paradigm for anthropology. *Ethos* 18: 5–47.

Csordas, T.J. 1994. Introduction: the Body as representation and being-in-the-world. In *Embodiment and Experience: The Existential Ground of Culture and Self*, edited by T.J. Csordas, pp. 1–24. Cambridge: Cambridge University Press.

Douglas, M. 1970. *Natural Symbols: Explorations in Cosmology*. London: Routledge.

Dumont, L. 1980. *Homo Hierarchicus: The Caste System and its Implications*. (Complete revised English edition. Trans. by M. Sainsbury, L. Dumont, and B. Gulati). Chicago: University of Chicago Press.

Fowler, C. 2004. *The Archaeology of Personhood: An Anthropological Approach*. London: Routledge.

Gell, A. 1998. *Art and Agency: An Anthropological Theory*. Oxford: Clarendon Press.

Gillespie, S.D. 2001. Personhood, agency, and mortuary ritual: a Case study from the ancient Maya. *Journal of Anthropological Archaeology* 20: 73–112.

Gillespie, S.D. 2002. Body and soul among the Maya: Keeping the spirits in place. In *The Space and Place of Death*, edited by H. Silverman and D. Small, pp. 67–78. Archeological Papers of the American Anthropological Association No. 11. Arlington, VA: American Anthropological Association.

Gillespie, S.D. In press. Corporate aspects of person and embodiment among the Classic Period Maya. *Estudios de Cultura Maya*.

Graham, I. and von Euw, E. 1977. *Corpus of Maya Hieroglyphic Inscriptions, vol. 3, part 1, Yaxchilan*. Peabody Museum of Archaeology and Ethnology, Harvard University. Cambridge, MA: Harvard University Press.

Grosz, E. 1994. *Volatile Bodies: Toward a Corporeal Feminism*. Bloomington: Indiana University Press.

Grube, N. 2004. Las antiguas biografías mayas desde una perspectiva comparativa. In *Janaab' Pakal de Palenque: Vida y Muerte de un Gobernante Maya*, edited by V. Tiesler and A. Cucina, pp. 225–261. Mexico City: Universidad Nacional Autónoma de México and Universidad Autónoma de Yucatán.

Houston, S.D. 2001. Decorous bodies and disordered passions: Representations of emotion among the Classic Maya. *World Archaeology* 33: 206–219.

Houston, S.D. and Stuart, D. 1989. The *Way* glyph: Evidence for 'Co-Essences' among the Classic Maya. *Research Reports in Classic Maya Writing* 30. Washington, DC: Center for Maya Research.

Houston, S.D. and Stuart, D. 1996. Of gods, glyphs and kings: Divinity and rulership among the Classic Maya. *Antiquity* 70: 289–312.

Houston, S.D. and Stuart, D. 1998. The Ancient Maya self: Personhood and portraiture in the Classic Period. *Res: Anthropology and Aesthetics* 33: 73–101.

Houston, S.D., Stuart, D. and Taube, K. 2006. *The Memory of Bones: Body, Being, and Experience among the Classic Maya*. Austin: University of Texas Press.

Inomata, T. and Houston, S.D. (eds) 2001. *Royal Courts of the Ancient Maya*. 2 vols. Boulder, CO: Westview.

Jones, A. 2005. Lives in fragments? Personhood and the European Neolithic. *Journal of Social Archaeology* 5: 193–224.

Jones, C. and Satterthwaite, L. 1982. *The Monuments and Inscriptions of Tikal: The Carved Monuments*. Tikal Report No. 33, Part A. University Museum Monograph 44. Philadelphia: University Museum, University of Pennsylvania.

Joyce, R.A. 1996. The Construction of gender in Classic Maya monuments. In *Gender and Archaeology*, edited by R.P. Wright, pp. 167–195. Philadelphia: University of Pennsylvania Press.

Joyce, R.A. 1998. Performing the body in pre-Hispanic Central America. *Res: Anthropology and Aesthetics* 33: 147–165.

Joyce, R.A. 2000a. *Gender and Power in Prehispanic Mesoamerica*. Austin: University of Texas Press.

Joyce, R.A. 2000b. Girling the girl and boying the boy: The Production of adulthood in Ancient Mesoamerica. *World Archaeology* 31: 473–483.

Joyce, R.A. 2003. Making something of herself: Embodiment in life and death at Playa de los Muertos, Honduras. *Cambridge Archaeological Journal* 13: 248–261.

Joyce, R.A. 2005. Archaeology of the body. *Annual Review of Anthropology* 34: 139–158.

Kantorowicz, E.H. 1957. *The King's Two Bodies: A Study in Mediæval Political Theology*. Princeton: Princeton University Press.

Kubler, G. 1984. *The Art and Architecture of Ancient America: The Mexican, Maya and Andean Peoples*. New York: Penguin Books.

Kus, S. 1992. Toward an archaeology of body and soul. In *Representations in Archaeology*, edited by J.-C. Gardin and C.S. Peebles, pp. 168–177. Bloomington: Indiana University Press.

Looper, M.G. 2003. From Inscribed bodies to distributed persons: Contextualizing Tairona figural images in performance. *Cambridge Archaeological Journal* 13: 25–40.

Meskell, L. 1996. The Somatization of archaeology: Institutions, discourses, corporeality. *Norwegian Archaeological Review* 29: 1–16.

Meskell, L.M. and Joyce, R.A. 2003. *Embodied Lives: Figuring Ancient Maya and Egyptian Experience*. London: Routledge.

Miller, M. and Martin, S. 2004. *Courtly Art of the Ancient Maya.* Kathleen Berrin, Curator. New York: Thames & Hudson.

Mosko, M.S. 1992. Motherless Sons: 'Divine Kings' and 'Partible Persons' in Melanesia and Polynesia. *Man* 27: 697–717.

Pasztory, E. 1978. Artistic traditions of the Middle Classic Period. In *Middle Classic Mesoamerica, A.D. 400–700*, edited by E. Pasztory, pp. 108–142. New York: Columbia University Press.

Pasztory, E. 1990–91. Still invisible: the Problem of the aesthetics of abstraction for Pre-Columbian art and its implications for other cultures. *Res: Anthropology and Aesthetics* 19/20: 105–136.

Proskouriakoff, T. 1950. *A Study of Classic Maya Sculpture.* Carnegie Institution of Washington Publication 593. Washington, DC: Carnegie Institute.

Reents-Budet, D. 1994. *Painting the Maya Universe: Royal Ceramics of the Classic Period.* Durham, NC: Duke University Press.

Reents-Budet, D. 2001. Classic Maya concepts of the royal court: an Analysis of renderings on pictorial ceramics. In *Royal Courts of the Ancient Maya*, Vol. 1, *Theory, Comparison, and Synthesis*, edited by T. Inomata and S.D. Houston, pp. 195–233. Boulder, CO: Westview.

Sahlins, M. 1985. *Islands of History.* Chicago: University of Chicago Press.

Sahlins, M. 1991. The Return of the event, again; with Reflections on the beginnings of the Great Fijian War of 1843–1855 between the Kingdoms of Bau and Rewa. In *Clio in Oceania: Toward a Historical Anthropology*, edited by A. Biersack, pp. 37–99. Washington, DC: Smithsonian Institution Press.

Schele, L. and Miller, M.E. 1986. *The Blood of Kings: Dynasty and Ritual in Maya Art.* Fort Worth, TX: Kimbell Art Museum.

Strathern, A. 1994. Keeping the body in mind. *Social Anthropology (Journal of the European Association of Social Anthropologists)* 2(1): 43–53.

Strathern, M. 1988. *The Gender of the Gift: Problems with Women and Problems with Society in Melanesia.* Berkeley: University of California Press.

Stuart, D. 1998. 'The Fire Enters His House': Architecture and ritual in Classic Maya texts. In *Function and Meaning in Classic Maya Architecture*, edited by Stephen D. Houston, pp. 373–425. Washington, DC: Dumbarton Oaks.

Tanner, J. 2001. Nature, culture and the body in Classical Greek religious art. *World Archaeology* 33: 257–276.

Turner, B. 2003. Foreword: the Phenomenology of lived experience. In *Embodied Lives: Figuring Ancient Maya and Egyptian Experience*, by L.M. Meskell and R.A. Joyce, pp. xiii–xx. London: Routledge.

Turner, T. 1994. Bodies and anti-bodies: Flesh and fetish in contemporary social theory. In *Embodiment and Experience: The Existential Ground of Culture and Self*, edited by T.J. Csordas, pp. 27–47. Cambridge: Cambridge University Press.

Turner, T. 1995. Social body and embodied subject: Bodiliness, subjectivity, and sociality among the Kayapo. *Cultural Anthropology* 10: 143–170.

Wagner, R. 1994. The Fractal person. In *Big Men and Great Men: The Personification of Power in Melanesia*, edited by M. Strathern and M. Godelier, pp. 159–173. Cambridge: Cambridge University Press.

Webster, D. 2001. Spatial dimensions of Maya courtly life. In *Royal Courts of the Ancient Maya*, Vol. 1, *Theory, Comparison, and Synthesis*, edited by T. Inomata and S.D. Houston, pp. 139–167. Boulder, CO: Westview.

14

Colonised bodies,
personal and social

Nan A. Rothschild

Introduction

Bodies are and were implicated in colonial activities at many levels and in multiple spheres. Both the colonised and the coloniser felt the impact of encounter, albeit in different ways. Archaeology as a colonial endeavour has also participated in the violation of past bodies, objectifying and dehumanising them, and while this continues to some degree, there is now an ethical stance among many archaeologists that involves an attitudinal change toward the remains of past peoples, minimising or eliminating further research on them. And these bodies themselves have become empowered in new ways both because of increased respect now provided them and also because as technology advances, new and significant forms of information may be acquired through minimally invasive research modalities.

In this paper I attempt to disentangle some of the complex effects of colonisation on past bodies. I see these effects as potentially significant at the individual/personal level and the social/corporate level, although these are intertwined. I will consider research conducted by a number of anthropologists and archaeologists in a variety of settler colonies, and will then focus on North America, primarily on native peoples; I also consider enslaved Africans who suffered the impact of an extremely repressive form of the colonisation of bodies. Perhaps most significant, it is clear that the body is a unique site for understanding the colonial experience. Archaeologists are privileged to have access to data from internal bodies, but these data must be analysed in a frame beyond the biological, incorporating the physical body into a social context.

What is a colonial encounter?

Initially it seems important to discuss what I mean by a colonial encounter. 'In its most neutral sense, a colonial setting is one in which, given two groups of people of unequal power, the more powerful one enters the other's territory to obtain material resources and labour power, using various forms of force and political/legal control mechanisms to achieve its goal, with an ethnocentric rationale for that invasion' (Rothschild 2003: 1). Colonial interactions always involve dominance, as well as the creation and elabouration of a hierarchy arraying racial and ethnic groups in relation to power.

Anthropology has spilled a lot of ink on how intercultural interactions proceeded and perhaps, more significantly, how to describe them. Some of the terms used – acculturation, diffusion, creolisation, culture contact, hybridity, boundaries and frontiers – are flawed as they assumed unidirectional change, and that European traits were adopted while indigenous ones were lost. They also ignored the agency of individuals and the complexity of change.

Creolisation is a term used to describe contact situations in which there is a blending and mixing of cultural traits (Ferguson 2000). It is more useful than other terms because it recognises that traits are not uniformly passed in one direction, from the colonial, or dominant, society to the colonised, dominated one. Many of the colonial contexts to which this model has been applied involve racial as well as cultural mixture; most occur in the southeastern United States and the Caribbean. The notion of hybridity is similar to that of creolisation in that it recognizes the racialised nature of cultural heterogeneity; for what are probably historical reasons, it has been used especially in Latin American settings, by archaeologists and others (Garcia Canclini 1995). The factors structuring adoption of new traits are complex; they are not random and need to be considered in local, historicised context. (Rothschild 2003: 6)

Some of the classic work on frontiers (Turner, Forbes) and boundaries confuses spatial and cultural margins. A number of recent writers, however, problematise these contact zones and demonstrate the complex and mutable interconnections between peoples. James Brooks (2002) in a study of nomadic and other groups in the colonial southwestern US notes the 'reality that in-group survival depended to some degree on social and economic interactions with out-groups' and that 'the exchange of culture-group members fostered accommodation, eroded linguistic and cultural boundaries, and concomitantly placed stress on the production and preservation of in-group identity' (op. cit: 26).

White's concept of the Middle Ground (1991) offers another elegant example of contact in process. The Middle Ground was not a place but an adaptation and a system of meaning that evolved between Algonkians and French, during the seventeenth and eighteenth centuries, in the 'pays d'en haut', from the Great Lakes west to the Mississippi. It served to allow communication between the two groups and overcome their mutual misunderstanding of one another, although it was based to some degree on 'creative expedient misunderstandings' of what each society believed the other wanted, their values and practice (White 1991: x). White provides a description of the events in this area and a picture of its complexity as indigenous groups moved west, dislocated by the Iroquois Beaver Wars, trying to forge ways of interacting among themselves, while simultaneously balancing Jesuit overtures, French fur traders' demands, and French requisitions for military support against the British (Rothschild 2003).

> The alliance endured not because of some mystical affinity between Frenchmen and Indians, nor because Algonquians had been reduced to dependency on the French, but rather because two peoples created an elaborate network of economic, political, cultural, and social ties to meet the demands of a particular historical situation (White 1991: 33).

Colonialism is ancient practice: the Romans in Europe, The Han in Asia, and the Aztec and Inka in the Americas are just a few examples of empires with colonies that long preceded the familiar European forms. However, I will focus on settler colonies, emanating from a variety of European countries in the seventeenth and nineteenth centuries. I make use of some insightful examples set in Africa, India and the Pacific, but will concentrate on a discussion of North America. In any conversation about the parties involved in these settings, it is important to recognise the essentialising characteristics of the categories 'colonisers' and 'colonised'; each of these classes includes a range of individuals and sub-groups (minimally partitioned by age, gender, rank and power within the system). Identities within these groups are fluid and multifaceted (Gonzalez 2005). However, it is also true that the encounter promotes (perhaps temporary) solidity within each group and consolidates an identity through opposition to other groups. For example, when the people we call Dutch arrived in the New World, they perceived themselves as residents of a particular province; only later did the United Provinces become Holland (Rothschild 1990). As well it is known that tribal identities were often assigned to indigenous people by Europeans (Fogelson in Beider 1990, cited in Hamilton 162).

Body surfaces and symbols

Moving to the main subject of this paper, much of the interesting work on individual or personal bodies, beginning perhaps with Douglas (1970), is focused on the corporeal exterior, and the means by which it served as both natural and social symbol. It is important, but difficult to disentangle the physical and social aspects of bodies, even when considering their individual rather than corporate aspect. As Burke notes, 'the material body is often in plain sight, but the social body, as an artifact of the self and a canvas for identity, is both indispensible and invisible' (1996: 4). A number of analysts have considered the body surface as a canvas on (or through) which to communicate a variety of messages (Meskell 1999; Meskell and Joyce 2003).

In a special issue of the *Annual Review of Anthropology* (2004) several authors wrote essays on this form of messaging, applying intriguing and variable interpretations. Reischer and Koo describe the body as text, which when read in a social context can provide interconnections between the individual and society; they distinguish between the body as symbol or as agent (2004). Van Wolputte concentrates on the fragmentation and multiplicity of bodies and the relationship between self and embodiment; he also sees the body as the meeting ground on which hegemonic and counter-hegemonic forces interact. 'It is a canvas on which major cultural, social and political changes are projected. On the other hand, it is a (if not the) major focus and objective of these changes' (2004: 260). And Schildkrout details a variety of inscriptions on the surface of the body: tattooing, scarification, foot binding, dental modification, piercing and painting, which function to define social boundaries. These are often instituted at socially crucial times and convey varying messages; some of these inscriptions are clearly more permanent than others. Colonisers sometimes left tangible reminders of violence (scars, whip marks, or as an extreme example, the removal of portions of the body). In general, anthropologists consider modifications to indigenous bodies, but, of course Europeans without scarification or tattooing are equally marked, especially to those who bear these basic identifiers. I will discuss the issue of dress below as it does not involve the kind of physical alteration that other modifications do.

The impact of colonial pressures on bodies also emerges in areas as different as the definition of beauty (slenderness or fatness, the customisation of the body through cosmetic surgery [Reischer and Koo 2004]); and the significance of hygiene (which does bridge the border between internal and external) and the consumption of toiletries (Burke 1996). As Burke notes:

> white attitudes toward black bodies inspired institutions that remade practices of the body, domesticity and manners. The bodily racism of settler society constantly lurked around the edges of the lives of those Africans whose social aspirations were most identified with 'modernity,' but the shifting and loosely defined 'hygienic ideals' of nineteenth-century Zimbabwean culture also continuously reinvented and reproduced themselves in everyday life... (1996: 215)

Some of the topics central to medical anthropology involve an approach to a problematised body; here again internal and external are blurred. I will not discuss these here, but they often involve the introduction of 'improvements' by a colonising power. I offer just a few tantalising examples: the transformation of the female body, mediated through the medicalisation of traditional obstetric practice in the Congo (Hunt in Van Wolputte 2004: 257); the late nineteenth-century introduction of notions of the connections between hygiene and health in a British nursery school (Strathern 2004); and the exploitation of bodies for organ harvest (Sharp 2006) or for sensationalised public display.[1]

Body interiors

The interior of the body as accessed through skeletal remains provides information that is not otherwise available through any other means. Although the internal body is invisible, it offers socially relevant information which archaeology is privileged to have access to. Important data on disease, illness, physical stress, work load and demography have been developed through these analyses. Meredith Linn (2002, 2003) analysed data from a series of site reports in order to demonstrate the effects of Spanish colonialism in North America. She covers a wide range of impacts, including the devastation of total demographic collapse in some cases, due to a combination of epidemic disease, dietary stress and the cruel exploitation of bodies for labour. Colonial encounters altered the body's physical structure, as seen in: bone hypertrophy and remodeling as a result of work load; the development of rugged muscle attachments related to new assigned tasks; and osteoarthritis developed because of forced labour. A study of pre-colonial and post-colonial skeletons from Pecos, New Mexico, for example, indicates a decline in women's humeral strength while men's increases as a result of Spanish policy which shifted the major task of agriculture from women to men (2003: 7).

Foraging peoples were less affected by colonisation than farmers were, in part because their diets were healthier to begin with, and they may have developed greater adaptability prior to contact (2002: 12, 15). However, an analysis of diet from isotopes (strontium and nitrogen; ca. 3–4 [2003: 11]) shows that foragers' bodies in California demonstrate the long-term effects of colonialism. They were healthier prior to missionisation than after it, apparently due to a decrease in consumption of marine plants. Missionaries focused subsistence tasks on herding and agriculture and presumably discouraged the gathering of marine resources and fish. These studies offer other insights: evidence of disease, reflected in decreased fertility, bone lesions, and dental enamel defects (hypoplasias and other dental indicators) from childhood nutritional stress (Figures 14.1 and 14.2). However, Linn concludes that the greatest impact on health comes from enforced social change instituted by the Spanish: their policy of population aggregation, which promoted susceptibility to epidemic disease; relocation and the enforced shift from foraging to agricultural production. Those indigenous people who remained the healthiest were those who lived in small groups, were mobile and had a dispersed settlement pattern, managed to eat nutritiously but also avoid intense or prolonged contact with the colonisers (2002).

Similar kinds of information are also derived from the analysis of over 400 sets of human remains from the New York City eighteenth century African Burial Ground (ABG) which provides data on demography, trauma, nutritional stress and the effects of malnutrition. A total of 70% of those individuals analysed

Figure 14.1. Porotic hypersotosis affects the cranium and inidcates anemia or other nutritional stress (from Clark Spenser Larsen [1998], Post-Pleistocene Bioarchaeology of the Agricultural Transition, 14th Annual International Congress of Anthropological and Ethnological Sciences, Williamsburg, VA, on-line)

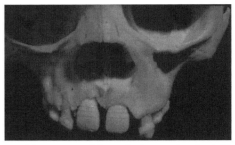

Figure 14.2. Linear enamel hypoplasias are bands visible on teeth as a result of childhood nutritional stress (from Clark Spenser Larsen [1998], Post-Pleistocene Bioarchaeology of the Agricultural Transition, 14th Annual International Congress of Anthropological and Ethnological Sciences, Williamsburg, VA, on-line).

had *dental enamel* hypoplasias, suggesting generalised stress in childhood. Children born in colonial New York 'within the condition of slavery were more vulnerable to health risks and early death due to nutritional deficiencies and illness than is evident for the childhoods of those who were likely to have been born in Africa' (Blakey and Rankin-Hill 2004: 331); these indicators were high in the ABG population 'regardless of age or sex' (op.cit: 398), and stress levels in ABG children were higher than those among contemporary populations of enslaved people in Maryland or in Barbados (op.cit: 313).

And the same kinds of skeletal indicators of work load just noted for Native Americans – oesteoarthritis, pressure facets, fracture, and hypertrophy of places where tendons and ligaments attach (op.cit: 403)

– were found in both males and females. Women had particularly high rates of lumbar oesteoarthritis (around 58% of the sixty-nine individuals studied), suggesting the effects of strenuous labour on the vertebral column (op.cit: 412); there were also many examples of cervical oesteophytosis, or deformation of vertebral elements, which comes from carrying loads on the head, or other activities involving heavy weight (op.cit: 442). There were also a large number of fractures in the population; the highest percentage were inflicted on the cranium (males –11%) or femur (females –12%). Cranial fractures usually indicate violence, although limb fractures need not as they are also found among labourers (Meredith Linn, personal communication, 2005). One young adult female had thirty-two fractures, a fifty year-old woman had ten, eight of which were perimortem, on the arms, legs and pelvis, and a male of the same age had twenty-three (op.cit: 450). Even adolescents were found to have fractures, some of which – especially cranial ones – were undoubtedly the cause of death (op.cit: 457). The most compelling burial is no. 25, a twenty to twenty-four year-old woman who had been shot, had blunt trauma force applied to the face (perhaps a rifle butt) and had her arm broken through simultaneously twisting and pulling. She appears to have lived for a few days after the beating (op.cit: 458). These bodies bear especially compelling witness to the relation between slave and master, and its associated violence. Other colonial contexts demonstrate similar, though perhaps less dramatic evidence of violence, through physical abuse, enforced social and dietary change.

The ethics of investigating skeletons

While it is clear that the information derived from

human remains is significant, one must consider how to balance these data with the invasive and in many ways colonial – and even violent – techniques of extracting information; that is, 'scientists' use bodies without permission and tend to treat the bodies simply as inanimate material, without considering their humanity (Hamilton 2004). Those whose bodies have been used this way, generally the powerless members of society, have been enraged by this approach. In North America there is now NAGPRA (Native American Graves Protection and Repatriation Act), which offers some protection for Native American remains stored in museums, and there have been varying responses by African Americans to the use of their cemetery populations for research.

Physical anthropologists and others are themselves divided in this post-NAGPRA world as to how to balance ethics and 'science'. Hamilton has recently compiled reactions to several issues (2004) and notes that there is a tremendous range of opinions expressed. The ultimate questions are: does the information generated scientifically from human remains outweigh concerns of religion, morality, ceremony and ethics presented by descendant communities (op.cit: 149), and, second, who gets to decide? In part these determinations should be based on the significance of the data generated. Some archaeologists note that certain kinds of information, such as issues of physiological stress or evidence of oesteoarthritis, as well as warfare, origins, population migration, can only be obtained from bones (op.cit: 144), as in the examples I've described.

A claim is sometimes asserted that research on Native American remains is of benefit to their descendants; however, a former U.S. Assistant Surgeon General, and longtime director of the Indian Health Service says: 'I am not aware of any current medical diagnostic treatment or procedure that has been derived from research on...[American Indian] skeletal remains' (Emery Johnson, cited in Hamilton 2004: 158). Some anthropologists believe that ancient skeletons belong to all people, that no single group has the right to claim exclusive use and that the limitation of access for purposes of study deprives mankind of important information (Buikstra 1981: 27, in Hamilton: 148).

And there is also the question of what to do about bodies that are 'unprotected', i.e., no one objects to their study? In some parts of the world there appears to be no concern with the study of human remains. Should we, as anthropologists, try to protect these past bodies against scientific incursions? Or do we accept the claim that research on skeletons implies the greatest of respect for these individuals (Buikstra 1983,

cited in Hamilton: 160)? Lest we gain the impression that all violation of bodies was conducted in colonial situations, let me mention some Native American practices – scalping, the use of skulls of the dead as emblems of conquest – that existed in the New World and elsewhere.

Clothing the social body

As we move back from the interior of the body to its surface, we reposition ourselves at the interface between the body and society (Schildkrout 2004), and move from the personal to the social body. There is much fascinating and significant work on the powers of clothing and its meanings in colonial settings. I will only discuss a few examples, set in India (Cohn 1989); Africa (Comaroff 1985) and the Pacific (Colchester 2003). Clothing and other superficial adornments (as opposed to treatments that modify the skin or other parts of the body) offer multiple ways to enact programs of action as well as identification, appropriation, imitation, mockery and resistance. Material things such as clothing and ornaments are themselves reconfigured and recontextualised in colonial situations. They are not just passively manipulated but become agents, acting to form new social contexts. Hair style may also convey a wealth of socially relevant data on marriageability or adulthood (in the American southwest), where the Spanish are known to have forcibly cut men's hair so that they appeared more European (Severin Fowles, personal communication 2006).

The fact of wearing clothing or not is the first relevant factor, with European appraisal of those who are not (partly or fully) dressed as offering themselves as sexual partners or possessing character traits such as sexual lasciviousness (Tcherkezoff 2003: 58–9). The reconfiguration of status hierarchies is manifest in dress, as some Pacific Islanders layered European and indigenous clothing (Colchester 2003), creating a material hybridity that challenged European attempts to categorise people. In some ways, putting on European clothing may be equivalent to removing important native markers of status, particularly indicators of lineage history and rank (Tcherkezoff 2003: 53; Bolton 2003: 128). Gender in particular is significantly coded by clothing and when both male and female bodies were covered, it meant 'obscuring in one action all the information about a person which they normally wore or embodied' (Bolton, ibid). However, dress didn't only indicate gender but mixed symbolic representations of social status with male-female designations. Some women, in wearing 'male' clothes signaled that they wanted to enact roles that had been assigned post-colonially to males (op.cit: 137).

There is a significant difference between cloth and clothing; the production of cloth is a multivalent act, bearing economic, social and political meaning. The economic dominance of the production of cloth was understood by Ghandi when he told Indian people that they would only be freed from British domination if they substituted their own home-woven cloth for that produced in the mills of Manchester (Cohn 1989: 343). This movement proved a direct and quite successful attack on the Empire, both on economic and symbolic levels. Thomas notes that when Samoan women began to produce clothing, the act did not necessarily transform the sewers in the way that missionaries believed it would (2003: 84). The latter wanted 'dress that altered the being of the convert,' not just a badge or flag that could be read (whether accurate or not) as indicating the acceptance of Christianity (and that incidentally might have been adopted to enable the acquisition of European wealth) (Thomas 2003: 90, 93).

Comaroff's (1985) classic study of dress among Tshidi in southern Africa focuses on the impact of Christianity on clothing in the form of uniforms worn by members of particular church groups. These uniforms were gender-specific but, more than that, held power; they were believed to act as shields in the way that Ghost-dance shirts did on the American Plains (1985: 201). The bodily demands of conversion also included the proscription of specific foods and medicines, and the Tshidi in particular held taboos against pork, alcohol and tobacco, which were seen as emblems of white colonial culture. The corporeal aspects of conversion are elaborated on further: this is a population among whom a high rate of malnutrition and physical morbidity existed, and who believed that the body's state serves as an index of being, 'providing a discourse upon their location in the social, material and spiritual world' (op.cit: 211). The dress codes form a bricolage; they are similar to cargo cults in taking on specific signals normally associated with colonial oppression and converting them so that they can be incorporated as benign or beneficent emblems (1985: 226).

The classification of bodies

The last topic I will consider is the social body and its classification, through the creation of racially and ethnically marked identities, such as black/white, enslaved/free and, in particular, a vast and basically unmanageable range of casta designations imposed

Typical Eighteenth-Century *Casta* List *

NON-CASTAS

1. Español
2. Criollo
3. Other Europeans

CASTAS

1. Español x india = mestizo[1]
2. Español x mestiza = castizo[1]
3. Español x castiza = torna a español
4. Español x negra = mulato[1]
5. Español x mulata = morisco
6. Morisco x española = tornatrás
7. Albino x española = tornatrás
8. Mulato x india = calpamulato
9. Negro x india = lobo[1]
10. Lobo x india = cambijo
11. Calpamulato x india = jivaro
12. Indio x cambija = sambahigo
13. Mulato x mestiza = cuarterón
14. Cuarterón x mestiza = coyote[1]
15. Coyote x morisca = albarazado
16. Albarazado x saltatrás = tente en el aire
17. Mestizo x india = cholo
18. Indio x mulata = chino[1]
19. Español x china = cuarterón de china
20. Negro x india = sambo de indio
21. Negro x mulata = genízaro[2]
22. Cambijo x china = genízaro[2]

Figure 14.3. Diagram of casta system shows 22 racial categories based on parents' classification (from Rothschild 2003).

by the Spanish in their colonies. My example is the borderland colony of New Mexico in the eighteenth and nineteenth centuries.

The Spanish *casta* system was instituted in all of New Spain including New Mexico (Bustamante 1989). It shows particularly well the permeability of the boundary between internal and external, social and individual bodies. It formed part of the colonial system of domination in which legal statuses were identified in an attempt to regulate social interaction, but more importantly to create groups of people with specific responsibilities and privileges in the political economy. These statuses regulated access to land, provided the basis of taxation, decreed who was available for labour (Jackson 1999: 3–4) and who was eligible for colonial office. Basically the system employed racial categories as cognitive labels referring to groups with contrasting positions in the socio-political system and the economic organisation of production (Seed, cited in Jackson 1999: 10). The Spanish believed in the idea of 'purity of blood (*pureza de sangre española*) and created a classification system involving twenty-two

Figure 14.4. Many sets of paintings were used to illustrate the casta categories (from Rothschild 2003).

different categories of mixed peoples, depending on the amount of Indian, African and European blood each had (Figures 14.3 and 14.4). The practice of Catholicism created humans (and marriage partners) out of heathen by the simple act of baptism, making women eligible as sexual partners and leading to genetic and social destabilisation. Once this situation was out of hand, the Spanish tried desperately to create order through racist census surveys and church records, applied by priests and local officials inconsistently. It was clear at the time that it was an arbitrary and unworkable system, subject to manipulation (Dominguez 1776, cited in Bustamante 1989: 74). By the end of the eighteenth century, the population was genetically quite mixed (Bustamante 1991: 162), although social differences validated by perceived physical differences continued in effect. Thus the casta system was organised initially on internal/genetic differences but then substituted external distinctions such as skin colour, class and manners as markers.[2]

The unworkability of the casta system should not be taken to mean that ethnic identity was not significant in New Mexico, but the labels that counted were few. They were applied both by Euro-Americans and Native Americans, but differently. I suspect that during the pre-Revolt period the Spanish would have perceived three groups of people: Indian, mixed or *mestizo* and Spanish (defined by relative whiteness, eliteness, the use of the Spanish language and a subscription to Spanish ideals). Spanish and *mestizo* would have lived in the same communities. These broad caste-like categories would have minimised differences which were highly relevant in Spain, such as place of birth, wealth and heritage. Subsequently, after the Pueblo Revolt of 1680, I believe Europeans would have perceived two major categories of people resident in New Mexico: Indians and Hispanos, a label which incorporated Spanish and *mestizo* into what is today called 'Hispanic', including primarily people born in Mexico and in the southwest who spoke Spanish, identified themselves as Spanish-descended, and had various combinations of Spanish, Indian and African ancestry (Rothschild 2003).

The Pueblos would have had their own perception of ethnic differences. There are no indigenous documents available, but my assumption is that their classification would have encompassed two groups: European-derived and Indian. 'The indigenous nations generally make a distinction between two sorts of prisoners, who get totally different treatment. The first are Creoles, whom they call *white men*, although some are every bit as dark as themselves. The others are other natives, whom they call *red men*' (Berlandier, cited in Brooks 2002: 185). These would have recognised differences in power and wealth within the category of 'Spanish', distinguishing church, government officials, and settlers. The Pueblos would, at the broadest level, have distinguished themselves from nomadic groups, although they were also very aware of differences among themselves. These differences were amplified by attitude toward the Spanish and missions, and re-shaped after the Revolt according to participation and group re-location or stability. As conflicts with the Spanish receded, factionalism appeared within each group (Preucel 2002; Rothschild 2003). The classification of indigenous peoples was complicated by several factors: illegitimate births, as well as the realignment and resorting mechanism of local slavery and rescue, and by intermarriage across ethnic lines which created ties of mutual obligation, fostering further exchanges of human and non-human resources (Brooks 2002:17, 30). Brooks suggests that seemingly timeless identities in the southwest like Navajo, Comanche, Ute, Kiowa, Pueblo and Hispano were the result 'of biological interchange, strategic reconstruction, and political invention, as sexual enslavement, market penetration, and state pacification policies closed some avenues of identity while fostering others' (2002: 37).

In California another set of Spanish missions is analysed by Voss (2005) and Lightfoot (2005) who highlight the variability within the meta-categories of coloniser and colonised. Voss suggests that identifiable groups who began as Castilians, Africans and indios, were overlaid by casta complexity, which ultimately reflected a 'pigmentocracy' (463), modified in part by manners, class, ancestry and material practice. Interestingly, the material record downplays differ-ence; Voss sees this as representing the formation of a new ethnicity (thus, ethnogenesis), a single regional category, Californio.

Historic documents note the signaling of mixed identities similar to those just described as Native American used European goods as markers. These echo my earlier discussion of the significance of clothing, dress and the decoration of the body which, as material elements, are capable of expressing social statements at varying scales. They are used as badges but may also create hybrid identities. Captivity narratives describe Mary White Rowlandson, an English woman who lived for months among several native groups who had captured her in Massachussetts in 1676, and her distress on seeing:

> A company of Indians [coming] to us, near 30, all on horseback. My heart skipped within me thinking that they had been Englishmen at the first sight of them, for they were dressed in English apparel with hats, white neckcloths, and sashes about their waists, and ribbons upon their shoulders (Kestler 1990: 49)

Her account also details the use of Holland lace from a pillowcase for an Indian child's shirt, and describes her master and his wife, dressed for a dance:

> He was dressed in his Holland shirt, with great laces sewed at the tail of it; he had his silver buttons, his white stockings, his garters were hung round with shillings, and he had girdles of wampum upon his head and shoulders....She [his wife] had a Kersey coat; and covered with girdles of wampum from the loins upward, her arms from her elbows to her hand were covered with bracelets... She had fine red stockings and white shoes, her hair powdered and face painted red (Kestler 1990: 58)

This description of a Narragansett couple in the seventeenth century suggests that they were manipu-lating objects which were valued by Europeans (British in this case) for conspicuous display in a ritual performance, although the hybridity of their dress is worth noting; they were also wearing wampum and face paint. It is evident that indigenous people were appropriating for their own use some European things that they found particularly significant. They were not masquerading as British but were accepting some elements of British dress which fit their own ideas of symbolic meaning. Note the colors mentioned (red, white, black) and the use of silver; white lace and ribbons would also have had analogues (deerskin fringe, bone beads, wampum) in their own semiotic system (Rothschild 2003).

Many European colonists are known to have worn items of indigenous apparel, although it is hard to know how common the practice was or what it meant. An eighteenth-century portrait of a British officer, Sir John Caldwell, shows him wearing 'an Indian headdress, breechcloth, leggings and moccasins, and Indian jewelry in his nose and ears' (Calloway 1997). A portrait is a posed setting; one can imagine Caldwell using the occasion to show off his acquisitions. Another contemporary portrait depicts a Mohawk in 1710 on his visit to London with facial tattoos, holding a string of wampum, but wearing English clothing. In this case

I suspect the outfit was probably meant to incorporate him, and by extension, the Iroquois into the British universe. Loren examines ethnic 'cross-dressing' in the American southeast, especially Louisiana, and the ways in which mixed practices of dress challenged orthodox codes of status, particularly among Europeans. 'Dress and the body were key aspects of colonial discourse because the practices of dress that distinguished self and the actions of colonial bodies...were often politically and sexually charged' (2001: 175). She suggests that mixed dress among both Native Americans and Europeans may have enhanced the wearer's ability to move freely within different political, social and economic situations (2001: 184), but it seems clear that there are multiple reasons for such hybrid accoutrements.

Conclusion

I have barely skimmed the surface of this complex and intriguing topic which could be the subject of entire volumes. It is evident that the specific parameters of individual situations create interesting complexities that might appear in, for example, expressions of social distance, forms of dress, burial practices and sexual encounters. Each group—coloniser and colonised—would have brought its own beliefs and behaviors to the connection and the impacts would be quite variable on both parties. Europeans as well as indigenous people would have inevitably had to rethink their self-images and the meanings and boundaries of their bodies. Whereas social scientists and historians assume that these impacts were more strongly felt by subjugated peoples, there were reciprocal effects on the settlers, taking different forms in different situations.

I hope I have made it clear that the body is an important site for the investigation of colonial impact and that archaeologists are uniquely placed to conduct this examination because we have access to multiple kinds of information from internal and visible bodies, from personal and social ones. Bodies themselves express total existence (Merleau-Ponty 2002); experience is inscribed on the body, behavior is embodied, and the body provides the site and central phenomenon of experience. All forms of mental and physical being are situated in the interface between the body and the world, where archaeologists and others may examine them.

Acknowledgements

A number of colleagues and friends provided references, data and/or read drafts of this paper. I am grateful to all of them: Nadia Abu-El Haj, Michael Cooper, Severin Fowles, Michelle Hamilton, Brian Larkin, Meredith Linn, Emily Rothschild, Lesley Sharp, Claire Smith and Paige West. All contributed to the completion of the paper and none can be blamed for its shortcomings. I would also like to express my appreciation to John Robb and Dušan Borić for organising the symposium and getting it to publication. Finally, my thanks to an anonymous reviewer for thought-provoking comments.

Notes

1   A current series of displays in different cities in the US, called 'Bodies: the Exhibit' shows preserved, skinless bodies of 20 individuals (per exhibit) as well as many body parts. The bodies are said to have been obtained from 'unclaimed individuals in China', thought to be prisoners who died in jail.
2   I am grateful to Meredith Linn for this insight.

Bibliography

Blakey, M.F. and Rankin-Hill, L.M. (eds) 2004. *The New York African Burial Ground Skeletal Biology Final Report*. The African Burial Ground Project, Howard University, for the General Services Administration.

Bolton, L. 2003. Gender, status and introduced clothing in Vanatu. In *Clothing the Pacific*, edited by C. Colchester, pp. 119–139. New York: Berg.

Brooks, J.F. 2002. *Captives and Cousins; Slavery, Kinship and Community in the Southwest Borderlands*. Chapel Hill, NC: University of North Carolina Press.

Burke, T. 1996. *Lifebuoy Men, Lux Women: Commodification, Consumption and Cleanliness in Modern Zimbabwe*. Durham, NC: Duke University Press.

Bustamante, A. 1989. Espanoles, Castas, y labradores: Santa Fe society in the eighteenth century. In *Santa Fe: History of an Ancient City*, edited by D.G. Noble, pp. 65–78. Santa Fe, NM: School of American Research Press.

Bustamante, A. 1991. 'The Matter Was Never Resolved:' The Casta system in colonial New Mexico, 1693–1823. *New Mexico Historical Review* 66(2): 143–163.

Calloway, C. 1997. *New Worlds for All: Indians, Europeans, and the Remaking of Modern America*. Baltimore, MD: Johns Hopkins University Press.

Cohn, B.S. 1989. Cloth, clothes and colonialism: India in the nineteenth century. In *Cloth and Human Experience*, edited by A.B. Weiner and J. Schneider, pp. 303–353. Washington, DC: Smithsonian Institution Press.

Colchester, C. (ed.) 2003. *Clothing the Pacific*. New York: Berg.

Comaroff, J. 1985. *Body of Power, Spirit of Resistance: the Culture and History of a South African People*. Chicago: University of Chicago Press.

Douglas, M. 1970. *Natural Symbols: Explorations in Cosmology*. New York: Pantheon Books.

Ferguson, L. 2000. Introduction. *Historical Archaeology* 34(3): 5–9.

Gonzalez, S. 2005. Envisioning the colonial subject: a Feminist and Indigenous approach to the archaeology of colonialism. Paper presented at AAA meetings, Washington DC.

Garcia Canclini, N. 1995. *Hybrid Cultures: Strategies for Entering and Leaving Modernity*. Minneapolis, MN: University of Minnesota Press.

Hamilton, M. 2004. *Seeking After Empire: Bioarchaeologists and American Indians in the New Millennium*. PhD dissertation, University of Tennessee, Knoxville.

Jackson, R.H. 1999. *Race, Caste, and Status: Indians in Colonial Spanish America*. Albuquerque, NM: University of New Mexico Press.

Kestler, F.R. 1990. *The Indian Captivity Narrative: A Woman's View*. Women's History and Culture; 2, Garland Reference Library of the Humanities; vol. 1179. New York: Garland Publishing.

Lightfoot, K.G. 2005. *Indians, Missionaries and Merchants: the Legacy of Colonial Encounters on the California Frontiers*. Berkeley, CA: University of California Press.

Linn, M. 2002. Marred bones: the Physical consequences of Spanish contact upon the native populations of North America. Ms. for Columbia University, Human Skeletal Biology.

Linn, M. 2003. Patterns of diet and activity: Fleshing out the Native American demographic collapse. Ms. for Columbia University, Human Skeletal Biology.

Loren, D.d. 2001. Social skins: Orthodoxies and practices of dressing in the early Colonial Lower Mississippi Valley. *Journal of Social Archaeology* 1(2): 172–189.

Merleau-Ponty, M. 2002[1962]. *Phenomenology of Perception*. London: Routledge.

Meskell, L. 1999. *Archaeologies of Social Life*. Oxford: Blackwell.

Meskell, L. and Joyce, R. 2003. *Embodied Lives: Figuring Ancient Maya and Egyptian Experience*. London: Routledge.

Reisher, E. and Koo, K.S. 2004. The Body beautiful: Symbolism and agency in the social world. *Annual Review of Anthropology* 33: 297–317.

Rothschild, N.A. 2003. *Colonial Encounters in a Native American Landscape: the Spanish and Dutch in North America*. Washington, DC: Smithsonian Institution Press.

Schildkrout, E. 2004. Inscribing the body. *Annual Review of Anthropology* 33: 319–44.

Sharp, L. 2006. *Strange Harvest: Organ Transplants, Denatured Bodies and the Transformed Self*. Berkeley, CA: University of California Press.

Strathern, M. 2004. The Whole person and its artifacts. *Annual Review of Anthropology* 33: 1–19.

Tcherkezoff, S. 2003. On Cloth, gifts, nudity: Regarding some European misunderstanding during early encounters in Polynesia. In *Clothing the Pacific*, edited by C. Colchester, pp. 51–75. New York: Berg.

Thomas, N. 2003. The Case of the misplaced ponchos: Speculations concerning the history of cloth in Polynesia. In *Clothing the Pacific*, edited by C. Colchester, pp. 79–96. New York: Berg.

Van Wolputte, S. 2004. Hang on to your self: Of bodies, embodiment and selves. *Annual Review of Anthropology* 33: 251–69.

Voss, B.L. 2005. From Casta to Californio: Social identity and the archaeology of culture contact. *American Anthropologist* 107(3): 461–474.

Weiner, A.B. 1989. Why Cloth? Wealth, gender and power in Oceania. In *Cloth and Human Experience*, edited by A.B. Weiner and J. Schneider, pp. 33–72. Washington, DC: Smithsonian Institution Press.

White, R. 1991. *The Middle Ground: Indians, Empires and Republics in the Great Lakes Region, 1650–1815*. Cambridge Studies in North American History. Cambridge: Cambridge University Press.

15

The challenge of embodying archaeology

Chris Shilling

Archaeology appears to be at a critical turning point in its dealings with embodiment. Widely acknowledged as a key topic in current theory, 'the body' has nevertheless been something of an 'absent presence' in the discipline. The concern of archaeologists with such issues as artistic representations of the human form, the relationship between embodiment and ascribed and performed gender roles, and the sensing body, has placed on the agenda matters that have become increasing important across the humanities and social sciences during the past few decades. In so doing, however, there has been a tendency for the body to be both tied and subordinated to *other* issues, often remaining rather opaque and entering into the archaeological field of vision only when manifest in ways that coincide with the representational, gendered or other antecedent concerns of its investigators. This tendency for the body to appear, only to fade from view as it undergoes one metamorphosis after another, has been evident in many of the articles and books on embodiment (both inside and outside of archaeology) that have focused their concern on issues which may be important yet which remain dominated by priorities and perspectives rooted in the discipline's established paradigms. The evidential bases of archaeology, moreover, add an additional dimension to the problem of corporeal recovery. In dealing with fragments of bodies past, or even with just fragments of the material cultures of bodies past, there is a hermeneutic challenge of interpretation and understanding here of a scale which is often greater than that which confronts those working within the field of body studies from other inter/disciplinary bases.

This does not, of course, mean that it is possible to achieve a wholesale recuperation and analysis of the body from some pure archimedean point. There is always likely to be a certain partiality or incompleteness to our investigations irrespective of the discipline/ theoretical framework/historical epoch with which we are associated, and explicit recognition of this helps to concentrate attention on what is and is not possible. Nevertheless, if we are to take seriously the body as a generative resource that can provoke new insights, it is important that the embodied foundations of social and cultural life continue to be acknowledged as an important issue *in their own right*. In this context, *Past Bodies* provides a welcome and sustained focus on body matters by including papers that address the range of human societies from the hunter-gatherers of the Upper Palaeolithic, to modern European populations, and that are informed by a diversity of body relevant theories and methodologies. These studies take a variety of forms – ranging from Bailey's analysis of the representational omissions characteristic of Neolithic figurines in the lower Danube, Sørensen's and Rebay's paper on the continued representational presence of the body after cremation, and Mitrović's account of the recovery and disturbing visceral presence of the recently slaughtered bodies of Kosovo Albanians in mass graves – but each explores how the multiple presences and absences of bodies discovered is consequential for what can be said about the embodied foundations of the cultures and societies under investigation.

In what follows, I shall begin by suggesting that *Past Bodies* includes within it valuable contributions to the issue of how we should conceptualise the embodied subject, contributions that take us decisively beyond the *homo clausus* images of human beings that still characterise many studies on the Western body.

I then examine how these contributions towards an archaeology of the body continue to face important problems in theorising corporeal presence and absence in relation to their epistemological, phenomenological and ontological concerns. These problems, I suggest, have consequences for the theoretical sources that are more or less adequate to the task of taking forward viable forms of 'body archaeology', and to the challenges that continue to confront its practitioners.

Visions of Embodiment

Since the 1980s, the field of 'body studies' has become increasingly influential across a growing range of academic subjects (Shilling 2003 [1993]). These studies have explored an impressive and sometimes bewildering array of issues related to embodied life, but they have generally been dominated by what are essentially Western views of what it means to both be and to have a body. There are important exceptions to this trend, and they have often emerged from anthropology (e.g., Csordas 1994; Okeley 2007; Stoller 1997; Strathern 1988), but the figure of the monadic subject continues to loom large in many investigations of embodiment.

This model of the body has been referred to by Norbert Elias (1987) as *homo clausus* (meaning the 'closed individual' or 'closed personalities'). Its roots exist deep in the division Western philosophy has traditionally made between the 'external' world and the 'internal' world of the individual mind. Formulated most influentially by Descartes, permeating the writings of Leibniz, and culminating in the thought of Kant, there is a preoccupation here with how individuals are able to 'reach out' from their enclosed minds and gain reliable knowledge of the social and natural world beyond them (including the minds of other, similarly enclosed individuals). To be human, moreover, is defined by the possession of a mind: the body exists as little more than a form of inertial drag on, or obstruction to, cognitive thought processes and decisions. Elias (1987: 130) points out that this model portrays people as 'thinking statues', isolated egos who are devoid of concepts, symbols, bodily customs and habits handed down from previous generations. In contrast to this *homo clausus* model, Elias suggests that we begin with a more processual and embodied vision of humanity which rejects the idea of a rigid and impermeable boundary between what occurs within and outside of the mind and body, and recognises instead that people are 'open' and bonded together in various ways and to various degrees. This view of *homines apertis* ('open people') allows us to explore how social and material relationships *re-form* the human body over evolutionary

and generational time (Mellor and Shilling 1997), while also being sensitive to cross-cultural differences in the embodied constitution of humans.

One of the major aims of the growing field of body studies has been to put the body *back into* social and historical analysis, and to take account of the corporeal basis of thought and action and the corporeal consequences of cultural forms and social structures. As such, there was a quite deliberate reaction against the cognitively driven portrayal of *homo clausus* dominant in Western philosophy. Instead of eradicating entirely the influence of this monadic subject, however, important studies have sometimes engaged in a version of *inverted Cartesianism*. Here, the body may replace the mind as the *focus* of study, but it remains either as a *physical casing*, that subjects people to external control, or a barrier that threatens to separate phenomenologically the individual from others. This was evident in Turner's (1984) theory of bodily order, for example, which drew on Hobbes's and Parsons's concern with 'the problem of order' in viewing the body as an object from the perspective of the social system. In continuing to posit a strong boundary between the external and the internal environment, and in continuing to separate analytically the mind from the body, the studies by Turner and others *reinvented* rather than solved the problems inherent in the *homo clausus* vision of humanity.

It is in addressing this area that *Past Bodies* makes its most significant contribution, providing evidence and argument that highlights the partiality of the traditionally Western *homo clausus* conception of embodied being. It accomplishes this primarily through the various ways in which its contributors demonstrate the *relationality* of embodied subjects. Borić's and Robb's introduction sets the scene for this in its discussion of the affinities between archaeology and Amazonian ethnography in recognising the constant processes of change that affect self-image. Fowler's concern with 'fractal thinking' makes a similar point in showing how the social and material webs of interdependence that characterise human life provide people with modes of classification that shape how they view themselves and their surroundings.

This relationality takes several forms but is perhaps most easily demonstrated in terms of relationships between people. Stoddart's and Malone's analysis of the rise and fall of collectivist and individualist approaches towards bodily display and disposal, for example, illustrates how the connections that people have with others in their community shape the type of identities reflected in dominant cultural practices. As such, Stoddart's and Malone's paper can be seen as an interesting contribution to Durkheim's argument that relationality remains important even in societies and social groupings in which individuality is prized. Durkheim (1973 [1898]; 1984 [1893]) makes this point in his analysis of how the 'cult of the individual' – involving a heightened respect for individuality – develops alongside an increasing *social* division of labour.

The relationality of embodied subjects is not, however, confined to the pattern of their involvement in *human* configurations. The papers by Robb and Miracle and Borić look at how the 'openness' of embodied subjects extends to the symbolic and material relations they have with *animals*. Indeed, Miracle and Borić outline a distinctive approach towards embodied hybridity in their analysis of animal-human association, substitution and transformation. Malafouris, in contrast, turns our attention to relational processes involving *inanimate* material culture by examining how objects can become incorporated into the body schema. Following a path investigated by the likes of Head (1920), Schilder (1978 [1935]), and Merleau-Ponty (1962), Malafouris suggests that key cultural products (in this case the Mycenaean sword) can shape the minds and bodies of those that carry them, and serve to illustrate the mutual determination of embodied subjects and the tools and products they produce. Joyce examines a similar issue in her argument that the formal characteristics of early Mesoamerican figurines were not simply 'representations' but constituted instruments of experience, incorporating within them the muscular movements, tensions, and even becoming bodily extensions of their creators. Joyce suggests further that these figurines reach beyond the individual, serving as a 'bridge' between the physical presence of the maker and the physical absence of the 'person' of whom the sculpture is an image.

The social and material relationality or 'openness' of embodied subjects is illustrated further in contributions that examine representations and practices of *political power* within group life. Historically, political conceptions of the relationship between the individual body and the social group or social body have been expressed through symbols and practices regarded as sacred. The notion of the 'King's Two Bodies' (the idea that the monarch's legitimacy was based on divine right and manifest in the king possessing a natural body subject to death and a sacred political body in which resided incorruptible sovereignty), for example, reiterated the doctrine of the 'mystical body of Christ' and was then reflected in secular form in the notion of the Head of State as someone who governs and represents the body politic (Kantorowicz 1957). Exploring such themes in a specific context, Gillespie's analysis of bodily representations in late classic Maya

sculpture provides us with an interesting case-study of symbols of power in a civilization spanning southern Mexico, Guatemala and Belize. Drawing on Joyce's (1996) research, Gillespie suggests that images of male rulers wearing items of female costume provided a symbolic example of the totalising and unifying capacities of leaders. In this context, symbolic or actual challenges to this transcendent power were not just a threat to the individual body of the ruler but to the *social body* itself and, as Foucault's (1979) analysis of monarchical power illustrates, were dealt with accordingly. Against this background, Tarlow's contribution constitutes a fascinating account of the history of Oliver Cromwell's head after his death; tracing how it was treated variously as an object of punishment, as a collector's item, and as a conversation piece and a family heirloom.

If taking seriously the relationality of embodied subjects to their social, animal, material and political environment highlights the limitations of the *homo clausus* model of individuals in relation to their boundaries, contents and identities, so too does it cause us to question the equation of death and finality that is key to the contemporary obsession with youth in consumer culture (Featherstone 1981). Sørensen's and Rebay's analysis of the transition from inhumation to cremation during the Middle Bronze Age in central Europe (in which the body was viewed as transformed rather destroyed), and Robb's account of the Huron practice of consuming and incorporating the bravery of one's slain enemies through cannibalism, provide just two examples of practices that call into question conventional Western medical accounts of death. Similar to many other contributions within this collection, there is a focus here on the transcendent potentialities of embodied subjects. In continuing to leave a mark on the experiences of others, on the cultural practices of a group, and on the physical landscape, death does not always represent a secular 'point zero' which is sequestered away from the living (Giddens 1991).

Knowing, Sensing and Being

In making what can be seen as a sustained assault on the 'closed', non-relational characteristics of *homo clausus*, via a series of interrogations into what corporeal presences and absences can tell us about embodied life, the contributors to *Past Bodies* also address issues relating to questions of epistemology (knowledges and representations of the body), phenomenology (the lived experiences of people's past) and ontology (the material bodily properties and capacities of our generational and evolutionary antecedents). These issues have been of central importance to the field of body studies since its origins, and also to those classical studies in sociology, history and other disciplines on which this field has drawn (see Shilling 2005), and they also serve to introduce us to some of the theoretical dilemmas that continue to confront those seeking to advance an archaeology of embodiment.

Epistemologically, the link between historical representations of the body and what these enable one to know about embodied life in a previous era has long been key to the work of archaeologists and is a central issue in this collection. What particularly interests me about the contributions that tackle this issue is that they explicate and explore the *varied* cultural and historical manifestations and importance of Douglas's (1970) theory of classification (Douglas suggests that the body is the most ubiquitous image of a social system and that ideas about the body tend to approximate to ideas about the social system). Bailey's study, for example, analyses how material culture mediates this body symbolism, while Stoddart and Malone look historically at how the individual body can be absent from, as well as present within, the belief systems of a group or culture. One of the main elements of Douglas's analysis is a consideration of how bodily discipline and order is related symbolically to concerns about the boundaries and integrity of the social body. In this respect, Robb's analysis of how the categories through which the Huron people think are associated closely with practices of both incorporation into and expulsion from the physical and the social body, Fowler's discussions of fractal thinking and Melanesian beliefs about corporeal partibility and exchange, and Miracles's and Borić's study of how beliefs pertaining to the chronic instability of the body can vary widely in different cultures and at different times, provide valuable additions to debate in this area.

Phenomenologically, the historical reconstruction of experience poses a far larger challenge, requiring an archaeological exercise in corporeal hermeneutics that is extremely challenging and has yet to be confronted fully. Nonetheless, papers by Joyce and Malafouris provide interesting ideas as to how this problem can be addressed. While Joyce seeks to trace back muscular experience and habits from the moulding of clay, Malafouris draws on science in suggesting that material culture impinges in a fundamental manner on the corporeal vehicles through which subjects engage with their world. *Ontologically*, we can see a similar process of analytical reconstruction in this volume. Malafouris' paper makes deductions about the cerebral architecture of the Mycenaeans, while Rothschild and Mitrović are able to draw on a

wider evidential basis. Rothschild's paper constitutes an extremely valuable addition to the literature on imperialism and colonisation by focusing on the effects of colonial rule on the bodies of those subject to it. Fanon (1984 [1952]; 1970), for one, has described in detail the powerful effects colonisation has on the body schema of the oppressed. Rothschild's study reaches deeper into the actual materiality of the body, however, in looking at archaeological evidence that shows how the bodily remains of the colonised 'speak' of disease, broken bones, dental enamel defects from childhood nutritional stress, osteoarthritis and other damage. As Rothschild concludes, these past bodies bear 'compelling witness to the relations between slave and master and its associated violence'. Mitrović's account of his time as a member of the Batajnica mass grave site provides a different example of the 'witness' provided by dead bodies. Concerned with identifying the causes of death, Mitrović's account provides us with a stark reminder that investigating the brute ontological materiality of bodies can be a vital part of our understanding of social conflicts in particular and human societies in general.

Issues of knowing, sensing and being are not, of course, entirely separate, and the contributors to *Past Bodies* provide us with plenty of evidence regarding their interrelationship. Osborne's critique of Gombrich's account of the shift in body representation that occurred in Greek sculpture, for example, insists that this break can only be understood adequately if we analyse it as related to a moment in the history of the 'real body'. Representational shifts do not just happen, in other words, but are frequently connected to associated changes in people's bodily capacities and the corporeal modes through which they experience the world. If we wish to interrogate transformations in symbolic and other forms of representation, we need to attend to *re-formations* of embodiment. Representations also clearly affect people's experiences of their own and other people's bodies. Thus, the contributions by Miracle and Borić, and by Robb, focus on how the categories used within a social group define the 'established' and 'outsiders', affect how people experience themselves in relation to outsiders, and shape the extent to which it is possible to empathise with the pain and suffering of others (for an extended discussion of the processes underpinning such relations, see Elias [1994]).

Theorising the Archaeological Body

The case studies in this volume provide us with stimulating explorations of corporeal knowing, sensing and being, but there remains the issue of which theoretical resources best illuminate these issues given archaeology's concern with the 'open' and varied relationships that exist between embodied subjects and the social bodies of the tribe, community or society. As Borić and Robb suggest in their introduction, this volume seeks to reposition the body as a central issue in archaeology rather than offer any detailed prescriptions as to the precise route that the discipline should follow in this respect. I do not think it inappropriate, however, to highlight some of the potential problems associated with the more popular theoretical resources that have been drawn on thus far (sometimes in archaeology but mostly more widely in the field of body studies). I will confine myself here to brief comments about the three most influential theories associated with social constructionism, phenomenology, and structuration theory.

Social constructionist analyses of the body have focused in the most sustained manner on how the body is objectified and rendered controllable through forms of representation. Human physicality here becomes a phenomenon that is regulated by political, normative and discursive regimes: the body, in short, is seen as a *location* for society. Studies which developed this view did much to initiate and consolidate the form taken by the corporeal turn in social theory, and helped make a valuable epistemological break from normative views of the body as a 'natural', purely biological phenomenon. Turner's (1984) structuralism, for example, identified representation as one of the four core problems faced by every social system. Later, post-structuralist studies such as Butler's (1990) *Gender Trouble* and (1993) *Bodies that Matter* emphasised the normative power of gendered modes of representation as key to the relationship between embodied subjects and social bodies. The influence of Foucault is readily apparent in such social constructionist writings. Foucault (1979) conceives of the body as 'the inscribed surface of events' and as 'totally imprinted by history'. There are no irreducible 'essences' that define people's identity or actions for all time, just 'inscriptions' of identity which change over time. These theories and others like them have proven effective at illuminating the significance of representational forms, and suggesting how the body is ordered and inscribed by power relations, and their influence is evident in some of the contributions to this volume. However, they frequently remain silent about how the body is possessed of capacities that mean it can be an active *source* of the social, and about the 'lived experience' of embodied action. Crucially, they also tend to erase any ontological existence the body has apart from specific societies, thus making it impossible to evaluate institutions in terms of their beneficial or detrimental effects on the body (something which is revealed as a fatal flaw when we consider Mitrović's paper). We can readily agree that social relations and forces shape human bodies in all manner of ways, but the 'strong' social constructionist theories considered here engage in a social or discursive reductionism that tends to erase the material history, phenomenology, and the agentic capacities of embodied subjects.

In response to this lacuna, the 1990s witnessed a rise in action-oriented and phenomenological studies about 'the body's own experience of its embodiment' (Frank 1991: 43). Leder's (1990) focus on the lived experience of instrumentally rational action is an important example of this genre. So too is Young's (1990, 1998: 147–8) feminist phenomenology which highlights the daily foregrounding of the female body within patriarchal societies in a manner which ladens women's bodies with immanence. Accounts such as these drew on phenomenology, on existentialist and on interactionist resources, to portray the body as a *source* of experience and of society. It is the phenomenology of Merleau-Ponty, however, that has been most influential in shaping calls for a 'carnal sociology', the founding assumption of which being that '"self", "society" and "symbolic order" are constituted through the work of the body' (Crossley, 1995: 43). For Merleau-Ponty (1962: 136), embodied subjects develop direction and purpose on the basis of the *practical* engagements they have with their surroundings and through the *intentionality* they develop as a result of the situatedness of embodied existence. This emphasis on the determining rather than determined nature of our embodiment, and on the universal bodily basis of meaning and knowledge, constitutes a major challenge to structuralist and post-structuralist theories. Despite its ostensible focus on the 'lived body', however, there is a paradox within phenomenology. Having been interpreted as analysing how people experience their bodies, this tradition is actually concerned with the bodily *basis* of experience. As Leder's (1990) study illustrates, it is quite possible, therefore, for the body to fade away within a phenomenological account of people's practical experiences of the world. In this context, it seems to be vital to contextualise phenomenological concerns within a wider framework that is able to explain the varying significance and existence that particular forms of bodily experience acquire over time. Particular social figurations may be conducive to the promotion of forms of *carnal knowing* in which the senses play a key role, for example, while the modern Western world's relative devaluation of the senses other than seeing has been accompanied by a much narrower validation of cognitive ways of apprehending the world (Mellor and Shilling 1997).

These analyses of the representationally ordered and 'lived' bodies provided the field with alternative lines of development, but replicated what many saw as a longstanding and debilitating division between theories of structure and agency. This division analytically collapsed structures into action, or actions into structure, and thus made it impossible to examine the *interaction* that occurred *over time* between existing social / cultural forms and new generations of embodied beings. Structuration theories developed as a means of overcoming this opposition. Based on assumptions about the mutually constituting nature of social structures and actions, the body was central to structuration theory's vision of society. Bourdieu (1984) and Giddens (1984, 1991) have been the most influential proponents of this theory of social life, while Grosz (1994) provides us with a distinct, feminist analysis of the mutual constitution of the body and dominant norms of sexuality. Despite their differences, these theorists claimed that the body was simultaneously a recipient of social practices *and* an active creator of its milieu. Structuration theories provide us with a 'middle way' between social constructionist accounts of governmentality and phenomenological accounts of 'lived experience'. The body, in short, is a *means* through which individuals are attached to, or ruptured from, society. Whether they provide us with *viable* alternatives, however, is questionable. While Bourdieu (1984: 466) asserts the facts of changing bodily dispositions, his argument that the *habitus* operates at the level of the subconscious makes it difficult to see how individuals can escape the dispositional trajectory assigned them. The emphasis Giddens places on changeability and reflexivity, in contrast, invests the body with an unconvincing permanence and malleability; it can be reinvented by the individual alongside their reflexively constituted narratives of self, and we get little sense of the corporeal limitations and fragility of human being. Finally, despite her concern to identify possibilities for change, Grosz's focus on the body's sexual specificity, and the additional 'investments of difference' made by society into the interiors and exteriors of bodies, seems to ensure the continuation of opposing male and female identities. The problem for structuration theories, in short, is that they tie the embodied subject, society, experience, identity and action so closely together that it becomes impossible to examine their interaction over time or the possibilities of social change that follow from this interaction. In these theories it is not that the embodied subject and material culture, for example, are relational or open to each other, but are *one and the same thing*.

If archaeology is to be able to examine the relative degrees of openness that exist between embodied subjects on the one hand and the social, animal and inanimate material culture around them, there is a strong case for suggesting that it needs to be able to recognise the distinctive properties of these phenomenon in order that it can appreciate their relationality over time. If we are to explore the relational character of the links that exist between the individual and the social body, for example, we have to understand the properties and capacities of *what* is involved in this relationship as well as how these properties and capacities may change as a result of their interactions over time. This cannot be done by theoretical approaches that entirely conflate the separate properties of the phenomena under discussion. In this context, there would be a considerable risk in extending Joyce's argument that 'it is artifical for us to separate human beings from figurines'. To take such an approach to embodied subjects and the material culture they produce would be to risk positing an identity between them which disallowed one from examining the different ways in which they interconnected over time. This is not to suggest that social constructionist, phenomenological and structuration theories are of no use, but as presently formulated there is a tendency for them to 'over reach' their explanatory capacity. In this respect, it is interesting to note that the most recent developments in body theory are seeking to incorporate their insights into distinctive frameworks which can carry forward our understand of embodiment.[1]

Conclusion

The humanities and social sciences now generally recognise the centrality of embodiment to the key issues that have long preoccupied their practitioners. Important questions remain about how best to conceptualise and theorise the importance of corporeality across distinctive cultures and through different historical epochs. Nevertheless, if we accept that embodied actors exercise their desires and actions 'under circumstances directly encountered, given and transmitted from the past' (Marx 1968 [1885]: 96), then the papers in this collection suggest that archaeologically related studies have an important role to play in advancing the field of body studies.

Note

1   See, for example, Crossley's (2001) attempt to synthesise Merleau-Ponty and Bourdieu, my own conception of corporeal realism (2005), how this can be supplemented

by pragmatism (2008), and the related study of body pedagogics (2007a, Shilling and Mellor 2007), Davis's (2007) explication of the partial combination of action-oriented and post-structuralist feminist theory, Turner's (2007) discussion of the existential problems associated with the potentiality of prolonged life in technological society, and Levine's (2007) extension of action theory to embodiment.

Bibliography

Bourdieu, P. 1994. *Distinction. A Social Critique of the Judgment of Taste*. London: Routledge.

Butler, J. 1990. *Gender Trouble*. London: Routledge.

Butler, J. 1993. *Bodies That Matter*. London: Routledge.

Crossley, N. 1995. Merleau-Ponty, the elusive body and carnal sociology. *Body & Society* 1(1): 43–63.

Crossley, N. 2001. *The Social Body*. London: Sage.

Csordas, T.J. (ed.) 1994. *Embodiment and Experience*. Cambridge: Cambridge University Press.

Davis, K. 2007. Reclaiming Women's Bodies: Colonialist trope or Critical Epistemology. In *Embodying Sociology. Retrospect, Progress & Prospects*, edited by C. Shilling, pp. 50–64. Oxford: Blackwell/The Sociological Review Monograph Series.

Douglas, M. 1970. *Natural Symbols. Explorations in Cosmology*. London: The Cresset Press.

Elias, N. 1987. *The Society of Individuals*. Oxford: Blackwell.

Elias, N. 1994. A theoretical essay on established and outsider relations. In *The Established and the Outsiders*, edited by N. Elias and J. Scotson. London: Sage.

Fanon, F. 1984 [1952]. *Black Skin, White Masks*. London: Pluto Press.

Fanon, F. 1970. *A Dying Colonialism*. New York: Grove Press.

Featherstone, M. 1981. The body in consumer culture. *Theory, Culture & Society* 1(1): 18–33.

Foucault, M. 1979. *Discipline and Punish*. Harmondsworth: Penguin.

Frank, A. 1991. For a sociology of the body: An analytical review. In *The Body: Social Process & Cultural Theory*, edited by M. Featherstone, M. Hepworth and B.S. Turner, pp. 36–102. London: Sage.

Giddens, A. 1984. *The Consequences of Modernity*. Cambridge: Polity.

Giddens, A. 1991. *Modernity and Self-Identity*. Cambridge: Polity Press.

Grosz, E. 1994. *Volatile Bodies*. London: Routledge.

Joyce, R. 1996. The construction of gender in classic Maya monuments In *Gender and Archaeology*, edited by R.P. Wright, pp. 167–195. Philadelphia: University of Pennsyvania Press.

Kantorowicz, E. 1957. *The King's Two Bodies. A Study in Medieval Political Theology*. Princeton, NJ: Princeton University Press.

Leder, D. 1990. *The Absent Body*. Chicago: University of Chicago Press.

Levine, D. 2007. Somatic elements in social conflict. In *Embodying Sociology. Retrospect, Progress & Prospects*, edited by C. Shilling, pp. 37–49. Oxford: Blackwell/The Sociological Review Monograph Series.

Marx, K. 1968 [1885]. The 18th Brumaire of Louis Bonaparte 1885. In *Marx/Engels. Selected Works in One Volume*, by K. Marx and F. Engels. London: Lawrence & Wishart.

Mellor, P.A. and Shilling, C. 1997. *Re-forming the Body. Religion, Community and Modernity*. London: Sage.

Merleau-Ponty, M. 1962. *The Phenomenology of Perception*. London: Routledge.

Okely, J. 2007. Fieldwork embodied. In *Embodying Sociology. Retrospect, Progress & Prospects*, edited by C. Shilling, pp. 65–79. Oxford: Blackwell/The Sociological Review Monograph Series.

Shilling, C. 2003. *The Body and Social Theory, Second Edition*. London: Sage.

Shilling, C. 2005. *The Body in Culture, Technology & Society*. London: Sage.

Shilling, C. (ed) 2007. *Embodying Sociology. Retrospect, Progress & Prospects*. Oxford: Blackwell/The Sociological Review Monograph Series.

Shilling, C. 2008. *Changing Bodies. Hubris, Crisis and Creativity*. London, Sage.

Shilling, C. and Mellor, P.A. 2007. Cultures of embodied experience: Technology, religion and body pedagogics. *The Sociological Review* 55(3): 531–549.

Stoller, P. 1997. *Sensuous Scholarship*. Philadelphia: University of Pennsylvania Press.

Strathern, M. 1988. *Gender of the Gift*. Berkeley, CA: University of California Press.

Turner, B.S. 1984. *The Body and Society*. Oxford: Blackwells.

Turner, B.S. 2007. Culture, technologies and bodies: the techno-logical Utopia of living forever. In *Embodying Sociology. Retrospect, Progress & Prospects*, edited by C. Shilling, pp. 19–36. Oxford: Blackwell/The Sociological Review Monograph Series.

Young, I.M. 1990. *Throwing Like a Girl*. Bloomington: Indiana University Press.